P9-DCH-917

A RIVER FOR
CHRISTMAS

A RIVER FOR CHRISTMAS

• THE STEPHEN GREENE PRESS •

AND OTHER STORIES

Ernest Schwiebert

with illustrations by the author

• PELHAM BOOKS •

THE STEPHEN GREENE PRESS / PELHAM BOOKS

Published by the Penguin Group
Viking Penguin, a division of Penguin Books USA Inc., 40 West 23rd Street,
   New York, New York 10010, U.S.A.
Penguin Books Ltd, 27 Wrights Lane, London W8 5TZ, England
Penguin Books Australia Ltd, Ringwood, Victoria, Australia
Penguin Books Canada Ltd, 2801 John Street, Markham, Ontario,
   Canada L3R 1B4
Penguin Books (N.Z.) Ltd, 182-190 Wairau Road, Auckland 10, New Zealand

Penguin Books Ltd, Registered Offices: Harmondsworth, Middlesex, England

First published in 1988 by The Stephen Greene Press
This paperback edition published 1989
Distributed by Viking Penguin, a division of Penguin Books USA Inc.

10 9 8 7 6 5 4 3 2 1

Copyright © Penguin Books USA Inc., 1988
All rights reserved

Some of the stories in this collection first appeared, in different form, in the
following publications: *Fishing Moments of Truth* edited by James Cornwall
Rikhoff and Eric Peper, published by Winchester Press; *Fly Fisherman*; William
Mills and Son Catalog; *Rod & Reel*; *Sports Afield* and *Trout*.

Library of Congress Cataloging-in-Publication Data

Schweibert, Ernest George.
     A river for Christmas and other stories / by Ernest Schweibert.
        p.   cm.
     ISBN 0-8289-0695-5
     ISBN 0-8289-0696-3 (pbk.)

     1. Fishing.   I. Title.
   SH441.S395   1988   88-11193
   799.1 — dc19   CIP

Printed in the United States of America
Set in ITC Garamond and Caslon Open Face
Designed by Deborah Schneider, Schneider & Company
Produced by Unicorn Production Services, Inc.

Except in the United States of America, this book is sold subject to the condition
that it shall not, by way of trade or otherwise, be lent, re-sold, hired out, or
otherwise circulated without the publisher's prior consent in any form of bind-
ing or cover other than that in which it is published and without a similar
condition including this condition being imposed on the subsequent purchaser.

Perhaps all this seems beyond the scope of a fishing book yet I do not think I should enjoy fishing in a country whose hopes and aspirations were unknown to me or whose people seemed remote from me.

—RODERICK HAIG-BROWN

Fishing is the least important thing about fishing.

—ARNOLD GINGRICH

· C O N T E N T S ·

Acknowledgments

Special thanks must be given to several outfitters and airlines for their assistance in the travel involved in these stories, and for which the carriers are due consideration. The outfitters include Mytravel International of Oslo, for its help in fishing the Alta, and Thomas & Thomas, in concert with Abelson & Dahlenson of Stockholm, who assisted with a trip to the Gaula. Travel to both Norwegian rivers was provided by Scandinavian Airline System, and SAS has proved exceptionally helpful, courteous, and comfortable service in the twenty-four years I have been fishing in Norway. The Mulcahy organization, which owns the Butler Arms and Ashford Castle, are due thanks for their help in Ireland, along with Aer Lingus for its excellent air service, and the Irish Tourist Board. Rex Forrester of the New Zealand Tourist Office, Geoffrey Thomas and Hugh MacDowell of Rotorua, and Richard Fraser of the Cedar Lodge at Makarora, are owed an immense debt of gratitude for their knowledge and generosity. Both Pan American World Airways and Air New Zealand have assisted in my eighteen years of travel to the Antipodes. Other thanks are due José de Anthorena, Carlos Nordahl-Olsen, Felipe and Mauricio de Lariviere, Riccardo Santa Marina, Guy Dawson, Laddie Buchanan, Gustavo Schwed, Jorge Berghmann, Harry Thompson, Walter Wood, Nellie Dawson Reid, and particularly her son, Douglas Reid, who is president of the ranchers throughout the Neuquen province of Argentina. Their assistance across thirty years of fishing in Patagonia has been without price. Travel has been provided on some of those expeditions by Panagra, Braniff International, Eastern, Aerolineas Argentinas, and the domestic Argentine carrier called Austral. Considerable debt is also acknowledged to Braniff International and LAN Chile in my eighteen years of travel there. Chilean anglers like Alfredo Heusser, Alberto Schirmer, Riccardo Vargas, and the famous Adrian Dufflocq have all been charming hosts and fishing friends.

American friends are due thanks too. Philip Wright of The Compleat Flyfisher helped with many floats on the Beaverhead and Big Hole. There were several seasons with Charles Fox, Jim Kell, and Ross Trimmer on Letort Spring Run. Ralph Wahl and Wes Drain were my mentors in arranging a wonderful time on the Stillaguamish. Anne Haig-Brown and Dan Callaghan were critical factors in our last visit with the late Roderick Haig-Brown in British Columbia.

Some stories collected here involve material that has been previously published elsewhere. None appears in this anthology in its originally published form. Each has been substantially revised and rewritten. The original stories remain the property of the author. Only first American and Canadian rights were granted on first publication. Several of these pieces are entirely new work.

Permission to modify material written over more than twenty-five years has been generous, and *Sports Afield* even helped to find lost articles in its morgue. The following publishers are entitled to considerable gratitude: the brief story called "The Perch Fisherman" appeared in slightly different form in *Rod & Reel*, Number Seven, Volume One in March–April 1980; the piece titled "The Night of the Gytefisk" appeared in *Fishing Moments of Truth*, collected and edited by James Cornwall Rikhoff and Eric Peper, and published by the first Winchester Press at 460 Park Avenue, New York, 1973, although it has been substantially changed; the Irish piece called "The Butler Pool" was retitled and modified as "The Softness on Butler's Pool" in *Fly Fisherman*, Volume Seven, Number One, Winter 1975; the Montana story called "The River of the Girdlebugs" was published in slightly different form at *Sports Afield*, Volume 175, Number Three, March 1977; the long story "The Rivers of Patagonia" was originally a short essay written after my first expedition in 1959, and published in the catalog of William Mills & Son, 21 Park Place, New York, 1965; the essay "Letort Soliloquy" is enlarged from a piece using that title which first appeared in *Trout*, Volume Twenty-Six, Number Three, Summer 1985; the relatively long "Kiwi Country" was also published in *Trout*, in two parts, appearing in Volume Twenty-Six, Number One, Winter 1985, and Volume Twenty-Six, Number Two, Spring 1985; the short story called "The Spider at Buttonwood Pool" appeared in modified form in *Fly Fisherman*, Volume Eleven,

• ACKNOWLEDGMENTS •

Number Five, May–June 1980; the steelhead piece entitled "Song of the Stilliguamish" was first published with considerable editorial reworking in *Sports Afield*, Volume 175, Number Three, March 1977; the travel essay entitled "The Ring of Kerry" was extensively changed when first published under that title in *Fly Fisherman*, Volume Fourteen, Number One, Winter 1982; the long eulogy called "The Orchard and the River" appeared in a partially truncated version in *Fly Fisherman,* Volume Nine, Number Three, March 1978; the short essay "Fishing Luck" was first published in *Trout*, Volume Twenty-Seven, Number One, Winter 1986; and the title piece of the entire anthology first appeared in considerably changed form in *Fly Fisherman*. It was called "A River for Christmas," and was found in Volume Nine, Number Seven, July–August 1978.

Each story is considerably changed. Any writer continues to learn and evolve and work.

John Groth
1908-1988

Art teacher, painter, storyteller and adventurer, writer, graphic designer, traveler, and combat correspondent who carried sketchbooks and crow-quill pens and sable brushes to five wars, and rode with the first reconnaissance patrol to enter Paris.

Groth was a gentle man who found himself in warlike times, fought in Germany with Ernest Hemingway—and sat sketching him with coffee washes and Chinese ink, while they were under artillery fire at Bleialt in the Hürtgen Forest.

Like Hemingway, Groth was a flyfisherman, and passionately loved the gentle sport. It was a privilege to have such a remarkable friend.

The Perch Fisherman

Fifty years have passed since that summer in the Great Depression when I explored the stone jetties and breakwaters that protected the campus from Lake Michigan and found the old men fishing for perch.

It was a simple time, in a summer that mixed pleasures and sorrows, and there was gratitude in our family that my father still had his teaching post. His textbook had sold just well enough that we could take a summer cottage in Wisconsin to escape the doldrums of late August.

But the first weeks of summer passed slowly, and our lives had a measured pace. Our neighbors were mostly shopkeepers, mixed with professors and instructors at the university. There was a minor executive at a local machine-parts factory, and an old attorney who still had some money from the Coolidge years and amused himself with politics. Our neighborhood had its craftsmen too, men who made tool-and-die patterns and elegant millwork and wrought-iron hardware. Others were walking from house to house, trying to sell cars and vacuum cleaners and insurance to people with no money. The mills and warehouses were empty. It was several years before I understood that the shabbily dressed men riding the freight trains were not actually part of their crews.

There was a retired doctor who lived down the street, his house surrounded by a jungle of lilacs and forsythia, and an old banker who lived in the Victorian house beyond our vegetable garden. His days consisted of cataloging memorabilia from Chateau Thierry and the terrible campaign of the Argonne Forest in 1918, and tending the flags he had brought home from France.

Sometimes we played baseball or simply explored the creeks and cornfields beyond the town, and sometimes we tried to sell lemonade. We started a schoolboy newspaper, wrote the copy listening to the ball games at Wrigley Field, and discovered what our fathers already knew too well—it was hard to sell lemonade and schoolboy news to people without steady work.

It was usually still cool in the mornings, when I woke to the noisy robins in the big maple outside my corner bedroom, but the evenings were best. There was radio news. Supper was usually at seven o'clock, and there was still enough light to play with friends when we had finished, when my parents stood talking and washing the dishes.

The nights grew dark quickly with the cicadas at their vespers in the trees. Finally it was too dark for our games, and we gravitated to the streetlights, talking and watching the swift choreography of bats dancing among the moths and fireflies until our parents called us home.

But it is seldom the children's games and talk that I remember now, thinking back across the years. My thoughts often return to our fathers in those summer twilights—sitting in the porch-swing darkness, talking in worried whispers beyond their bedroom walls, or stoically watering their parched lawns.

The men stood in the cool evenings, their cigarettes glowing in the dark, hosing grass and gardens withered in the ice-wagon heat of August. Each hose was attached in a leaking necklace of spray at its spigot, a tiny fountain misting where frayed tubing was clumsily wrapped with electrical tape. The hissing spigots, and the angry guttural spoutings until nozzles were finally adjusted, mixed with the music of katydids and twilight crickets. The sounds were heard softly through the neighborhood, first in one yard and then another along our entire street. My father's hose was a delicate sibilance under my windows, watering the vegetables and rose trellises and peonies, its nozzle spraying a soft bell-like film that splattered gently in the night.

There was sorrow that summer, since we went to the burial services of a childhood playmate. It was my first funeral. It was terribly hot that afternoon, and a dry wind eddied through the cornfields. The cicadas made it almost impossible to hear the minister at the cemetery, or the brittle soil that rattled across the coffin.

Three weeks later, walking back from fishing bluegills in a stone railroad culvert, I took the shortcut through the cemetery. It is impossible to forget the feelings of dread when I passed the fresh grave, or the faint scent of the withered roses that surrounded its headstone.

Just before sleep, my childhood speculations about death mercifully drifted to the summer cottage in Wisconsin, where I fished off the dock for pumpkinseeds and perch. There were frequent daydreams of fishing throughout the summer. When such daydreams filled my waking hours, I sometimes walked to watch the perch fishermen on the jetties at Lake Michigan.

The lake was usually windy and rough. Its whitecaps rolled and broke across the dark water offshore, and my parents refused to let me fish on its breakwaters. It was probably wise, since angry waves often rose and fell sullenly across the jetties themselves. The perch fishermen were a puzzling clan. They seemed strangely like the hollow-eyed men who furtively rode the trains, and their lives had a curious rootlessness. Sometimes I followed them to their campsites along the railroad, studied the stratigraphy of their cook fires while they were fishing, and found their pitiful cache of bottles in the weeds.

The perch fishermen were often working men whose jobs were lost when the mills and factories closed, but a few were unmistakably cut from other cloth, exiled from the fabric of their earlier lives. Their frayed clothing betrayed them. The men emerged like moths in good weather, carrying their rudimentary tackle and brown paper bags. They gathered on the breakwaters like *Corixa* beetles at the margins of a spatterdock lagoon, seeking out sheltered places in the sun. The men tethered their corroding minnow pails in the gentle wash behind the jetties and set their lines while they dozed or drank raisin-grape muscatel.

Their methods were both sophisticated and simple. Shiners and sticklebacks and dace were fished on silkworm gut and elegant little Kirby hooks. Their lines were braided linen. When the lake grew particularly rough, the fishermen used pear sinkers or lead shot to keep their bait riding properly in the waves. They spread the shot with their penknives and set them with their teeth. Some also used such esoteric equipment as brass-plated music stands, each fitted with a small clip to hold the line and a tiny bell to signal a biting perch.

The fishermen ate some of their catch. Fish skeletons were often found at their campsites, perch averaging ten to twelve inches in those years, and I often saw them carrying sash-cord stringers into the railroad yards. The perch were mostly skillet fried, but some were mixed with carrots and new potatoes and onions stolen from our gardens, and boiled over their campfires. Sometimes I watched them chumming and seining baitfish in the creeks and lagoons, and they sold both perch and bait to get wine money.

Bad people, my mother warned me sternly. *There is always work for people who really want to work!*

Perhaps she was right about a few, but history also tells us she was mostly wrong, and there was one fisherman who made me doubt her judgment. It was too filled with certitude. The old man who puzzled me most was almost always fishing the jetties, sometimes ignoring the weather and poor sport, and I found him sitting there often.

The old man was disheveled and dirty, but his frayed clothing had obviously been expensive. His British shoes were cracking and parchment thin and scuffed, their heels lopsided and worn, and were laced with grocery twine. His suit bagged comically at its knees. It had once been a fashionable pinstripe with a matching vest, suitable in a bank or brokerage firm that had failed to weather the times and had probably locked its doors with a ragged line of frightened people in the streets.

Several buttons were missing. His soiled topcoat had a torn silk lining, and there was a hole worn in the crown of his homburg. Its crown had been pinched too often, putting it on too many times for too many years. The regimental stripe was badly frayed from too many knottings, its silks bearing the colors of a fine eastern university.

The fisherman was sleeping when I found him sitting on the break-water, in a sunny corner sheltered from the wind. Chill whitecaps covered the entire lake. The old man's topcoat was neatly folded and partially concealed a cheap bottle of wine. The expensive hat was tilted across his eyes, and his mouth hung slack, showing several gold crowns. He was snoring noisily. His brass music stand was tightly wedged into the rocks. The line clip and bell were mounted, but his line was not hooked into the clip.

Mister! I shook the old man gently as he snored. *Mister!*

He stirred grudgingly and mumbled something unintelligible from under his hat. His arms pulled his topcoat into a pillow, and the wine bottle clattered into the sun, rolling to his feet. He was snoring again.

Mister! I shook him harder.

Finally he lifted his homburg, blinking his eyes and squinting into the sun. *I was dreaming*, he said grumpily. *It was a good dream and you interrupted it.*

I'm sorry, Mister.

What did you wake me for?

Mister, I said, *your gear is rigged wrong.*

What's rigged wrong?

Your line's not hooked up. I said, *Your bell won't ring if a fish bites.*

It doesn't matter, he replied.

Why not? I asked.

I'm out of bait, the old man covered his eyes with his hat and sighed heavily, *and out of hooks too.*

No bait and no hooks?

You'll understand when you're older, he sniffled noisily, *but I don't want a fish to interfere with my fishing.*

It was a puzzling observation, since I was only seven years old that long-ago summer on the jetties, but it seems obvious that I had met my first Oriental philosopher.

The Night of
the Gytefisk

Skree-jah! the terns screamed. *Skree-jah*!

The midnight sun hung low on the northern horizon, strangely bright at two o'clock in the morning. The ghillies decided to stop for lunch. No one fished except in the twelve-hour twilight that passed for night. The boatmen skillfully worked our slender Karasjok riverboat ashore, and its graceful Viking-shaped prow grated on the gravelly shingle. Such boats have been used by river Lapps for centuries and are perfectly suited for salmon fishing.

It was quite cool for July, and a brisk wind riffled the great pool at Steinfossnakken. The ghillies built a fire on the beach, and I studied the midnight sun on the waterfalls that spill like Yosemite from the escarpment at Sautso, their plumes a thousand feet above the river. Cooking smells of bouillon and hot coffee eddied on the wind, and we sat on the mossy boulders, listening to the muted thunder of the Gabofoss Rapids a mile upstream.

Skree-jah! the terns cried.

The graceful birds were catching *Metretopis* flies that were hatching from the river, and I watched their hovering and fluttering before they dropped like ospreys to seize the mayflies with a rapier-swift strike of their beaks. Grayling worked softly to the hatching flies. The grayling ran between two and three pounds, but we were after bigger game. Three salmon lay gleaming in the boat, wedged crosswise to ballast its slender lapstrake

7

hull. The best had been taken at Mostajokka, bright with sea-lice and thirty-three pounds. The smallest went twenty-one, less than average for the river. When it had cartwheeled awkwardly on its first eighty-yard run, the ghillies had laughed contemptuously and called it a grilse.

The thick sandwiches and hot soup warmed our bodies, and we sipped coffee laced with cognac, watching the river. Two wiry Lapps went past in the mail boat, bound for the Sautso camp at Sirpinakken. The Lapps waved and we waved back. We were in no hurry, with three fine salmon in the boat, although we would fish another two hours before reaching the middle camp at Sandia.

It was my second night at Sandia, and in the morning, the mail boat was scheduled to ferry me upriver to Sautso. The Sandia camp had been built for the Duke of Roxburgh in 1873, its simple log frame almost unchanged in more than a century. There are two bedrooms with private baths. Its sitting room has a fireplace, and four trophy fish between forty and fifty pounds. The trophies were taken by the Duke and Duchess of Roxburgh, and the room has become something of a shrine. The fishing house at Sandia sits high above the river, with a grassy clearing that reaches down from its porch to the boat landing.

The river itself begins in the treeless snowmelt plateaus and escarpments of the Finnmarksvidda, two hundred miles above the polar circle in Norway. It lies eight hundred miles north of Oslo, at the latitude of Point Barrow in Alaska. The valley floor is thickly forested, while the Finnmarksvidda is a granite highland that bears the lakes and grinding scars of the Pleistocene glaciers that shaped most of northern Europe. These arctic barrens are a world of scattered taiga and immense tundra moors, pockmarked and scoured with dark peat-stained tarns. The river gathers in the lichens and pothole seepages below Kautokeino, the settlement that is considered the capital of Lapland. The district shelters a number of Lapp encampments, with their pyramidal log roofs and storehouses on stilts and turf cabins. The settlements are permanent sites where the Lapp herdsmen winter with their reindeer. They migrate with their herds each spring, carrying their skin-covered pole shelters on the treks. The Lapps are patient and hardy. There is both wry humor and sadness in their coppery faces, deeply wrinkled by the weather at such latitudes—it is a swiftly vanishing tribal way of life.

The river rises slowly in its lacework of glacial ponds and burns, mixing and gathering until it finally spills into a series of deeply scoured gorges, fifty miles north of Kautokeino. Its first twenty miles are lost in steep-walled faults and chasms, filled with the spilling of countless waterfalls. Salmon are thought to spawn in these headwaters, using the labyrinths of impassable cliffs and rapids. Below the little gorge at Sautso, the river changes completely.

Between Sautso and its estuary, the river is a symphony in three movements. Below the first tumbling chutes at Svartfossnakken and Bolvero, its moods are almost pastoral, sliding into the two-mile mirror of smooth water below the fishing-camp at Sirpinakken. Such *pianissimo* passages change swiftly at the Velliniva Narrows, eddying into the deep half-mile lake that ends in the Gabofoss Rapids. The river plunges wildly through truck-sized boulders there, dropping almost eighty feet in less than a quarter mile.

Downstream from the Gabofoss portage, the river gathers itself again. It spills into the swirling amphitheater at Steinfossnakken, and its famous Sandia beats begin. The Sandia beats are a stairsteps of boulder pockets and brief holding-lies, rather than salmon pools in the classic sense. These reaches of river spill into brief, connecting rapids before swelling and spreading into another pool. Sandia ends in the moss-walled gorge above Battagorski, where the river fights its way through cottage-sized boulders. The river has claimed many lives here, its angry music filled with brass and kettledrums and cymbals.

The forests become dense at Battagorski, thriving on the sheltered valley floor. There is a magnificent salmon pool there, deep and smooth flowing above the great boulders that hide in its Stygian currents. It is a favorite midnight-lunch pool. Twenty-five summers ago, I watched Sampson Field hook a heavy salmon at Battagorski. It took a Silver Durham with a strike that wrenched his two-handed rod into a tight circle. The fight began as a stubborn tug of war. The ghillies worked hard to hold the boat against the strong current, and Field leaned back into the fish. It was sullen and strong. It did not jump and it steadily forced the boat downstream. The oarsman was sculling hard, his face tightening into a grimace of pain, watching the mossy boulders slip past. The current hissed past their long-boat, its stern trailing a thickly eddying line of foam, and it drifted inexorably toward the rapids.

The big salmon was winning. It forced the boat into the swiftly gathering currents and bulled off into the chutes downstream. We still had not seen the fish and scrambled to follow in a second boat. The salmon was still taking line. It was exciting to follow down the rapids, watching the boatmen fight to stay alive and stay with the fish, and changing priorities in the wild chutes. The war lasted almost a mile, until it ended in a rocky backwater and the ghillie waited like a heron with the gaff.

Field pumped the fish close. The ghillie stared into the dark tea-colored currents and spume. Suddenly his shoulders tightened and he

struck, swinging the great fish aboard. It was dispatched with a priest while
Field rummaged through his tackle bag for the scale.

Twenty kilos! he said excitedly.

Forty-four pounds, I said and shook hands with him. *Congratulations!*

It was some fight, Field nodded.

Battagorski is a huge pool, its eddying depths brooding and mysterious, tracing fingerprints of foam. Its salmon lies mark the beginning of
the classic Jøraholmen beats. These lower pools include such famous water
as Gargia and Bradstraumen, where I watched the Duchess of Roxburgh
boat a forty-six pound cockfish in 1963. Bradstraumen is also the pool that
surrendered a forty-nine pound salmon to Charles Ritz in 1954, fishing as
a guest of Herbert Pulitzer, and Ritz wrote knowledgeably about the river
in his book *A Flyfisher's Life*. Ritz fished two seasons at Jøraholmen and its
sweeping salmon pools, where the river finally winds through a valley of
farmsteads and forests to the villages at its mouth. The estuary itself is
unimpressive. Its shallows spread across a series of gravelly channels a
hundred miles south of Hammarfest and its North Cape. Bossekop is the
village at its mouth, its cheerful houses a brightly painted collage of color
scattered along its hillsides. The fjord itself is more sprawling than scenic.
It was not always so peaceful, because its sheltered moorings held German
pocket battleships forty-five years ago, during the bitter convoy campaigns
between Reykjavik and Murmansk. The river is the finest salmon fishery
in the world.

It is the storied Alta.

The Alta has been fished since the Duke of Roxburgh first sailed his
yacht into its fjord in 1862 and discovered that the river teemed with big
salmon. Roxburgh shared its sport for many years with the Duke of Westminster, who was famous for both salmon fishing and his liaisons with
the French couturier, Coco Chanel. Roxburgh built the Sandia and Sautso
camps in Victorian times, but in earlier seasons his parties fished from
steam yachts moored off Bossekop. The beats were fished in rotation,
splitting the rods into four groups. Each party was patiently ferried and
poled to Sautso, where they camped and floated back to their luxurious
quarters on the yachts. When the first party reached the middle beats at
Sandia, the second was ferried past them to the upper river, and the third
group soon followed. These parties poled and portaged along the river
throughout July, fishing back from Sautso to the comfort and cuisine of
the yachts, stopping at rough camps along the river.

It was a time of great wealth and privilege.

Alta has been fished in our century by a parade of celebrated anglers.
The Duke of Windsor and his equerry, the Earl of Dudley, were regulars

on the river more than a half century ago. The Duke and Duchess of Westminster fished it steadily until his death in 1953, except during the Second World War, when German forces occupied Norway.

The Roxburgh family fished the river for more than a century, except for the war years, and the late Duke of Roxburgh had fished it every summer since childhood. The family seat was the Floors Castle at Kelso-on-Tweed, which commands the great salmon pool where the Teviot joins the Tweed. Roxburgh fished its spring runs from early childhood, sailed to fish the Alta for an entire month each summer, returned to shoot grouse in the highlands, and fished the autumn salmon run on the Tweed in Roxburghshire.

It's been wonderful, Roxburgh admitted over supper at Jøraholmen on the Alta. *It's been a life spent rather well, I think.*

Death duties and other changes in British life eventually ended British control of the river at midcentury. Anglers like Admiral Edward MacDonald, Herbert Pulitzer, Charles Ritz, Tony Pulitzer, Seward Johnson, Carter Nicholas, Anderson Fowler, Edward Litchfield, Robert Pabst, Ted Benzinger, Ralph Strauss, Roger Gaillard, R. R. Donnelly, Sampson Field, Peter Pleydell-Bouverie, Peter Kriendler, Robert Graham, Thomas Lenk, James Graham, Ogden Goelet, Cornelius Ryan, Robert Goelet, George Coe, Lee Wulff, General Lawrence Kuter, Charles Vaughan, General Thomas White, Walton Ferguson, Warrington Gillett, Sir Thomas Sopwith, Nathaniel Pryor Reed, Sir James Pearman, Earl Worsham, Philip Kingsland Crowe, and Admiral William Read—who successfully flew an NC-4 flying boat across the Atlantic before Lindbergh—became pilgrims to the Alta fishery over the past thirty-odd years.

Its fishing is unique. Twice in the past century, the river surrendered more than thirty fish to a solitary angler in a single night's sport. The Duke of Roxburgh took thirty-nine in 1860, and James Harewood killed twenty-six 16 years later. Major Courtney Trotter caught twenty-nine weighing 615 pounds in 1925. The following season, the Duke of Westminster boated thirty-three salmon weighing 792 pounds in twelve hours. Such catches averaged approximately twenty-three pounds. Sampson Field holds the modern record, with seventeen fish from the storied Gargia in a single night—all taken with flies and averaging just under thirty pounds, and the Alta surrendered eleven salmon weighing better than forty pounds that season.

Charles Ritz has written about such sport in *A Flyfisher's Life*, and I have heard him sing its praises from the little bar just off the rue Cambon, in his famous hotel at the Place Vendôme in Paris. *It is simply unique*! Ritz insisted excitedly with Gallic gestures and staccato speech. *There are no mountains except the Himalayas, no oceans to equal the Pacific, no fish like the Atlantic salmon—and there is only a single Alta!*

Ritz was right. Like a rock climber who has not tested his skills against Dhaulagiri or Annapurna in Nepal, and like the hunter who has not seen the Serengeti, the salmon fisherman dreams of fishing the Alta. Although I had boated a half-dozen fish over twenty pounds on three brief visits to Jøraholmen, I had been awestruck by a brace of cockfish weighed at its ghillie's hut that weighed over forty pounds in 1963. Those trophies had been taken by the Duchess of Roxburgh and Peter Pleydell-Bouverie, who had served with the British Western Desert Force, elite commando troops that gathered intelligence behind German lines in Africa. The Alta has the smell of history.

Valhalla! Ritz insisted over lunch with Robert Pabst and Ralph Strauss at the River Club in Manhattan. *It's the Valhalla of salmon fishing—and once you have tasted it, nothing in your life is the same!*

My first night at Sandia was something of an accident. I had been fishing the Reisa, and it had been so poor that we decided to leave three days early. When I arrived at Bossekop, there was a message telling me to come immediately to Sandia. Its party was a rod short, since one of the fishermen had become ill, and I had been asked to fish out his last day. It was not so much a day of fishing I had been offered, since the salmon I might catch belonged to the river owners and were worth considerable money. The night's fishing proved wonderful. Although I felt a little like a Danish trawler, I took ten salmon averaging twenty-three pounds with a ten-foot Garrison that had belonged to the late Paul Hyde Bonner.

The boatmen arrived after lunch to ferry me farther up the river to Sautso, and we motored upstream through famous pools like Ronga and Mostajokka to the foot of the boulder-strewn portage at Steinfossnakken. We changed boats there. The ghillies carried my duffle and baggage between them on a heavy pole, past the wild torrent of the Gabofoss rapids to the lip of the Gabofoss waterfall itself. I carried the tackle and a small duffle of fly-tying gear. Gabofoss thundered past in its chill explosions of spray, its roar blotting out all thought and other sounds, filling the morning with its icy breath. The rocky trail was traversed slowly, and finally we reached the Sautso stillwater.

We spooked a great fish lying off the upper boat mooring, and its wake disturbed the rocky shallows. The old boatman stood looking at the towering cliffs, squinting into a surprising midday sun.

Sautso is a paradise, he said.

Several terns circled and screamed, capturing salmon fry in the shallows. We rested before loading my baggage into the second Karasjok

• THE NIGHT OF THE GYTEFISK •

longboat and started upstream toward the Sautso camp, crossing the smooth flowage that lies between Sirpinakken and the Gabofoss Rapids.

The Sautso camp stands astride the small tributary at Sirpinakken, under the thousand-foot escarpments across the river. Its fishing house is simple and rough. It was also built by the Duke of Roxburgh just after our Civil War. There is a sitting room with log walls sheathed in wainscoting, two bedrooms with rudimentary baths, a small kitchen, and quarters for a cook and serving girl. The ghillies sleep in a Lapp turf cabin near the river. The sitting room wall had a pale pencil-tracing of the fifty-nine pound salmon caught by Admiral William Read at Steinfossnakken in 1962. It had been taken with a 3/0 hairwing Abbey dressed for the admiral at William Mills & Son. The salmon tracing was primitive and faint, in great danger of fading away. I reverently retraced its muscular outlines on the wainscoting with black fly-head lacquer, like the delicate brushwork in Japanese calligraphy.

The afternoon was still bright when the cook informed me that supper was scheduled for seven o'clock. Fishing would start at eight. Black curtains kept the light from the sleeping quarters, but I slept only fitfully, dreaming of giant salmon. Sleep proved difficult all week with the day's clock turned upside down. Supper is actually breakfast, since the fishing starts at eight and lasts until midnight, when the ghillies break to eat lunch, drink coffee, and plan tactics for the rest of the night. The midnight break is welcome. Depending on the night's sport, the fishing can last until five o'clock. Whisky is also welcome after an entire night on the river, and a wonderful cold buffet is always waiting too. Breakfast is transformed into an early-morning supper, and the anglers sleep through the morning until the late afternoon. Clocks are set for three o'clock, leaving a leisurely time to prepare tackle and dress flies. Cocktails come again at six, with dinner at seven o'clock, while the ghillies prepare their Karasjok longboats for another night's fishing.

The dice cup was brought out over coffee. We rolled dice, and my boat was awarded the upper river from Toppen, where the river finally escapes its impenetrable gorges, to the pretty pool called Dormenin. It is among the few wadable pools on the entire twenty-seven miles of river. We carried my tackle to the boat after supper, and I clambered eagerly aboard, trying hard to conceal a wildly swelling sense of excitement.

The motor caught quickly and we circled out. We traveled upstream swiftly, hand-lining the longboat around the Svartfossen Rapids and past the rocky chutes called Bolvero and Jagorski. Toppen lay still farther, flowing smooth and almost still between low cliffs that rise straight from the river. The ghillies put me ashore on the rocks and lined the boat farther upstream to the last mooring. They secured it there. The boatmen built a fire, brewed a pot of fresh coffee, and filled their pipes.

We pulled the boat over the fish, they explained in Norwegian. *We must give the salmon time to forget us.*

The coffee tastes good, I nodded.

Finally we doused the fire and started fishing. We clambered down through the boulders and pushed off, rowing furtively upstream. We waited quietly and I checked my tackle again. Leader knots are critical on fish averaging between twenty and thirty pounds. The pool seems quite deep, its secrets hidden in tea-colored depths. The ghillies had selected a big Orange Blossom, a silver-bodied hairwing dressed on a 3/0 double. Alta is a big-fly river. The current was swift and smooth against the opposite wall of rocks. It was a roll-casting place with another cliff of rhyolite behind us, and I had to loop the big fly only thirty-five feet to cover the fish. Their lie was tight against the cliffs. The boatman at the bow rowed patiently, measuring the current's speed and letting our boat drop about two feet downstream between each successive cast. It was obvious that he used outcroppings and other benchmarks to calibrate his work. It required great strength and discipline, mixed with intimate knowledge of the river. His skills were remarkable.

The fish were holding in a classic lie. I worked through ten casts against the cliffs, locking the line under my index finger with the rod-tip held low, pointing toward the fly as I patiently followed its swing. Our salmon tactics were basic.

But the Alta boatmen have evolved some footnotes over the century. The ghillie seated at the stern works a single scull to sweep the boat's stern with the fly-swing. The fisherman stands at the middle of the boat, bracing his legs against a cross-thwart shaped to cup his knees.

When the fly-swing came around toward the stern, I lifted the rod over the ghillie to extend its teasing half-circle, letting it work well behind the boat. The boat's stern followed smoothly, controlled perfectly by the ghillies, and deftly came back into line. My pickup was roughly parallel to the boat, and I false-cast once, changing direction into the final cast itself. It was beautiful fishing teamwork, rhythmic and metronome smooth, and I have not seen its equal elsewhere.

Before picking up each cast at the end of its fly-swing, I let it hang there swimming in the current a few seconds. Several six-inch pulls followed in a retrieve of about ten feet. Sometimes a fish following a swinging fly will take it when the fly-swing stops. Sometimes a fish will follow through its entire swing, circling under the fly when it stops, and take when its final retrieve is started back toward the boat. The ghillies believe the big Alta fish follow a fly surprising distances, and experience on the river confirms their judgment.

Salmon fishing is discipline and patience. Anglers must cover half-mile riffles with hundreds of patient, concentric fly-swings. The mind drifts and daydreams with the steady drumbeats of muffled oarlocks and casting, and I had started to think of other things when there was a big swirl.

Laks! said the ghillie softly.

The fish had rolled at the fly without taking, and the boatman stroked hard to hold our position, helping me repeat the cast.

He comes again! the ghillie hissed.

The entire current had bulged when my fly worked past, and there was literally a bow-wave showing, but there was still no weight. The fish had still not touched the big Orange Blossom.

Did you feel anything? he asked. *Did you feel him?*

No, I said.

Cast back to him again, he whispered.

Sometimes a fish can be teased into taking by changing the fly-swing. It was possible that my fly was swimming through too fast, perhaps faster than it seemed. The third cast dropped and settled into its swing, and I slowed the teasing rod-tip, stripping about six inches of line into its bellying quarter-circle. It slowed the fly just as it reached the salmon's lie, until it seemed to hang momentarily, and the fish was hooked.

There had been no warning, no bulging swirl when the fish rolled to follow. Its weight was surprising. The rod had simply snapped down as the bellying line sliced back against the current, and there was a tail splash when the fish bored deep and sounded.

Good fish! I thought wildly.

Several times it threatened to leave Toppen, working deep under the boat and bolting back into the shallows at its tail. Each time we patiently worked it back into the pool. It was almost thirty minutes before we finally controlled its strength. The boatman worked us back against the cliffs, between some sheltering rocks, and I pumped the salmon close. The ghillie in the stern reached with his gaff, deftly wrestling a thirty-pound henfish over the gunwale, and dispatched it. He washed the priest and laid our prize across the boat.

Det var findt! he grinned.

We rested the pool again, holding the longboat among the rocks while the boatmen smoked their pipes, and I ate a little Toblerone chocolate. We took a second twenty-pound fish farther down the pool, landing it easily after its first run threatened to reach the rapids.

Below the broken quarter-mile at Toppen lies the Jagotku Pool, the swift boulder-filled chute where the late Joe Brooks took a forty-pound cockfish, sharing a rod with his host, Warrington Gillett. The boatman walked our craft down the shallows while I waded and fished through Jagotku. It did not seem a likely holding-lie. But when the fly worked past a giant boulder, almost skittering across the choppy spume, a third salmon slashed out to seize it. The fish fought well but did not try to reach the chutes farther downstream, and it surrendered almost meekly. It weighed twenty-two pounds, and the boatmen came running to help just before I tailed the fish myself.

We laid the fish crosswise in the boat and decided to stop fishing. It was almost midnight, and it was getting overcast and cold, although it was still surprisingly bright. The fire on the rocky bar felt good. The boatman gathered more firewood while the ghillie laid out the midnight supper, making fresh coffee and heating a thick cauliflower soup. There were smoked reindeer and sausages and dill-cured salmon, and we finished with thick rose-hip jelly and cookies. It was quite cold when we doused the fire and launched the boat again.

Svartfossnakken was next, a sprawling rough-water pool where the river turned sharply toward the west, gathering itself to plunge into the Svartfossen Rapids. Their currents looked fierce, tumbling through a long sickle-shaped curve at the base of the mountain. Huge boulders and scour lines high above the river bore witness to the volume of its spring spates. The rapids are almost frightening downstream. The boatman held us expertly above the chute, back-rowing with seemingly effortless skill, while I covered the pool. We hooked another salmon after changing flies, and the boatman fought to hold our position, while I tried to force the fish. It proved foolish and the fly pulled out.

The ghillies quickly saw that I was not unhappy, and we laughed together, deciding to rest the pool. It was already almost two o'clock. We had three fish in the boat, and that was considered par on the Sautso water.

We hooked a second fish at Svartfossen almost immediately. It was a smaller fish, perhaps twelve pounds, and I suspect it was a stray from the Eiby tributary on the lower river. It fought well, but unlike the others, it lacked the weight to use the river and beat us. The fish was quickly boated.

Grilse, the ghillie teased wryly.

The boatmen lined their way down through the Svartfossen Rapids while I walked downstream through the boulders to Dormenin. It was our last salmon pool that night. Dormenin is the only real greased-line pool on the entire Sautso water, and I changed reels while the ghillies brought the boat downstream. Fishing from the shore, I moved a fish twice from a shallow lie where I once saw Ralph Strauss lose an immense salmon when the knot failed at the fly. I tried the fish for thirty minutes, but it did not show itself again. Another fish rolled farther downstream. The boatmen arrived, and I got aboard to fish the place it had porpoised, where the pool slides into Ovre Harstrommen. It was cold and starting to rain, and we fished through without moving another salmon. Dormenin was the bottom pool of our first night's beat.

It had been a good night, and we were ahead of the three-fish average at Sautso, although the Eiby stray was small. The boatmen were pleased with our night's work. It was four o'clock and still dark and overcast. When we reached the camp at the Jotkajavrre tributary, the ghillies were studying the sky. The smooth expanse of the Sautso was lost in misting rain.

Russian weather, the boatman said.

It will be stormy, the ghillie agreed, *but tomorrow we have Gabo and Velliniva to fish*.

Good pools? I asked.

Excellent pools, the ghillie said. *Velliniva is our favorite*.

It was raining hard before we finished eating and went to bed, and we fell asleep to its steady kettledrum pounding on the roof. I had stayed up long enough to dress several big Orange Blossoms. With the black curtains drawn tight, I fell asleep gratefully, listening to the rain.

It was late afternoon when the serving girl awakened us, but it was still gloomy and dark. The overcast had settled between the ragged escarpments until it hung like a shroud, a hundred feet above the river. Our breakfast omelets and goat cheese and brislings were ready, and the ghillies sat unhappily in the kitchen, staring at the barometer.

Russian weather, they muttered.

It did not feel like a fishing night. *The barometer dropped right through the glass last night*, I said. *It's really low*.

Ja, they agreed sourly.

It was raw and cold when we loaded the boats. We traveled slowly upstream to the gravel-bar island at Dormenin, rigged our tackle in the rain, and started at Ovre Harstrommen. The boatmen looked dour and sat staring at the current. The night grew more gloomy, its overcast settling until great scraps of mist drifted through the trees. It was raining harder now. We shouldered into our ponchos and slickers, watching the tea-colored river. It was rising slightly and looked murky. The ghillie had pointed happily to a freshly tied Orange Blossom, the pattern that had killed well the night before, and insisted on knotting it to the nylon himself.

Since the ghillies share in the salmon which are sold, they seldom trust knots tied by others. The boatman worked us patiently into position, his leather oar pads squeaking in the rain, while we fished the sixty-yard pool.

Nothing! I said quietly when we had fished it out. *Too gloomy for fishing.*

Perhaps it's a gytefisk night.

What's a gytefisk?

It's a really big cockfish, the ghillie explained. *Some nights we catch nothing, even on the Alta—but when we finally catch something on such nights, it is often a big gytefisk!*

And nothing else? I asked.

Ja, he nodded. *We get the gytefisk when others will not take the fly.*

Pray for a gytefisk night! I laughed.

Ja, they smiled.

We worked back to the top of the pool. The currents seemed like strong tea but were still clear enough for fishing. It seemed wise to change flies, selecting something like a bright yellow-hackled Torrish. It was obviously visible in the tea-colored shallows beside the boat, with its canary-bright throat and silvery body. The Torrish was dressed on a 2/0 double, and it had been given to me by Clare de Bergh over lunch with Charles Woodman in Oslo.

They had been fishing the Jøraholmen beats with Seward Johnson, Anderson Fowler, and Carter Nicholas two weeks before, and Clare de Bergh had outfished them all. She had boated thirty-seven salmon weighing 987 pounds, including a superb Alta cockfish of fifty-seven.

Every bloody one took the Torrish, she laughed and handed me the fly. *You take the last one and try it.*

I'll try to dress copies, I said.

The dressing was a pale hairwing version of the Torrish that some anglers call the Scalscraggie. It had looked enticing in the Wheatley box, set among a covey of somber patterns like the Ackroyd and Black Doctor and Black Dose. The ghillie seemed lukewarm about my choice, but he took the fly and clinched it to the leader, preening its feathers and wing. We fished it carefully through Ovre Harstrommen without moving a fish. It was raining harder when we reached Nedri Harstrommen. It is a strong hundred-yard reach of water named for its heavy flow. The ghillies worked us expertly into position, and I stripped off line to cover the pool.

Good place? I asked in Norwegian.

Ja, they shook their heads. *We do not hook many salmon at Harstrommen—but the fish we hook are usually big.*

Gytefisk pool, I suggested.

Perhaps, they said.

It was almost prophetic. The line worked out into the darkness and rain, dropping the pale Torrish sixty-five feet across the currents in the throat of the pool. I lowered the rod and let the fly settle deep before it worked into its bellying swing. There was a heavy pull and the line came sullenly taut.

Fouled on something, I said.

It's not possible, the ghillie shook his head. *There's nothing out there.*

Gytefisk? I suggested.

The ghillies said nothing and looked grim. The boatman worked steadily to hold our position, and we stared at the throbbing line. It still felt snagged. The rod strained into a sullen circle. Both men seemed unusually concerned at the tenor of the fight, and suddenly I understood. The stalemate ended when an immense sow-sized fish cartwheeled awkwardly in the rain, landing with a gargantuan splash.

My God! I gasped.

The reel surrendered line in a wild series of ratchety jerks. The boatmen seemed almost stunned. The fish burst halfway out again in a huge gout of spray, broaching like a whale just off our boat, and fell heavily again.

Thirty kilos! the ghillie hissed.

The boatman nodded, pulling hard at his oars. Both men began chattering excitedly, more agitated than I had seen them with fish between twenty and thirty pounds, and we settled into the grim business of fighting such a fish in heavy water with a single-handed rod. The salmon shook its head angrily, turned almost majestically downstream, and gathered speed. The current was a powerful flood. The fish was strong too, ignoring any rod pressure we could apply, and it took a full hundred yards of backing with almost ridiculous ease. Its run was a little frightening, and I sighed with relief when it finally stopped. The fish still seemed like a snag. The boatmen used the time to maneuver into better position, and we crossed the middle of Nedri Harstrommen into the quiet shallows, a little below the fish. I worried about changing our angle so radically but dismissed those doubts when the fish began head-shaking. It moved upstream and shook itself angrily again.

The fish finally stopped, and I had just started to pump-and-reel like a tarpon fisherman when it turned and slowly left the pool. Its strength was still awesome. There was nothing we could do except follow, and it had simply shouldered us aside, floundering into the rapids downstream.

How big did you think he was? I asked.

Thirty kilos, they said.

But thirty kilos is over sixty-five pounds! I calculated its metric weight wildly. *Sixty-five pounds!*

Storlaks, the ghillie agreed.

The backing was dwindling too fast. Both ghillies worked desperately to follow, rowing and poling to keep the line free of the rocks. It was a wild half-mile trip with little control over the salmon. It escaped the pool downstream too, forcing us through the pools called Battanielo and Banas, until it finally stopped in the throat of Sirpinakken.

More swift water lay below, but it was tumbling and broken, and we came chuting through with the fish still hooked. The fight went better in the lake-sized shallows above our camp. The fish had started to porpoise, circling the backwater stubbornly, fifty yards out. It had finally seemed to weaken. The steady rod pressure forced it closer and closer, muting its weakening runs. I forced it into the Jotkajavrre backwater until there was line on the reel again, its dark green covering the pale backing. The fish circled closer still, until the leader knot was visible just under the surface. It foundered weakly and we gasped.

Thirty kilos, the ghillies were awestruck.

The fish bolted again weakly and stopped. It stripped off fifty feet and faltered, and I turned it back toward the boat. The boatman stroked patiently to hold our position. The ghillie slipped his gaff free, moved soundlessly into position, and sat waiting. The fish bulged to the surface, rolling and working its gills. It was floundering and beaten. The giant salmon was almost in reach of the gaff when it worked its jaws yawning until the fly came free.

Damn! I groaned.

The fish drifted just beyond our reach and the ghillie threw his gaff angrily. The boatman slumped exhausted at his oars, like a beaten sculler at Henley, and stared helplessly as the fish gathered its strength. It shuddered and turned back into the river, pushing a giant bow-wave like a half-submerged submarine. Alta ghillies are used to huge salmon and are usually so taciturn and laconic that their anger startled me.

The big cockfish was gone.

Our riverkeeper explained later that the biggest salmon killed on the Alta was a sixty-pound cockfish, and the boatmen were convinced that our fish was bigger, perhaps a new record for the river. The existing record-fish was caught by the Earl of Dudley, who came to the river while serving as Royal Equerry to the late Duke of Windsor.

Lord Dudley became one of the wealthiest peers in the United Kingdom before his death in 1969. He died in Paris and had lived abroad for many years, dividing his time between country houses in France and the

Bahamas. The family seat was in Worcestershire at Dudley Castle, and its original title dates back to 1604. Dudley held extensive lands, but his family's great wealth lay primarily with its holdings of iron and coal, and the ancestor who developed a coal-fired iron smelter in the late seventeenth century. The earl was brusque and unpopular with the Alta ghillies, so intensely disliked that he is the only fisherman who was ever tipped into the river, belly flopping over the gunwale of his Karasjok boat at Kirkaplassen. The ghillies only smile when asked about Dudley's baptism, executed with a deft shift of balance.

The Earl of Dudley was a difficult man, the riverkeeper explained. *We have fished with dukes and kings and princes all our lives—and we know that equerries are little more than ghillies in the world of palaces.*

The great fish had easily won. It had carried the fight through several pools, down more than two miles of river, and it had fought an hour and forty minutes. My boatmen had wanted to share a new record fish and displace the Earl of Dudley. We sat quietly in the boat, trying to gather ourselves, knowing we had lost the salmon of a lifetime. It was starting to rain again, with mist hanging only fifty feet above the river. The night held little promise.

Let's quit, I suggested.

Nei, the ghillie shook his head stubbornly. *We hooked a gytefisk!*

Let's try another pool, I agreed unhappily.

Goddanieni lies just below the fishing camp, where a foamy current-tongue works two hundred yards along the rocky talus slopes under the Steinfjeldet escarpment. Its eddies slide past a boulder fall into a similar holding-lie called Goddanielo. We worked patiently through both pools, because they had been quite productive a few days earlier, but the only fish was a two-pound breakfast grayling. The Sautso flowage is filled with such fish, but even its flotillas of grayling were not dimpling to the swarming *Anisomera* midges that night. It was even more discouraging to find the grayling dour.

It's dead, I shook my head unhappily. *It's so dead the grayling are still sleeping too.*

We must fish the Velliniva, they said.

It's your favorite pool?

That's right, the ghillie smiled. *It's the best pool at Sautso—and we must fish it on such a gytefisk night.*

Let's go, I agreed.

Velliniva is not really a pool, but a beautiful hourglass narrows in the Sautso flowage. Ancient rock slides have pinched off the river, leaving immense puzzles of boulders in its bed. It was quite still and strangely quiet.

The Gabofoss waterfall was clearly audible downstream. The mist was clearing swiftly at midnight, and we built a cook fire in the trees. The river boils and slides past the truck-sized boulders at the throat of Velliniva, and there are broken ledges that stairstep across the current, forming its tail-shallows. It is the last taking-lie before the Gabofoss, at the bottom of the Sautso beats. Gabofoss is a place I have never liked. When a salmon is hooked there, the boatman cannot hold the boat by rowing, and the ghillie starts the outboard to tow the fish upstream. It seems foolhardy to row steadily only a single cast away from a chute that spells certain death.

Both ghillies often row simultaneously at Gabofoss, watching the chute warily to judge their remaining margin of safety. We finished our midnight supper among the trees above Velliniva, and the night grew almost soft and mild. It seemed better for fishing. But we fished both Velliniva and Gabofoss without moving a salmon and returned to rebuild our fire. We talked about giving up, sharing the last of our chocolate and coffee. The weather was getting better.

Let's fish through again, I said.

We always fish through Velliniva again, the ghillie smiled.

It was already two o'clock. The pool was a polished mirror, and it grew strangely warm. The overcast grew bright orange and gold, with a morning sky that seemed robin's-egg blue. Flies were hatching and the arctic terns were back. The pool had come to life swiftly.

Let's fish, they suggested.

Our fatigue was forgotten, and we drifted stealthily into position, dropping a quartering cast eighty feet across the current. The ghillie smiled and nodded, and I lifted the fly into another cast, mending line as it settled across the flow. The bellying fly-swing stopped on the third cast, and a huge swirl erupted just before I felt the salmon. There was a second bulge as the line tightened across the current, a swelling that carried swiftly down the pool, with a huge coppery flash in its depths.

It's not like the fish we lost, I babbled excitedly, *but it's big!*

Twenty kilos, they guessed.

The fight went well. Twice I felt the line rake huge boulders that had calved off from the cliffs into the narrows. The boatman rowed hard to work us away from the principal holding-lie in the throat of the pool, and the fish came slowly. It seemed well hooked. It jumped twice, and I thought I could see my fly firmly seated in its jaw. It came stubbornly when I pumped it away from the main currents, and it did not jump again. It spent its remaining strength running upstream against the line belly. The ghillie gaffed it cleanly in twenty minutes.

Twenty kilos, we confirmed.

It was a fine cockfish, just beginning to lose its polished sea armor to the first bronzish cast of spawning. It was sleek and hard muscled and strong. It weighed just under twenty kilos, pulling my Chatillon scale to the forty-three pound mark. The ghillie bled the fish and laid it across the thwarts. It seemed like a perfect climax to the night's fishing, but the ghillies stopped me when I started to strip down my tackle.

We have our gytefisk, I said.

Nei, they insisted. *We have hooked two gytefisker tonight—they are taking well, and we still have two hours left to fish!*

Fine, I laughed. *We'll fish.*

Fifty yards below the lie where the first salmon had taken the fly, the currents had quickened perceptibly above the sunken boulders. The boatman pulled hard at his oars and changed his rhythm to hold us against the flow. Both men watched the pool intently. It was obviously the primary taking-lie, and I began to drop my casts closer together. Terns were busily working the shallows. The morning grew brighter until the cliffs were visible through the mist, strangely pink and violet, and it was getting almost warm. The overcast was gone, and the mist was burning off quickly.

Norwegian weather, I thought.

We were six casts into the pool before I dropped the Torrish well across the current, rolling a big mend before the line could settle and sink. I pointed the rod at the fly and held its tip low, teasing it with a subtle rhythm. The currents bulged behind the fly, welling up until a fifteen-foot circle drifted and died in the current, but I felt no weight until the fish flashed full length in the throat of the pool. It rolled powerfully, well hooked and strong, showing its guillotine-sized tail. It flashed again in the depths of the pool, bolting suddenly upstream until the line ripped through the water. When it jumped, writhing almost six feet from the river and falling straight back on its tail, I was almost certain that I had seen the bright-canary hackles of the Torrish.

My God! I shouted. *It's huge!*

It was another big cockfish, cartwheeling full length across the pool, until it fell with a heavy splash. The terns screamed in protest. The big fish jumped again, porpoising and splashing belly-down like a giant marlin. It held briefly in the heaviest current, shook its head sullenly, and bolted a hundred yards upstream into the Sautso stillwater. We followed it grudgingly to recover line and control our playing angles on the fish. The backing was almost entirely on the reel, when the big salmon turned back with sudden, explosive power and bulldogged angrily past the boat. The big Saint Andrews rattled and growled and shrieked, surrendering line as the fish gathered speed, and the pale backing blurred out through the guides.

We turned desperately to follow. The fish was still running wildly, and I was worried that it might foul the line in the boulders and ledges deep in the belly of the pool. It threshed powerfully through the ledge-rock shallows, riding their chutes into the stillwater below Velliniva. The fish had traveled a rough chute so filled with broken ledges that we did not follow and circled farther out to use a quiet channel. We negotiated it safely, lucky the fish had not stopped to sound among the worst rocks, and our luck still held. The fish had circled back while we were coming through with the boat, and the slack line had settled deep, fouling in a shoal of rocks. But the fish had largely spent its strength before it fouled the line. It lay resting in quiet water, too tired to break off. The boatman rowed furtively toward the stones while the ghillie probed and freed my line with his boat pole.

It took several minutes to work the line completely free, but the fish was still hooked and held quietly on the bottom. With the line untangled from the stones, it stirred itself to make a few strong runs that stopped. It was possible to turn the fish now. It flashed and writhed. I pumped it back until it rolled weakly at the surface, and I worked it close, holding my breath.

The big gaff sliced home. The great fish came wrestling in over the gunwale, and when the priest had stilled its struggling, we saw that it was bigger than our first salmon at Velliniva. It weighed more than forty-six pounds, and I stood beside the boat when we came ashore, staring in disbelief.

Gytefisk natt, the ghillies teased.

Kanskje, I agreed happily. *Men dette gytefisk natt var stor findt—tusen takk for alt!*

Ingen årsak! they said.

But our night at Velliniva was still not over. The ghillies brewed the last of the coffee, and we shared the cookies and Toblerone chocolate and last pieces of sausage. It was almost an anticlimax when we hooked another fish in the throat of Velliniva, and it steeplechased wildly toward Gabofoss. Its fight was explosive and berserk, too wild to last, and the fish spent itself quickly. Its last run lasted less than forty yards, circling almost blindly behind a shoal of rocks. It fouled the line weakly too, but it failed to break off, and the ghillie easily worked it loose with the boat hook. It tried to bolt again, but I snubbed and forced it back, until it floundered and circled our boat.

It's a pretty good fish too, I said.

Changing rod angles, I fought the fish in quickly. It seemed smaller and I forced it. The fish was still surprisingly strong, but it drifted weakly to the surface and the ghillie gaffed it. It twisted and writhed angrily. The ghillie deftly parried its struggles and killed it with a single blow. It weighed just over thirty-nine pounds. The ghillie laid it beside the brace of cockfish in the boat, and we sat quietly.

The ghillie scissored the Torrish from my leader and studied it. It had lost both junglecock feathers. Its hairwing was ragged and thin, showing the scarlet and bright blue and yellow hairs still left. The bucktail fibers were brittle and bent, and the canary hackles were matted with slime. Its dark ostrich butt was missing. Two long spirals of loose tinsel wound free of its body, and the working thread was worn thin, showing the hook. The fly had done its work, although I had never made copies, and I stood looking at the big cockfish in the boat.

Gytefisk night! I thought happily.

The ghillie climbed high on a mossy boulder, held the withered brightly hackled Torrish above his head, and threw it out across the pool. *It belongs to the river now*, he said.

The Butler Pool

Ballinskelligs lay chill and pewter colored under its breakfast fog, and a fine rain misted across the dining-room windows at the Butler Arms. The fog hung in the improbable palm trees outside. Gulls circled and cried. My breakfast was eggs and smoked mackerel and English marmalade. It was fine weather for salmon fishing, and I had taken a beat on the Butler Pool.

It is a famous salmon fishery.

Beyond the hotel, the smooth water of Lough Currane reflected the wild mountains of Kerry. Their treeless barrens were lost in the overcast that shrouded the entire Irish coast, and there were nesting swans in the broken skerries off Church Island.

The ruins of a small tenth-century chapel stand there with several beehive cairn dwellings. Lough Currane is justly famous too, perhaps the finest sea-trout fishery in Ireland, and its headwaters also sustain surprising runs of salmon. Fishermen travel throughout Europe to cast their flies at Lough Currane, drifting its shoals and shallows. Three-fly rigs are common. Several spawning tributaries feed the lake, but it has a single outlet, a swift half-mile river called the Cummeragh. Its pretty Butler Pool lies just above the sea.

You've got the Butler? Noel Huggard is hotelier at the Butler Arms. *We've had some bright fish coming.*

It might fish well, I said.

The weather looks good, and the glass is steady enough, he agreed. *But sometimes salmon are moody.*

The overcast could help, I suggested.

It's possible, he said.

The ghillie was already waiting when I reached his whitewashed cottage and sat watching his cats playing on the stone walls. *Good morning, sir*! He pulled off his houndstooth cap. *'Tis a fine morning we'll be having.*

You think it should fish well?

Been a bit moody of late, the ghillie put his fishing bag and gaff in my car, *but our weather's been too bright—this weather should change our luck, and we've plenty of bright fish.*

How many have been caught? I asked.

Few salmon, sir, the old ghillie admitted unhappily. *Perhaps two or three salmon in the past three weeks—but we've some fine sea trout coming through into the lough these days.*

Pretty thin odds, I thought.

The Butler Pool and the sprawling white villa above the fish-trap weirs belong to John Mulcahy, a wealthy American who retired to his mother country and bought extensive holdings across Ireland. Mulcahy has built a surprisingly large hotel at Waterville, with a costly golf course in the cliffs above Ballinskelligs, but the fishermen in the village are in his debt since he closed fish-trap weirs first used by medieval monks. These ancient weirs have decimated the sea trout and salmon for centuries, but fish migrate freely through the pool today, destined for the drainages beyond Lough Currane.

Mulcahy was at Ashford Castle, his beautiful hotel in the headwaters of Lough Corrib, where the late John Ford filmed *The Quiet Man*. We were met outside the villa by the old grounds keeper, who walked with us to the Butler.

We've been expecting you, sir, he said.

How's the fishing? I asked.

Been a bit dour, the grounds keeper shook his head. *The pool is filled with fish, but they're not taking well.*

Bright fish?

Plenty of bright fish, sir, he nodded. *You'll see them rolling and flashing in the Butler.*

The overcast might help, I said.

It might, sir.

The ghillie studied the morning sky. *'Tis better with a touch of softness in the wind*, he said.

Softness? I puzzled.

'Tis a word we use for rain, the ghillie laughed. *Our Irish salmon take the fly better with a bit of rain in the wind.*

Salmon everywhere, I said.

The Butler lay just below the villa, and we walked down through the gardens to fish it. Two salmon flashed silver in its throat. Above the mossy rocks that line the tail of the pool, another fish rolled and jumped. The outlet plunges steeply through the boulders into Ballinskelligs, where an armada of gulls roosted silently in the rocks.

My fly books were filled with flies. *What should we try?*

Blue Charm, sir.

Another salmon flashed deep in the belly of the pool, catching the light on its polished flanks, rolling just above the bottom. *It's a fine old pattern*, I agreed happily. *Let's give it a try.*

'Tis a fine dressing, sir, the ghillie said. *Our salmon like it.*

The Butler Pool flows swiftly between its fish-trap weirs and its outlet, which spills directly into the salt. Its perimeter is lined with low masonrywork. The bottom consists of pale grapefruit-sized cobbles. The swift current spills under the bridge at the lake, flows through the monastery weirs, and shelves off suddenly into about eight feet of water. The throat of the pool is strong and full, until it widens like a bell jar into its waist. The main body of the Butler is slightly more than a full-line cast across, a little more than a hundred feet, including the leader and fly. The primary current tongues lie along the garden walk. Fish lying there are easily covered with relatively short casts, although they see more people walking there and are often shy. Such fish are better covered from the opposite bank, taking care to mend often in the slack shallows to get the proper flyswing. Two big stones lie deep in the lower reaches of the pool, their presence betrayed by their eddying currents. Both salmon and sea trout lie there. The tail of the pool narrows below the big stones, its currents swelling to spill swiftly through a rocky chute into the bay.

Its fish can lie anywhere, from the shelving throat to the rocky tail shallows, flowing glassy smooth into its final chute. Salmon and sea trout were clearly visible. Although we fished it through patiently, the little Blue Charm failed to move anything.

Well, I reeled up with a growing sense of disappointment, *it looks like our bit of softness didn't change their mood.*

It might still rain, the ghillie said quietly.

I've got more faith in the fishing log, I said. *Only three or four salmon the past few weeks make some pretty long odds.*

Aye, sir, he said. *We'll see.*

Our picnic hamper from the Butler Arms held smoked trout, several pieces of roast chicken, hard-boiled eggs, cheese, freshly baked bread, rolls, hot coffee, a large bottle of Perrier, and four dark bottles of Guinness. The small cooler held ice, stemmed wine glasses, strawberries, and a bottle of Macon Lugny. Noel Huggard clearly understands fishing.

We carried our lunch down to the gardens and sat on the fish-trap wall, watching a few salmon pass through into the lake upstream. The weather was still mixed. We sat eating in a fickle sun, while rain squalls hid the mountain spires of Great Skellig and Skellig Michael. The halfhearted sun bathed the village across the bay, but Ballinskelligs itself lay pewter-grey and still.

Where did the Butler get its name?

'Tis simple enough, sir, the ghillie replied. *Seven generations of Butlers worked this ground on the Ballinskelligs—and their farmhouse stood where the great house stands.*

Pretty barren country, I said.

Aye, sir, the ghillie agreed. *'Tis not the richest ground in Kerry, but the fish traps were bounty enough for centuries.*

I'd forgotten that.

When lunch was over, and we returned to fish the pool, several fish porpoised and flashed deep. It stirred our blood again, and my casting quickened its rhythms. Although we prospected through my fly book several times, using patterns selected by the ghillie, we took nothing.

Once I thought a salmon had shifted its holding-lie and had started to drift toward the fly, but the faint boil that disturbed the current was fleeting. *You're just dreaming*, I muttered. *Just dreaming.*

The pool fished through several times without surrendering a salmon, and I walked back slowly to the bench where the old ghillie sat waiting. My back and shoulders ached. It seemed hopeless to fish it through again, and I started to take down my tackle.

But, sir, the ghillie stopped me. *We've still our allotted time.*

We haven't moved a fish, I said.

Aye, sir, he agreed. *'Tis a hard thing to hope and hope again—but try fishing through again, sir.*

Well, it's only fifteen or twenty minutes.

'Tis time enough, he said.

It was getting almost dark and dour. The misting rain settled across the gardens, strangely mixed with a fitful sun, and scarcely wetting our faces. My fly books were filled with flies we had already fished, but I searched them again, hoping to find a change-of-pace pattern. I finally settled on a single-hook prawn fly dressed with startlingly bright orange hackles, a slender rusty-colored tail that extended well beyond the hook, and golden pheasant plumage layered over its body of scarlet seal's fur dubbing and oval tinsel.

Why not? I thought suddenly.

'Tis a bit gaudy, sir, the ghillie frowned, *but it might just work.*

Working quickly now, but covering the current tongues along the garden wall, I mended to let the line belly deep and gently teased the fly. When each cast had completed its swing, undulating and swaying against the masonrywork, it was time to take a step downstream and cast again. The technique covers the fish in series of concentric fly-swings. It is still classic salmon-fishing technique everywhere, its rituals codified a century ago in the books of Kelson and Pryce-Tannat and Scrope, but it still failed.

Without changing flies, I worked farther down the pool, concentrating on the dark, bulging slick behind the big stones. My third cast beyond the stones came bellying through lazily and stopped, and a strong pull telegraphed back into the slender rod.

Salmon! I was stunned.

You see, sir! the old ghillie came running awkwardly. *'Tis hope that catches fish—hope and a bit of the softness to change their moods!*

Perhaps, I admitted.

My reel protested until the fish went cartwheeling and threshing across the pool, sounded on the rocky bottom, and stopped there stubbornly. Twice it worked boldly upstream to the swift throat of the pool, holding effortlessly in the foaming chute itself, but surrendering some of its strength to both the current and my straining butter-yellow Leonard.

Our luck has changed, I thought happily.

Suddenly, the fish wheeled in a run that stripped line the entire length of the pool, and it exploded past the shallows. It had plunged into the outlet before I could gather myself and follow, its speed making pursuit impossible. It was difficult to follow across the tidal stones, with their slimy coating of phytoplankton and kelp. The line was fouled in the rocks.

Twice I saw the fish wallow and break water in the brackish shallows, where the river surged through the rocks and died. The ebbing seas rose and fell. Its struggling seemed to echo back through the line, but when I tried to clear my backing from the wave-polished stones, a squall broke along the coast. Cold rain lashed across the bay, pounding against my shoulders. The wind smelled sharply of the sea, and I knew the fish was gone. There was no softness in the bitter rain, and when I picked my way back carefully through the tidal rocks, the harsh laughter of the gulls rose above the keening of the wind.

The River of the Girdlebugs

It was early autumn in Montana, with the aspens bright yellow in the Bitterroots after the first hard frosts. The proprietor of the tiny general store was also the postmaster in his crossroads town. There were stray cattle on the highway.

While the postmaster stamped letters and sorted mail, sitting in his red undershirt and suspenders, his opinions on his neighbors and politics and everything else were delivered with the sharp rhythms of small arms fire. The winters in the Big Hole country are fierce, and the silences store up a harvest of talk. When the gossip ebbed into talk of fishing, the old postmaster interrupted a harsh monologue on marijuana and shaggy haircuts and beards, and told me about the Beaverhead.

Big Hole's too dry to float, the postmaster sold a rancher's wife a sheet of stamps, *but the Beaverhead is getting just right—they're storing water at Clark Canyon with the haying started.*

Good fishing? I asked.

Maybe the best brown-trout water in Montana, the postmaster was busily stacking cereal boxes and canned beets, *and when there's not too much water coming, it's pretty hot fishing.*

Can you wade it? I took a six-pack.

Olympia's pretty good beer. The old man took the beer money in his teeth and went outside to pump gas into a rancher's pickup.

Oly's okay, I said.

Beaverhead's mostly too deep to wade. I followed him dutifully back into his store. *It's so thick with willows you can't bank fish it.*

Keeps the fishing good, I nodded.

The river has a surprising history, since it was the route traveled by Lewis and Clark in their first attempt to cross the Continental Divide in 1805. Its headwaters lie in the Centennial Valley, draining west toward the Monida Pass through the Red Rocks country. These windswept spaces are rich in phosphates and sedimentary geology, making the Beaverhead itself unusually fertile with fly life. Its flats are often lush with undulating fountain moss and elodea. Such fertility and character make it a sanctuary for large brown trout, which hide in the weeds and the brushy willows along the banks.

Before you fish it, the postmaster suggested, *stop at Sneed's in Dillion and get some flies.*

What kind of flies? I asked.

Girdlebugs, he said.

Girdlebugs?

Don't you laugh at Girdlebugs, the old man filled his pipe. *Hottest fly on the Beaverhead.*

Why do they work? I asked.

Who cares? He shook his head. *Maybe they look like helgrammites or something.*

Who named it the Girdlebug?

Got its name in Dillon, the old man explained. *It was a pretty tough town in those days, between the train crews and cowboys.*

Dillon's still pretty tough, I said. *But what's that got to do with Girdlebugs?*

I'm getting to that.

Are we talking about girdles? I interrupted. *Honky-tonk girdles?*

That's right, he laughed.

Honky-tonks?

We always had plenty of saloons and honky-tonk girls and tenderloins in our heyday, he explained. *We still have a few.*

You telling me the rubber legs and feelers on the first Girdlebugs were pulled from a saloon girl's girdle? I protested.

That's what they tell me, he said.

I don't believe it.

Believe it! the postmaster cackled. *We still got some pretty tough towns in Montana.*

You've got that right, I agreed.

You get over to Dillon and fish, he said. *You see anybody sober over there, you write me a postcard or something.*

Don't you think that's a little strong?

What's a little strong?

Last time I drove through Dillon, I said jokingly, *I saw a little girl pushing her baby sister down the street in a carriage.*

She was sober? the postmaster asked.

Both sober, I said.

But both hung over, he cackled.

It was three weeks later when I arranged to float the Beaverhead with Philip Wright, an old fishing friend from Colorado who moved to Montana to run float trips in the Big Hole country. The aspens were already stripped in the high country, and the cottonwoods were changing too. There was fresh snow in the Bitterroots, and the empty hayfields were white with frost. It was still cold when we loaded Wright's van and secured its boat rigging. It would get hot after lunch.

Got some Girdlebugs? he asked.

We need them today?

It's the hot pattern on the Beaverhead, Wright pushed the van hard through the winding Big Hole Canyon. *We'll get some at Sneed's.*

Rubber legs and feelers? I joked.

They're pretty crude, he admitted. *Pretty much a big chenille-body nymph with white rubber legs and feelers.* We reached the interstate and rolled south into the empty buffalo-grass country toward Dillon.

How do you fish them? I asked.

Like a big stone-fly nymph, Wright explained, *but you tease them to work the rubber legs and feelers.*

We wrestled the boat into the river just below the Clark Canyon Dam, where Lewis and Clark cached supplies. The river split below a cribbing bridge. Wright maneuvered his boat expertly into the swift channel in the willows. Coming through the chute, we passed a deep back-eddy in the brush, and a two-pound brown struck hard.

Brushpile trout, I laughed.

You're getting the picture, Wright worked to help me fight the fish. *When they're spilling water at Clark Canyon, it kills the willows and alders along the banks, and the good fish hide in the brush.*

That's how they stay big, I said.

We took fish steadily that morning, fat browns averaging twelve to fifteen inches. The Beaverhead carried us swiftly past the interstate bridge into the open sagebrush hills that line the valley beyond. Rocky buttes and outcroppings lay in the distance in some places, looming directly above the river in others. Wright is famous for the best river lunches in Rocky Mountain country. His wicker hamper is a cornucopia of treasures. There was a thermos of perfectly chilled *gazpacho*, cheddar and Gruyère and goat cheese, Cornish hen sandwiches with bean sprouts and dill sauce, and chocolate mousse in delicate pastry *tuiles*. The cooler held juices and beer, and a chardonnay from a small Mayacamas vineyard.

Wright spread a checkered cloth under the scrubby apple trees below an abandoned ranch, and we settled back for a midday nap.

You run a happy ship! I sighed.

It was late afternoon when we launched the boat again. Shadows were already lengthening across the river, and a heavy strike surprised me in a dark-flowing run under the brush. The fish felt strong. It splashed and wallowed in the shadows, fighting sullenly until it was forced grudgingly into the sunlight. It worked deep along the boat, surprised us when it bolted suddenly under the gunwale, forcing the rod into the flow. Finally we reached a quiet backwater, and Wright circled in with a series of deft strokes, netting the trout after a brief fight.

That's some fish! I said happily.

Best brown we've had on the Beaverhead this summer, Wright said. *He'll probably weigh six or seven pounds.*

The Girdlebug strikes again!

Our float ended in a cool stand of cottonwoods, where a huge monolith of rhyolite stood towering above the river. We hauled the boat ashore and roped it to the camper. The twilight lingered in the empty basin beyond Dillon, and the lights of the town lay behind us. The basin reached fifty miles from the Pioneers to the rolling Tobacco Range, with the frontier capital at Virginia City in the mountains beyond, and the dark summit on the horizon was Sphinx Mountain.

Let's celebrate, Wright suggested.

Celebration sounds like a good idea, I agreed happily, *but it looks like a hellish long trip to find one around here.*

Grogan's, he said.

The saloon stands half-hidden in the cottonwoods along the Big Hole, a simple cow-country bar crowded with cowboys and their girlfriends, mixed with a few ranchers and truckers. There was an old Chesapeake Bay retriever behind the potbelly stove. The regulars were drinking beer with shots of whiskey.

What'll you guys have?

Beers, I said.

Well, Wright reached for his glass, *let's drink to a great day's fishing!*

Amen! I said happily.

We stayed for another round, and when I paid the check, two cowboys swiveled on the stools to watch. Both men were grinning. The bartender had laid almost a dozen quarters on the bar in change. The coins lay glittering and when I scooped them toward my fingers, several fell and rolled across the floor. The big Chesapeake got up lazily and collected six quarters in his jaws.

Mister, the cowboys were laughing. *You got yourself some trouble.*

Dog likes cash! somebody said.

Think he'll swallow it?

Reckon not, the cowboys ordered another pitcher of beer, *but it looks like that dog's got a mouthful of your wages.*

Sweet-talk him, mister!

Well, I shook my head, *I'm not quarreling with a Chesapeake over a few quarters.*

Makes sense, Wright said.

Mister, the cowboys sat watching the retriever, *you could follow him around a few days if he swallows them quarters.*

They'll turn up, the bartender grinned.

Thanks, I said drily.

The crowd sat there waiting, watching the big Chesapeake watching me. When I turned to leave, it waddled lazily over to the bar. Its huge paws spread against the polished mahogany, and the bartender stroked its head. The crowd sat perfectly still. The big retriever disgorged my quarters like a change machine. The crowd roared with laughter, and the bartender wryly collected my coins.

Christ! I shook my head.

I went outside and found Wright busily checking the boat rigging on the camper. *That's some dog in there*, he laughed. *How does it feel to get ripped off by a retriever?*

Silly, I said.

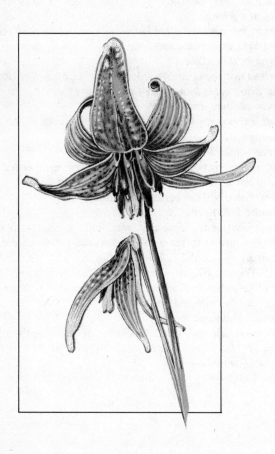

Fathers & Sons

My father went fishing on his birthday. There is nothing particularly un-usual about birthday fishing-parties in our family. He retired many years ago from his post in Washington and found he no longer liked the rigors of our northern winters. But he was also no particular lover of beaches and sun. College teaching years were still the things he loved and remem-bered best, and it did not surprise me when he married again and finally bought a small house in a college town in the South.

My mother died fifteen years ago. We took the body west after she died and buried her in a windy buffalo-grass cemetery in the ranching town where she was born. The prairie was startlingly green. Her father was a frontier rancher, and we buried her beside him.

The high plains are empty and treeless. It had been buffalo country, and their skulls and salty wallows were still found when her father first arrived from Virginia. There had been Arikara and Pawnee too, and my grandfather used to tell me about a wolf hunter who had mustered out of the cavalry at Dodge City. It is still hard country and it broke a lot of people. I had always thought that my mother hated it and had married an eastern college professor to escape its summer heat and almost constant wind, and winters so bitter they could wither your heart. But I was wrong about her feelings. She surprised us before she died, when she made me promise to bury her beside her father in the Smoky Hill country.

My father married again six years ago.

His wife is much younger, and there are faint echoes of my mother when her health was still good, except for the soft Georgia accent. His fishing birthday took place on the headwaters of the Chattahoochee, at a little town in the mountains above Atlanta. It was October and the hard-woods were brightly colored. It was impossible to get there, since I had two weeks' work in Santa Fe, but I called the hotel to cover the bill and arranged a bottle of Niersteiner at dinner. My father did not catch anything and complained that other fishermen were using worms and canned corn, but the weather was good. The birthday was a great success, and he made reservations for the following year.

My son was twenty-one that spring. My father came north to Washington before that birthday, since he still serves as a consultant appraising old manuscripts at the Folger Library. My son stopped off to fish with me at Fishing Creek, in the mountains of Pennsylvania, when he came home from college. The fishing there was good.

What should we organize on your birthday? I asked at lunch along the river. *Want a party?*

Is grandpa coming? he asked.

He's in Washington, I said. *He's coming.*

Let's just take him fishing.

His birthday weather was cool and clear. Puffy clouds sailboated past the Delaware Water Gap, on the kind of early summer morning that George Inness chose to paint landscapes there more than a century ago.

Shad fishermen were working the brushy channels of the Delaware beyond Phillipsburg. The trees along the river were lush and fully leaved, but high above the Water Gap, the trees on the Kittatinny Ridge were still only skeletal and budding. Shadblow was still blooming across the summits, in the broken talus slides exposed to the wind. It was warm enough along the Delaware itself for waterskiing, and a fast boat roared past, its skier trailing big roostertails of spray.

Beyond the Water Gap, the little Brodheads flowed low and clear. Every stone and pebble was clearly visible at Henryville. It was still and warm in late morning. Leafy sycamore patterns of light flickered lazily across the bottom.

Nothing hatching, I said. *Let's have lunch and fish it later—don't try to fish it blind.*

My father started rigging his tackle, and my son carried the wicker basket and cooler to the picnic table. The table stands under a giant oak. The sycamores line the opposite bank, shading the smooth currents that work past their pale roots. It is a lovely reach of water.

We sat under the trees and watched the river. There was little activity, except for a few soft rises deep under the sycamores. The picnic lunch was good, and the Trimbach was spicy and perfectly chilled.

Happy birthday! we said.

Several caddis flies fluttered over the riffles upstream, bouncing and hop-scotching to lay their eggs. The wind stirred faintly, rustling the leaves on the sycamores and smelling of rain. It was cooler and several fish started rising. Their splashes were quick and wild.

Grandpa, Erik stood up. *Let's get your tackle and try some fishing.*

Where will we fish? my father asked.

It's still pretty bright, I said. *Don't fish the pool yet—your best chance is fishing the broken pockets upstream.*

What fly? my father asked.

Something that floats high, I said. *Something grandpa can see.*

What's that? Erik interrupted.

I'd try a caddis, I replied. *Something that floats high in the pockets.*

Elk-Hair Caddis? Erik asked.

Exactly, I said.

But what body color? he smiled.

Olive.

My son finished rigging his grandfather's rod, seated the little Hardy reel, and strung the four-weight line. I nail-knotted a fresh leader to the line, and my son pirated a fresh hairwing caddis from my fishing vest.

Thanks! He rolled his eyes.

His grandfather was looking upstream from the picnic table, watching the sporadic rises. *It's pretty fast water*, he said, *and it's full of pretty big rocks—I'm not sure I can still wade it.*

Erik can help, I said.

Don't worry, grandpa, Erik said gently. *I'll wade along with you, and I won't let you fall.*

My father laced his worn English brogues, wading shoes bought at William Mills & Son before my son was born. They started upstream slowly together. My father gets cold easily, even with a heavy wool shirt and pants, but my son chose to wade wet with khaki shorts and the new felt-soled wading brogues he received last Christmas.

The shallows above the picnic table were rocky and swift. My father felt his way haltingly and turned to ask for a wading staff. We found him a stout shaft of driftwood in a high-water tangle of vines and wild roses. They worked slowly upstream past the withered birch stumps that had given the Birches Pool its name. It was the place where Edward Ringwood Hewitt first tried the dry-fly method, on a day recorded in his classic book *A Trout and Salmon Fisherman for Seventy-Five Years*. Hewitt had come when the Henryville water on the Brodheads was fished by famous pro-fessors, fishing writers, celebrities, politicians, and several presidents. My son helped his grandfather past the big birches, working carefully along the boulders that once shaped Hewitt's pool. It is storied fishing water. My son supported his grandfather by his wading belt and shoulders, while the old man probed cautiously among the stones with his staff.

It took them a long time to work out into casting position. *Erik*, my father was watching the pockets intently. *You hold my stick.*

I'll hold you too, grandpa.

My son pointed to a swift run under the alders, where the current bulged and paused above some big stones. It always held fish, and a trout had been working there sporadically. We waited until it rose again. My father saw it rise and tried a few casts. His fly dropped behind the fish, but when it fell perfectly, the trout drifted back until the fly dragged.

Try him again, Erik said.

Erik reached across to lift his rod into a loose mend, lengthening the drift, and the fish took the fly. My father did not see its soft rise. It did not come to the fly again, and they worked farther upstream. Another trout was rising sporadically thirty feet upstream in a pocket of tangled willow roots. It took several minutes of cautious probing in the rocks before they had a casting angle. My son looked back at me and I grinned. The fish took the fly after several casts, but my father missed it. They worked still farther upstream but failed to take a fish.

Can't fish anymore, my father waded out. *Guess I'm too old.*

But he had hooked a fish. It was lying against a big sycamore root just below the throat of the run. It had broken him off, taking a length of fresh nylon tippet.

Our fishing was excellent at twilight, but my father was cold and too tired to fish. He sat patiently at the picnic table, knowing he could not wade in the fading light, while we took several good trout. Driving back to Princeton, we talked about other seasons at Henryville.

Erik, my father said, *when you come back next week, try to get that fish against the root and get my fly back.*

I'll try, he promised.

We fished the water again two weeks later, with more egg-laying sedges and fish working steadily. My son strung his rod quickly and started upstream. *Where you going*? I asked. *Thinking about grandpa's fish?*

He stopped and grinned sheepishly.

Try him, I said.

My son worked upstream, taking some small fish in the swift run below the Birches Pool. The river had dropped a few inches in two weeks. Fish were not holding in the same lies. I slipped into the pool downstream and became preoccupied with a fish working softly under the big sycamores. My son shouted and his rod was dancing.

Same fish? I shouted.

Don't know, Erik yelled back, *wasn't lying in the same place.*

He played the fish cautiously, parried its bolting runs and splashing, and coaxed it patiently from the currents. It tried to reach the swift throat of the pool, and he stopped it. It started to circle weakly.

How big?

Fifteen or sixteen inches, he shouted. *Might be grandpa's fish!*

He coaxed the trout close and netted it deftly. When he stilled its threshing in the meshes he started to laugh.

What's so funny?

You're not going to believe it! he yelled downstream excitedly. *It's grandpa's fish—it's really grandpa's fish!*

You're joking! I said.

I'm not! he insisted. *It's his fish!*

He worked the matted fly free and quickly released the trout. The hook was already rusting out after only two weeks in the fish's jaw, and its fragile point had broken off.

We still have the fly.

We called and told my father that Erik had caught his fish, and he vowed to go fishing again on his birthday. He was sold on the hairwing caddis, and I tied him a dozen before he went back to fish the upper Chattahoochee. We heard from him that week, telling us that he had caught a trout on his birthday and had taken reservations next year.

My father is ninety-three.

The Rivers of Patagonia

In calling up images of the past, I find that the plains of Patagonia cross before my eyes.

—DARWIN

Darwin touched the barren Atlantic coasts of Patagonia aboard the HMS *Beagle* in 1834, when his ship's party went ashore at Carmen de Patagones. The settlement is still there at the silty mouth of the Rio Negro, in the coastal pampas five hundred miles south of Buenos Aires. Carmen de Patagones and the rust-colored Rio Colorado farther north were already known as benchmarks of the arid Argentine frontier called Patagonia.

Darwin joined an Argentine cavalry party briefly, was fascinated with these coastal pampas and their fierce Araucan tribes, and first encountered the ostrich still called Darwin's rhea. The HMS *Beagle* was a British hydrographic ship preparing charts of these remote coasts, and Darwin was serving as ship's naturalist on the expedition. The ship worked steadily south toward Cape Horn, and the treeless barrens at the Strait of Magellan, stopping to send a whaleboat party almost a hundred miles up the Rio Santa Cruz. When the party encountered an Araucan war party, it panicked and returned downstream to the *Beagle*. The ship's company finally wintered at the river's mouth, caulking and patiently refitting its hull, and

Darwin had been forced to retreat from Patagonia without sighting the Andes.

Robert Parker and Harry Longabaugh left the United States in 1902, when detectives working for the Union Pacific pressed them hard. Their colorful outlaw names were Butch Cassidy and the Sundance Kid. They sailed from New York to Buenos Aires with Etta Place, on a steamship called the *Soldier Prince*, and bought an *estancia* in Patagonia with money from a Great Northern train robbery in 1901.

It was in the southern province of Chubut, about thirty miles from Bolson, in a lush valley of poplars and wild roses called the Rio del Tigre. They built a log-framed house that still stands in the *coihue* and *maitenes* trees, and stayed there with Etta Place for several years. It is still wonderful country for livestock, and Cassidy described it perfectly in clandestine letters to his relatives and friends in Utah. When a tough Pinkerton operative tracked them successfully to Bolson, they sold their *estancia* on Lago Cholilla and left, trying again on a windy pampa at Rio Pico.

They did not die in Bolivia.

Patagonia was still a half-wild frontier reaching a thousand miles south, to the barren Strait of Magellan, until after the First World War. Its fierce tribes were never entirely defeated, and small bands simply retreated through the Andes into Chile. During these early years, an Argentine naturalist named Francisco Pertito Moreno had a dream of transplanting trout and salmon to the big swift-flowing rivers of Patagonia.

Before the Treaty of Versailles, the fish were already thriving in the headwaters of the Rio Negro. The bold experiment had worked. The fisheries had swiftly become some of the finest in the world after Moreno's first plantings of fry in 1904. Stories of wonderful sport began to reach Europe and the United States, stories that were quickly proved true. Some fishing writers seeking to explore exotic landscapes were fascinated, and others were wary of traveling across the entire world to the Argentine. The first to explore these waters was the British writer who lived in British Columbia, the famous Roderick Haig-Brown. His wonderful anthology *A River Never Sleeps* had just been published, and it was obvious that Chile and Argentina were a rich lode still waiting.

Haig-Brown was finally sent by Panagra Airways to fish these waters after the Second World War. His guides to the rivers of Patagonia were Gustavo Schwed, who lived in a charming cottage perched in the *coihue* trees above Lago Nahuel-Huapi, and the rancher Guy Dawson at San Martin de los Andes. Both men were wonderfully knowledgeable tutors about the region, men who also introduced me to the headwaters of the Rio Negro ten years later. Haig-Brown gathered his travels through these beautiful mountains and windswept foothills in his book *Fisherman's Winter*, but it was not my sole introduction to the Argentine.

Boyhood dreams are filled with thoughts of storied rivers draining remote parts of the world. Patagonia was always such a remote and romantic place. Its empty spaces and smooth Wyoming-like foothills rise steadily toward exotic rain forests in the towering Andes, where the rivers are born. The mountains are filled with huge fjordlike lakes and volcanoes, and are drained by river systems rich with trout and salmon.

It was boyhood reading that triggered my dreams of Patagonia. The epic book *The Voyage of the Beagle*, and its accounts of Darwin's work and observations, had intrigued me for years. Darwin described the flora and fauna of Patagonia with a growing sense of wonder and amazement. His writings evoke a world of hostile, totally uncharted coasts teeming with elephant seals and armies of penguins. The flat savannas of the coastal pampas were shared by half-wild livestock and ostriches, and primitive tribes dressed in *guanaco* skins. The bird life was overwhelming and totally unfamiliar. There were rain forests of curious beeches and flowering trees and bamboo, and there were wild tribes who lived half-naked in the remote mist-shrouded wastes that lay below the Strait of Magellan.

Patagonia was both wonderful and forbidding, a mysterious continent-sized wilderness reaching south toward Cape Horn from the blood-colored Rio Colorado, like our frontier before barbed wire.

It was the British writer W. H. Hudson whose books fascinated me too. His best-known book was *Green Mansions*, which was made into a film, but I liked his other titles better. Hudson had been born in the Argentine. His collected stories included *The Purple Land* and *Tales of the Gauchos*, and I could not resist the centaurlike horsemen with richly ornamental knives and the three-weight weapon called the *boleadoras*, although *bolas* are what we called them. Argentines quickly corrected that mistake thirty years ago, when I asked to purchase hide-covered *bolas* at a saddlemaker's shop in Buenos Aires.

It is not called the bolas, they said.

But that's what it's called, I protested.

We don't know where you gringos got the term bolas, they chided me gently, *but we call it boleadoras.*

But what're bolas? I asked stubbornly.

Bowling balls, they said.

Hudson wrote compellingly about the Argentine horsemen, solitary *ombu* trees that travelers believed were sacred on vast grass-covered plains, savage Araucan war parties attacking frontier settlements, and the unthinkable *estancias*—almost feudal empires of 150,000 to 1,500,000 acres that reached for miles and miles without fences, controlling entire regions and watersheds.

It was reading such stories, and the writings of others who followed, that led me toward this remote and romantic place at the bottom of the world. It was *Fisherman's Winter* that sealed my fate, and I made my first trip to Patagonia thirty years ago.

Patagonia proved itself everything I had imagined in those boyhood daydreams. It is better known these days. Outfitters are putting too many people on its easily accessible rivers, and their sport has eroded steadily. But on the big *estancias* and in its remote provinces, Patagonia remains a half-wild frontier. Its legendary sport still exists behind locked gates in many places.

The rivers of Patagonia hold the snowmelt of mountains and glaciers across the fifteen-hundred-mile face of the Andes, between the foothill vineyards at Mendoza and the treeless wind-seared barrens of Tierra del Fuego.

The most famous waters are scarcely secrets today and lie between Zapala and San Carlos de Bariloche. They hold both trout and landlocked salmon. The watersheds include the Neuquen and Limay, which join hundreds of miles east of the Andes to form the mighty Rio Negro. These are big rivers, too big for fly-fishing where they are still capable of sustaining trout. Their tributaries offer some of the finest trout fishing in the world, and I have returned again and again over the years. It is difficult to forget rivers like the Malleo, with its weedy flats like a Hampshire chalk stream in the shadow of Lanin, a towering Japanese-looking volcano. The Chimehuin is a brawling foothill river that rises full-blown from the outlet of Lago Hue-chulafquen and winds past Junin de los Andes through its half-desert valley toward the Collon-Cura. It is the most famous trout fishery in South America, and it is fished hard today. The Quilquihue is a small wading-sized river that drains Lago Lolog and winds from the cypress lagoon at its outlet to join the Chimehuin at Cerro de los Pinos. The Caleufu rises in the dense rain forests south of San Martin de los Andes, gathering its currents from icy alpine headwaters like the Falkner and Filo-Hua-Hum and Hermoso. The beautiful Traful is almost impossible to describe, with its towering megaliths of rhyolite and emerald pools, and landlocked salmon holding like pewter-colored ghosts in pools with colorful names—Campamento, Cipreses, Pool of Plenty, Grotto, and the boulder-filled Nellie Blood.

Such names alone exert their own alchemy, mixing English with poetic Spanish and the half-forgotten music of Araucan. The river names are poetic too. Their poetry seems perfect in this netherworld of active volcanoes and tree-fern forests and desert, saltpeter lakes filled with flamingos.

Their poetry has echoes across the entire world. The mountains behind Zapala hold Lago Quillen and the headwaters of the Alumine. The
high Mamuil Malal Pass into Chile lies between the Lanin volcano and the
shattered caldera that conceals Lago Tromen. Huaca Mamuil is a forest
lagoon that holds brook trout that could make a Maine guide tearful, and
there are still larger brook trout in the Tromen itself. There is a single
monkey puzzle tree below Tres Picos, a beautiful *Araucaria* that travelers
firmly believe is sacred, and where they have built a little shrine. I once
left a fully dressed Jock Scott embedded in its rough bark—wedged between its silver coins and corroded cartridges and other offerings.

The little Malleo is a particular favorite. It is not a river that holds
immense fish, although there are big browns in its lower reaches, but it
has great charm. It tumbles through a small postpile gorge just above San
Huberto, the sixteen-bed *hosteria* run by my old friends, Carlos and Carmen Nordahl-Olsen. Their family controls most of the river, since it flows
through their big *estancias*, Tres Picos and Santa Julia. The upper river
flows from a reedy outlet at Lago Tromen, but the principal source of its
fertility is a beautiful spring creek called Mamuil Malal, which bubbles up
through lava outcroppings and fissures under the volcano.

Farther south lies Junin de los Andes, an old cavalry post with a dusty
marketplace and transplanted monkey puzzle trees, and shuttered adobe
houses in the quiet poplar-lined streets. Its simple Hosteria Chimehuin
was a headquarters of great anglers for many years, including the famous
José de Anchorena and Prince Charles Radziwill. Its innkeeper was the
colorful José Julian, a short little Lebanese who was affectionately called
the Turk.

Why do they call him a Turk? I asked.

They don't know any better, Radziwill explained. *Argentines think all
Arabs are Turks.*

Julian once took me to his *refugio* in the headwaters of Lago Heu-
chulafquen, crossing the river on the old single-lane log bridge at the
Boca Chimehuin. We encountered the Chilean angler, the late Alfredo
Heusser, on the tiny Rio Blanco. Heusser had a twelve-pound brown caught
in the first pool above the big lake. Our antique 1936 Ford struggled as
we climbed steadily toward the Lanin Volcano, winding higher along the
gravelly corniche that crosses its steep shoulders, hundreds of feet above
the lake. The old Ford kept slipping out of gear, and I sighed and tried
not to look down. We kept running off the road into the brushy shoulders
when we met another vehicle, which I found strange until Julian explained
that we had no brakes and crossed himself. The old man kept repeating
something to himself in Spanish.

Que? I asked.

Poco pan! Julian grinned through dark *tinto*-stained teeth. *Mucho vino!*

Little bread, I nodded. *Much wine*.

The old innkeeper is gone now, and his sharp-tongued widow still operates the Hosteria Chimehuin, but something is missing today. Anchorena and Radziwill no longer stay there. Without them at supper, and the circle of famous anglers who traveled to join them, the simple room no longer has the smoky lamplight and steamy windows that I once compared to the stories of Dickens. Old friends are gone, and its moods have changed without their hearty laughter. I stopped off this past season for a *pisco* sour. It was late afternoon, with an April wind stripping the tall poplars outside, and I sat quietly studying the old photographs of friends on the walls. The simple room was gently filled with ghosts.

The Chimehuin flows past the cavalry post, and the big grove of poplars where *estancias* from the entire Neuquen province camp each summer for a festival of livestock and horsemanship. The river loops past the village, where the girls from the bordello that serves the soldiers wash their bedclothes in the pool jokingly called Las Senoritas. It was difficult to fish through the Senoritas on those fall mornings, concentrating on a series of concentric fly-swings, with the dark-eyed girls watching and washing laundry and giggling.

The river completely circles the entire village, winding between the treeless hills past the *carneceria* at its outskirts, with its fresh hides and sheepskins hung drying in the wind.

Below the little Currhue, and the fine reach of river below its stony mouth, the river lies tight against the smooth wind-polished hills. Las Manzanas lies several miles downstream where the river finally winds back to the road. The scrubby apple trees that gave the pool its name were planted by frontier Jesuit missionaries. Downstream on the Thompson *estancia* lies the beautiful cliff pool called La Marquesa, and the last time I fished it, I lost an immense brown in its wild throat. The pool is an old favorite over many years, and I first fished it with Guy Dawson in 1959.

There are beautiful pools below the Quilquihue on the big Larminat *estancia* called Cerro de los Pinos. The river forces through the lava chutes and cliffs that I have always called Las Barrancas and slides into the famous Black Bridge Pool. The river winds and braids into a series of serpentine channels here, and I have sometimes had excellent dry-fly sport on this water. Still farther downstream, the Chimehuin lies under the high bluffs we called Los Morros, in a series of quarter-mile pools that continue into the huge Putkammer *estancia*, where the river finally joins the bigger Alumine.

The Chimehuin is big water and justly famous.

The Quilquihue is a beautiful little river in itself, and it can surrender remarkably big fish at times. It is filled with spawning rainbows in the spring, fish that linger in the river well after Christmas. It receives a healthy spawning run of browns at Easter, fish that arrive from the Chimehuin like the rainbows and can also drop back into the river from Lago Lolog. Twenty-four years ago, I took a fish of almost ten pounds in the first pool above the Chimehuin, and when I told an Argentine friend about the fish, he simply nodded.

The Quilquihue is a little river, he said. *But it can hold sorpresas.*

It does hold surprises, I thought.

High in its headwaters, in the steep-walled Lago Lolog, the big browns and rainbows cruise the shallow outlet long before daylight. Its skillet-shaped *boca* is empty once the sun is on the water. The chill depths of the upper lake are fed by the Auquinco, and its shelving *boca* is prowled by trophy brook trout in the fall. Many years ago, I stood there awestruck while a giant, humpbacked brook trout ambushed transparent *Galaxias* at its drop-off.

The Chimehuin and Alumine join to form the Collon Cura, a labyrinth of winding channels in a huge, brushy basin with chalk-colored bluffs. It was seldom fished twenty years ago, and we never saw other anglers in those years. Few campsites held signs of recent use. It was Guy Dawson who first took me to the Collon Cura, climbing into the arid hills at Estancia Chimehuin, with volcanic ash billowing behind us for miles. We caught more than a hundred two-pound rainbows and a few larger browns, in spite of the bright weather. Because it has several access points, the Collon Cura is heavily fished today, with float trips sponsored by American travel organizations. Such floating has led to bitter feelings among the landowners, with often unwitting fishermen carried through their *estancias* by guides who are not really welcome there. The Collon Cura is among the few that can sustain such pressure, since the floating is still nothing like the flotillas that crowd the Madison and Big Horn in Montana, but there are more parties each season.

The little Quemquemtreu has its wellspring in the Chapelco Grande, a range of foothill mountains just east of San Martin de los Andes. It has a big spawning run of rainbows from the Collon Cura each spring. Estancia Quemquemtreu and Estancia Enfantado, on the beautiful Caleufu farther south, were once part of a gargantuan cattle ranch called Gente Grande. It dwarfed the King Ranch in Texas and included the entire Collon Cura Valley, with its Pampa de Alicura highlands. Estancia Caleufu lies at its heart, in a valley of big treeless mountains, and belongs to my old friend, Douglas Reid.

The Caleufu itself rises in the *coihue* and bamboo forests of the high Andes, in watersheds above Lago Hermoso and Lago Falkner. Falkner is named for a Jesuit priest who was among the first to explore the region. Lago Hermoso holds big brook trout too, and its outlet is the Rio Hermoso. Its five *bocas* spill into Lago Meliquina, which Haig-Brown enjoyed for its landlocked salmon. Meliquina is headquarters for José Navas, the famous Argentine fly maker, and his mottled-olive Matona is among the best patterns in Patagonia. Haig-Brown describes his visit in *Fisherman's Winter*:

> José thought we would find some fishing in the Aquarium, a shallow part of the lake where big rainbows cruise among the weedbeds and rise to a surface fly, or off the mouths of the Hermoso, at the head of the lake, where there was a chance of Sebagoes and brook trout as well as rainbows.

Below the lake, the beautiful little Meliquina winds through a country of lava cliffs and cypresses, with cataracts that tumble wildly through cooling fissures and faults in the valley floor.

Its sister watershed starts with the half-mile flowage called Rio Falkner, which connects Lago Falkner and Lago Villarino. The Rio Villarino is a relatively short river too, flowing into a third lake called Filo-Hua-Hum. Its outlet is the swift little Filo-Hua-Hum, and it joins the Meliquina at the Casa de las Piedras to form the Rio Caleufu, at the foot of the winding switchbacks that rise toward the Cordoba Pass.

The Caleufu spills eastward through its rocky *barrancas* into a stag-shooting property held by André de Ganay, the Count of Chateaubriand. *I always thought a chateaubriand was a steak big enough for two*, a fishing friend observed wryly along the Caleufu, *and I find out it's some guy from Paris*! The river flows fifty miles through big country, like the Musselshell and Judith country in Montana, joining the Collon Cura thirty miles above the Rio Limay.

Paso Cordoba hides a river of startling beauty, the salmon-filled Rio Traful, which flows between Lago Traful and the Limay at Confluencia. The mountains here are volcanic and strange, with batholiths and basalt chimneys eroded by centuries of *pampero* winds. The first Spanish cavalry parties to explore the region were awestruck and called it the Valle Encantado—the Enchanted Valley.

The Traful has a mixed character. It rises in the swelling outlet of the lake, under the rocky outcroppings and cliffs that look like images from a delicate Oriental scroll. Above the sweeping cliff-face pool called Piedra Roja, the river is a series of silken, chalk-stream reaches over pale gravel and undulating weeds. The pools hold browns and surprisingly good rainbows, but it is the landlocked salmon transplanted from Maine in 1904 that make the beautiful Traful so fascinating. Traful is a primitive Araucan name whose meaning is blurred. Some scholars believe it describes blue shadows and mists, and others think it talks of the spirit world. The river still fishes quite well. Too many salmon were killed over the years, in both the river and its lake, and the fishery steadily declined. Several years ago, the Argentine National Park Service asked me to help them obtain a fresh shipment of fertile eggs from Maine. The shipment was disappointingly small, cut at the last moment by short-sighted decisions in Augusta, with an aircraft of the Argentine Fuerza Aerea waiting to fly its precious cargo south. The salmon ova were hatched and reared to smolting size at the Traful. The silvery smolts were taken to the center of forty-mile Lago Traful and released. The owners of the river finally decided to restrict the fishery to flies only and stopped killing its salmon. It cost them some well-known friends in Argentine fishing circles. But between the transfusion of fresh genetic stocks and the privately enforced regulations, the river has steadily improved. I fished it three days last April and caught and released nine landlocks in the upper pools at Arroyo Verde. The fish averaged smaller than the Traful salmon ran in 1959, but they are back in surprising numbers. I took silvery landlocks at Campamento, Cipreses, Nellie Blood, Horseshoe, and the Federico—which produced a ten-pound henfish my last morning on the river.

The Traful is still breathtaking. Its upper pools have such clarity that it is difficult to judge their depth. It demands the wisdom of cautious wading. The river has haunted me since I first saw it thirty-odd years ago, interrupting both daydreams and sleep, and I have even dreamed about pools that do not actually exist. I still think about our first campsite on the river just above the Minero, in a copse of cypresses and copper beeches, where springheads trickled from the cliffs in the ferns and flowers.

Above the forty-mile lake itself, looping through impenetrable forests of *colihue* and copper beeches and *notro* trees, is the lovely Pichi Traful. It holds few fish in its still currents above the lake, looping parallel to the cypresses along the beach to slide quietly into its *boca* shallows, tight against the mountain. Salmon feed on spawning baitfish in these shallows in the spring, mixed with a few rainbow kelts. Big brook trout forage off Pichi Traful in the autumn, fat char averaging three to four pounds. Pichi Traful has rich echoes for me, because I took my first trout in Patagonia there. We were camped in a meadow about two miles above the lake, and I fished upstream at twilight. I found nothing until I reached a deep pool densely hung with *colihue* and cypresses and tree ferns. Parakeets and *bandurrias* chattered noisily. I took two six-pound rainbows there on a big Donnelly Variant and brought one back to our camp for supper.

Guy Dawson had a bottle of Argentine *blanco* chilling in the shallows, and we toasted the big rainbow with the wine. *Congratulations,* he said. *It's a fine beginning!*

Two hours south from Arroyo Verde lies San Carlos de Bariloche, a village standing bright and tile-roofed across Lago Nahuel-Huapi, under Tronador and Cerro Catedral. The road follows the Rio Limay from Confluencia, through the Valle Encantado and its beautiful Anfiteatro to the Boca Limay. The first time I saw Nahuel-Huapi, it was only weeks after Villarica had erupted in Chile, and its ashfalls had changed the colors of the huge lake. It was bright and cool, with big, puffy clouds sailboating briskly across a February sky. The lake was lightly riffled, dappled with palette-knife patterns of pewter and lavender cloud-shadows, and the sun was bright on the icefields of Tronador.

Lago Nahuel-Huapi is huge. It sprawls some eighty miles from the arid pampas at its outlet to jungle-looking inlets like Boca Pireco and Boca Totoral, deep in the rain forests of the Andes. It has a half-dozen fjordlike arms. Its Araucan name means Islands of Tigers, and cougars are still plentiful in Patagonia. Its timbered islands are dark against a shimmering landscape of water, sometimes turquoise-and-silvery with sunlight, and sometimes somber and stormy with line squalls gathering at the alpine threshold of Chile.

San Carlos de Bariloche is like a village in the Tyrol, with its winter skiing and casinos and its scenic corniche above the lake. It has lovely hotels like the Tres Reyes and Casco and the steep-roofed Tunquelen, with its flower gardens and big trees and views of the Andes. It has wonderful restaurants too—the Munich and Vizcacha, and the beautiful Grisu—to watch the moonlight dancing on the lake long after midnight, drinking *pisco* sours and listening to soft Brazilian music.

Nahuel-Huapi lacks major rivers feeding its thousand-foot depths. Its fjords are incredibly beautiful, with steep mountains rising directly from the water and icy torrents spilling everywhere. There is the narrow-walled Lagoon of Sadness, its name taken from the tears of its countless waterfalls. The outlet of the Rio Nirihuau has surrendered a lot of big rainbows over the years, with the better-known Boca Limay itself, such as the shiny fourteen-pound *plateada* I took there years ago with Laddie Buchanan. There are big sow-fat brook trout off icy tributaries: the Millequeo, Colorado, Huemul, Bonito, Pireco, and Totoral. Such fish travel in big schools in the fall, squaretails the size of oarblades, with opal mottlings and bright ruby spots and orange fins. Many years ago, I watched a local Correntoso angler beach a brook trout better than ten pounds at the Boca Totoral, and I once lost a similar fish at the mouth of the Rio del Machete.

Boca Correntoso is the largest tributary feeding Nahuel-Huapi. It has a charming country hotel high above the lake, where the half-mile Rio Correntoso spills its swift currents a hundred yards into the lake. It is famous in the spring for its big trout and landlocked salmon, and a launch trolling out of Correntoso boated an immense thirty-six pound salmon in 1936. The fish has never been listed in the record books, although it easily surpassed the twenty-two pound world record from Maine.

Why isn't it listed? I asked.

Who knows? Guy Dawson replied. *We caught several bigger fish on the Traful too.*

But why isn't it listed?

You people keep the records, Dawson said drily. *Maybe you think our scales don't work—maybe you think we can't count.*

I'm ashamed, I said.

There are happy memories of the little Hotel Correntoso, fishing under its dining-room windows after dinner and exploring the outlets at Lago Correntoso and Ruca Malen. The hotel staff was filled with fishermen, including its headwaiter and wine steward, who had served as a cabin boy aboard the *Graf Spee* at Montevideo.

Thirty years ago, the roads south from Bariloche were still completely unpaved, and sometimes hung precariously from log-cribbing high above lakes such as Lago Mascardi and the Laguna de las Moscas. It is a district called the Cinco Lagos, a world of volcanoes and glacier-green lakes and thick forests of mossy-trunked *alerces* and *coihue* trees. There are good brook trout in the Lago Gutierrez, and in the other lakes in the Manso watershed, although I have never taken one over three pounds. Lago Mascardi is the largest of these lakes, a pale aquamarine lake fed directly by the melting glaciers on Cerro Tronador. It is also fed by the outlet of Lago Guillermo, which spills steeply into Mascardi from the south. There is a simple *hosteria* perched high above the lake there, and I took a good rainbow in the Boca Guillermo under its dining room, after a boisterous lunch with the late Sascha Turbanoff. Turbanoff had served in the horse guards of Czar Nicholas, and his father had been the royal ambassador to Japan. The colorful Russian had been visiting his father in Japan, on leave from his regiment at Saint Petersburg, when his entire family was butchered in 1917.

Captain Turbanoff left Japan after his father's death, eventually finding his way to Argentina, and took work teaching horsemanship and dressage.

• A RIVER FOR CHRISTMAS •

The old Russian was past eighty when I last saw him, but he still fished the rivers with great vigor and was newly married to a beautiful Argentine less than a third his age.

It's an old question, I sat drinking Stolichnaya with him that afternoon, *but how do you explain your health and longevity?*

Young wives! he laughed.

Boca Mascardi is the smooth tule-lined outlet of the sprawling U-shaped lake itself. It is a beautiful flowage, weedy and startlingly tourmaline blue, and it sometimes hides a crocodile-sized trout or salmon that has been lurking like a muskellunge, hovering over the fountain moss.

It is the Rio Manso there, tumbling beyond the outlet into thickets of bamboo and *maitenes*, and forests hung with sepulchral garlands of parasite mosses. Parakeets and black ibises and *checau* birds are everywhere, calling shrilly and darting swiftly through the trees. The narrow road clings to the cliffs on timber cribbing-frames, several hundred feet above the Laguna de las Moscas. Three other lakes are visible from the shoulder of the mountain. The Hosteria de los Cinco Lagos stands on Lago Hess and keeps boats on these waters. It is often too hot to fish them in summer, but they all hold good fish. My favorite is the Laguna de las Moscas, which is more a weedy flowage thickly lined with fountain mosses and reeds. It has wonderful populations of damselflies and big sedges, and it has excellent twilight rises of fish. The Manso road ends at the Cascadas de los Alerces, a thundering waterfall that seems to disappear into its mist-filled gorge. Spray drifts thickly, wetting the trees like a steadily drizzling rain. The falls are an explosion, falling into a terrible pit, cold and frightening and filled with mist. There were torrent ducks in the swift ledge-rock shallows just above the falls.

Correntinos! Turbanoff pointed.

The Manso vanishes into its precipitous gorge for almost fifty miles, collecting the discharges of the Rio Villegas and Lago Martin. It flows through Lago Steffen, winding back sharply toward the Pacific. The Rio Foyel joins the Manso under the icefields of the Cerro Ventisquero, and the river circles north again, tumbling through the Paso Cochamo into Chile.

Rio Puelo also rises in the Argentine and flows to the Pacific. Lago Puelo lies near Bolson, below the beautiful *estancia* called Las Golondrinas. It is wonderfully fertile country. The dusty roads lie under trees thickly laced together, like the naves of leafy cathedrals, lined with wild roses and blackberries. Rivers like the Ternero, Azul, Repollo, Epuyen, Turbio, and Alerzal all gather in the Bolson basin, spilling into Lago Puelo and draining north through the *cordillera* to join the Manso. These river drainages are puzzling, their broken geometry a senseless labyrinth of rift geology and faults. Both the Puelo and Manso flow into Lago Taguatagua, its brackish outlet reversing its currents with the changing tides. It is a superb fishery, with big sea-run browns running from the Pacific, and stray landlocked salmon from Argentina.

The country farther south is drained by the Futaleufu, where the narrow-gauge railroad finally ends at Esquel. Forty years ago, the few American mining engineers and cartographers who had seen Esquel considered it their badge of membership on the Argentine frontier.

When you've seen Esquel, it was said by a retired American engineer who had worked a gold lode in the Rio Tecka country, *you're an old hand in Patagonia*.

I've seen Esquel, I thought.

Paul Theroux wrote about traveling to Esquel on the narrow-gauge railway in his book *The Old Patagonian Express*. There are many disturbing things about the book. Theroux described a primitive settlement in a treeless frontier, evoking images of antique trackage dying in empty pampas-grass plains. Esquel was perhaps that primitive fifty years ago, but when Theroux wrote *The Old Patagonian Express*, it had become a major military center with glass-walled office buildings, large hotels, a warehouse-sized bowling alley, ski lifts, discotheques, and daily jet service.

Theroux tells us that he found treeless foothills and pampas when his antique train finally clattered into Esquel, and that its Patagonian landscapes were his ultimate yardsticks of emptiness.

The empty pampas-grass country he sought lies farther south less than a hundred miles, and there are echoes of the old Patagonia in the thousand miles between Esquel and Cape Horn. Jaramillo is a huge *estancia* about sixty miles south of Esquel, and I spent an entire day exploring its holdings in a battered Land Rover. Its treeless world was overwhelming, with lush pampas grass and rough jeep tracks reaching toward the horizon. Great herds of cattle were foraging in the grassy *arroyos*, and there were chalky saltpeter lakes that were alive with waterfowl and flamingos. We drove for miles and miles without seeing fences, and in the distance we could see the mountains.

It's like our frontier, I wrestled the vehicle across a mud sculpture of deep ruts. *It's like Wyoming before barbed wire—with nothing but the Oregon Trail scarring its prairies*.

Esquel is the fulcrum of a remarkable region. Like the Manso country south of Bariloche, its Futalaufquen drainages are inexplicable networks of chasms and seismic rifts and fault geology. The Rio del Tigre valley was the refuge chosen by Butch Cassidy at the government land offices in Buenos Aires in 1902, and the outlaw leader lived there several years with

Etta Place and Harry Longabaugh, in the most colorful *ménage à trois* in American frontier history.

The Rio Cholillo and Rio Blanco join to form the Futaleufu, finally spilling into Lago Rivadavia. It is sometimes called the Rivadavia below the lake, and in the strange mottled-bark forests above Lago Futalaufquen, it is called the Rio Arrayanes. Lago Menendez lies still farther to the west, its glacial tributaries gathering in the icefields along the spine of the Cerro Chato. The Laguna Cisnes lies above Lago Menendez, and its outlet is a famous fishery—the classic Boca del Cisnes.

Lago Futalaufquen is shaped like a wine goblet, spilling its contents between the Situacion mountains and the Cordon de los Piramides. There are Disney-colored *arrayanes* forests at Futalaufquen too, and its outlet is called the Rio Frey. It winds twenty miles to Lago Situacion, joined from the west by a chill watershed draining the high *cordillera* itself, and big mountains such as Castillo and Cuerno. Situacion has since been enlarged by building a power project, threatening the only landlocked salmon fishery that might equal the storied Rio Traful. The principal tributaries of the reservoir are curiously named. It seems the Spanish explorers who chose the poetic names throughout Patagonia lost contact with their muses at Lago Situacion.

The cartographers simply gave numbers to a watery chain of lakes and rivers there, unwittingly adding the Rio Numero Uno, and Numero Dos and Numero Tres in turn, to the roster of the world's fisheries.

Esquel lies in the foothills toward the east. The Rio Percy and Rio Esquel flow south to join the Futaleufu at Trevelin, a settlement of Welsh farmers and ranchers who have occupied its fertile river bottoms for more than a century. The Futaleufu is sometimes called the Rio Grande there, because it flows in immense, thigh-deep flats that offer excellent dry-fly fishing. The Futaleufu penetrates the *cordillera* of the Andes under the glaciers of Cerro Conico, its rift valley reversing sharply north again into Lago Yelcho in Chile. Yelcho is like a Norwegian fjord, a narrow thirty-mile lake trapped in a fault valley between the Cordon Plomo and the icefields of the Cerro de los Cuatro Piramides. Its outlet is the storied Rio Yelcho.

Thirty miles east of Esquel is the beautiful Arroyo Pescado, a British chalk stream rising inexplicably from an arid, brushy basin in Patagonia. It is a spring creek to dream about, winding like a tule-lined slough to join the sluggish Rio Tecka. It is filled with big selective trout. The Cerro Tecka is a foothill plateau where the Welsh settlers mined gold, but the Pescado wells up from its volcanic crevices and fissures, a mythic pot of gold alive with rainbows.

The family that owns the stream is Welsh, having sailed to Argentina aboard the *Mimosa* in 1865, along with 120 other Welsh families. They were ardent Welsh nationalists and religious dissenters. One wealthy member of the family operated a large general store that also served as a bank. When Cassidy and Sundance were displaced by the Pinkerton investigator from the Rio del Tigre country, they took Welsh names and tried to start again a hundred miles below Esquel. Later they robbed the Welsh trading post, and its owner was shot and killed. Many people in the region believe his killer was the colorful Cassidy himself, but Cassidy usually left such things to others in his Wild Bunch, and history tells us that the Welshman was probably a victim of the Sundance Kid.

The country where the Wild Bunch tried ranching again lies above Rio Pico, and their stone house is still there, with long views of the surrounding countryside. Many years ago, when I was exploring for trophy brook trout, I traveled there several times. It was rumors of big brook trout that first took me to Rio Pico.

I sought out a fisherman who owned a store there. *Tiene fontinalis aqui?* I asked after several glasses of whisky.

Si como no, senor! he said. *Pero quien quiere fontinalis?*

I left his bar much later, puzzled by a fisherman who did not share my fascination with big brook trout and had asked why anyone would bother fishing for them. It was several years before I fully understood such things. Patagonia teemed with big fish, and among the fishermen who trolled its big Andean lakes, a trout was simply a trout. *With rainbows and browns of fifteen pounds quite common*, I thought, *why bother with brookies that seldom go ten?*

Argentine biologists taking ova and sperm from trapped fish tell me they have weighed, stripped, and released brook trout that went between seven and eight kilos. Such fish weighed fifteen to seventeen pounds, and I believe their stories. They are men of probity and seldom fish themselves. Lago General Paz lies in both Argentina and Chile, a sprawling fifty-mile lake shaped roughly like a thresher shark, its tail forming a sickle-shaped fjord reaching deep into the mountains of Chile. It has brook trout of gargantuan size. There are four alpine lakes called the Lagunas de los Enganos, just north of Lago General Paz. The Enganos are connected and drain into a shallow emerald-green inlet on its roadless north shore, and its fertile shoals and drop-offs often hold schools of big brook trout. The mouths of its Chilean tributaries are excellent too, but it is wild country and difficult to reach them. Several years ago, I spent a week hunting big squaretails there in the late fall, fishing the *bocas* at Lago General Paz and exploring the marshy creek mouths of the Laguna de los Niños. The fish are clearly there, but the weather that trip was fickle and bitter cold, and

I was finally driven out by an April blizzard that threatened to trap me in a doorless log-walled *puesto* on the Rio Corcovado.

The Corcovado winds almost two hundred miles, flowing counterclockwise toward the stormy Pacific. It is called the Carrenleufu on some maps, and most Chilean charts call it the Rio Palena. It drains Lago General Paz, collecting the icy waters of the Huemul, Frio, Gredo, and Hielo before flowing through the Andes into Chile. There are deep gorges and steep-walled valleys beyond the border, and its principal Chilean tributaries are short mountain rivers like the Claro and Tranquilo and Salto, and the poetically named Rio de los Torrentos—the River of the Torrents.

Seven hundred miles still lie between the Corcovado country and the wintry seas off the Cabo de los Hornos, where the continent finally ends. It is still an empty frontier. There have been many times in these latitudes when I wished that Paul Theroux had traveled farther south, perhaps sleeping in the little jail at Calafate because the village offered no other place to stay.

There was a smoky saloon at Rio Pico when I stopped off in the rain to buy several bottles of wine. It was filled with *gauchos* and construction workers and truck drivers. Trucks and horses stood waiting outside. The room was noisy and crowded, but when I came inside and brushed the rain from my coat, everyone stopped talking and stared. There were no women. The men watched silently as I crossed the room to the bar. It was a little frightening. The talk stopped until I ordered a drink and asked about the wine, and the room erupted again with laughter and talk.

Theroux should stop here, I thought drily. *It's the real thing—but he'll need to bring his own railroad!*

There are more big brook trout in the Rio Senguerr and the Rio Belgrano, although most are average in Argentine terms, running only two to three pounds. The Andes are filled with snowfields and glaciers farther south, in the wilderness country below Lago Buenos Aires, a region holding the largest temperate-zone glaciers on earth. The Rio Pico and the Rio del Cisnes both rise in Argentina, in the south of Provincia Chubut, and flow to the Pacific above Puerto Aisen. Many Argentine rivers born in the snowfields below forty-five degrees latitude fail to reach the Atlantic and simply dessicate and die in the dry barrens east of the Andes—the little Rio Perdido is typical, and it vanishes in volcanic sinks west of Trelew.

Antoine de Saint-Exupéry wrote about the early mail pilots who flew the coasts of Patagonia sixty years ago. Books such as *Night Flight* and *Southern Mail* drew extensively on his experiences in Patagonia, when pilots risked their lives in fragile fabric-covered biplanes to carry the mails between Bahia Blanca and Rio Gallegos.

• THE RIVERS OF PATAGONIA •

The glaciers of Patagonia are fifty miles across at Lago San Martin, in icefields surrounding the Cerro O'Higgins, reaching south almost three hundred miles into the mountains of the Torres del Paine. Their icy drainages are too milky with glacial sediments to sustain much aquatic life, but there are some fish. Lago Buenos Aires is a chalky blue, filled with icebergs and draining to the Pacific. Its fish are restricted to spawning in a single clear-water tributary, the little-known Rio Ibañez in Chile, where immense brown trout gather in March and April. Lago San Martin is a labyrinth of ice-choked mountain fjords that also drains to the west, although the topography suggests that the lake once drained toward the Atlantic, through the marshy *cañadones* at Tres Lagos and Mata Amarilla. The arid basins between the Meseta del Viento and Corpen Aike were unmistakably carved by ice-dam floods discharged from Lago San Martin across thousands and thousands of years. Ice dams eventually built such extensive terminal moraines that the lake overflowed and cut a fresh outlet through a narrow fault that became the Rio Pascua.

Lago Cardiel lies forty miles east of Lago San Martin. Its present altitude is approximately fifteen hundred feet. Cardiel is shrinking imperceptibly in its empty, treeless basin and has no outlet today. It is fed by the Rio Cardiel and a series of spring-fed tributaries that trickle from the Meseta de la Muerte. The empty amphitheater of its basin is tormented by almost ceaseless *pamperos*, winds that gather fiercely between the glaciers and the foothill barrens, but the lake is famous for big brown trout that migrate to spawn in the Rio Cardiel.

Lago Viedma is another big Andean lake draining the icefields of the Cordillera Fronteriza. Its outlet in Pleistocene times probably shared the intermittent Rio Chalia with Lago San Martin. Its primordial outlet eventually filled in until the rising water forced a new channel to Lago Argentino, thirty miles farther south. Glacial tributaries like the Viedma, Huemules, and the Rio de las Vueltas keep the lake milky blue. The Vueltas drains a rift valley that undoubtedly joined San Martin and Viedma thousands of years ago. The spawning grounds for Lago· Viedma are found in clear tributaries such as the Rio Condor and the Rio Guanaco, and the Rio de los Cangrejos. The Rio Leona empties from Lago Viedma, flowing south into Lago Argentino at Estancia Leona.

Lago Argentino has several glacial tongues calving directly into its icy *brazos*, and these steep-walled arms are so choked with icebergs that the big lake seems like Glacier Bay in Alaska. It is still possible to observe the glacial cycles at its outlet that changed the Yellowstone and Big Hole watersheds of Montana in Pleistocene times. Lago Argentino is steadily collecting great shards of ice across its outlet, damming the lake until it rises between fifty and a hundred feet. Pressure builds steadily too, until the lake finally breaches its glacial dam. It has happened several times in the past century, sometimes so explosively that tidal surges of flood water have violently scoured the valley of the Santa Cruz downstream. Its battlements and sandstone cliffs and *barrancas* all bear witness to the violent erosion of such flooding. Their surges have deeply carved the yoke-shaped estuary of the Santa Cruz, where Darwin wintered with the HMS *Beagle* and its crew. There is a huge meat-packing plant at the site today.

Like the Santa Cruz, the Rio Coig and Rio Gallegos have late-summer runs of silvery sea-run brown trout. The Coig and Gallegos are the last watersheds to reach the Atlantic above the Cabo de las Virgenes, and the barren windswept coasts of the Estrecho de Magallanes—the stormy Strait of Magellan.

The sea trout were brought to these latitudes by homesick Scottish *estancieros* after the First World War, and the fish have steadily distributed themselves throughout coastal streams across southern Argentina and Chile. Both the Coig and Gallegos lack glaciers in their headwaters. Neither is subject to the fierce ice-dam spates that plague the Santa Cruz, but both rise farther south in arid, silty basins that trigger frequent turbidity. The principal headwater tributary of the Gallegos is called the Rio Turbio. The foothills also have extensive coal deposits, and there are active mines along the Chilean frontier. Several tributaries of the Gallegos rise in Chile, and its sea trout ascend their drainages to cross the frontier and spawn.

Fifteen years ago, I was working in the region with a Chilean team involved in planning a new national park at Torres del Paine. It is among the most beautiful places in the world. The Torres themselves lie about 250 miles above Punta Arenas, the Chilean provincial capital of Magallanes, and I found myself sitting at the bar in its comfortable Hotel Cabo de los Hornos. There was an American missile frigate passing slowly offshore, and the bartender was mixing a *pisco* sour.

What brings you to Punta Arenas? he shook it briskly.

We're working at Torres del Paine, I said, *but I've been farther south than Punta Arenas on other trips.*

Where's that? he poured my drink.

Ushuaia, I replied.

Tierra del Fuego, he nodded. *What took you to Ushuaia?*

Trout fishing, I explained, *and I've been fascinated with coming to Patagonia since boyhood.*

Why Patagonia? he asked.

Patagonia, I sipped the *pisco* sour slowly. *Darwin and Magellan and Martin Fierro.*

You've seen Junin de los Andes?

Years ago, I said.

Well, you've done it, he smiled.

Done what?

Patagonia, he said. *That's the Strait of Magellan out there—Patagonia stops right where you're sitting, at my bar.*

The great *llanuras* of Patagonia reach south almost two thousand miles from the Rio Colorado to the Strait of Magellan, and south of Lago Argentino its immense pampas-grass prairies reach across the border into Chile. The Llanuras del Cazador lie east of Lago Sarmiento, and the famous Cerro Castillo sheep station lies in the grassy foothill bottoms of the Rio de las Chinas. The fertile Llanuras de Diana lie farther south at Puerto Natales, their gentle hills reaching east toward Rio Gallegos. It has been livestock country for more than a century, its giant stations producing remarkable tonnages of wool and meat for shipment to Europe. Stations such as Springhill and San Gregorio and Viamonte control millions of acres—and the famous Maria Behety has a unique hangar-sized shearing barn capable of sheltering ten thousand sheep.

The brushy hillock country above the Strait of Magellan is drained by a score of rivers holding brown trout. Sea trout ascend many of these drainages in late February and March. Few people fish them, except when the trout are visibly spawning in the fall. These plateau rivers include the Rubens and Penitente, which rise in the brushy uplands of the Cordillera Chilena, and smaller streams like the Chico and Zurdo farther east.

The Torres del Paine are among the most spectacular peaks in the Andes. They explode abruptly from the Llanuras del Paine, a flat pale-grass bottom lying less than two hundred feet above the sea. The Torres are a series of thrusting turrets and spires that measure slightly less than seven thousand feet, rising more dramatically than our Tetons.

It was overcast and cloudy the morning we started toward the Torres del Paine from Punta Arenas, with rain squalls pushing through the narrow fjords and passages from the Pacific. The country was surprisingly flat. There were brushy *mogotes* and hillock ridges and pothole lakes. Just beyond the town, we picked up three hitchhikers wearing bright yellow rain slickers, a young boy and two girls who spoke workable English. We were startled to find they were from Tel Aviv.

Where are you going?

Puerto Natales, they said, *and then to Rio Gallegos in Argentina.*

What brought you so far from home?

Butch Cassidy, the boy said.

Our American bank robber? I asked.

That's right.

I think he worked a little farther north, I smiled.

We know about Bolson and the Rio del Tigre years and Rio Pico, he shook his head. *But they were in Punta Arenas too.*

What for? I asked.

They robbed the bank in Rio Gallegos, he said, *and they were hiding out when they came across the border into Chile.*

Punta Arenas also has banks, I interrupted.

It's possible, he admitted, *but they told everyone they intended to build a big meat-packing plant at Punta Arenas—and the governor of Magallanes entertained them lavishly.*

That's pretty funny, I said.

We left them at the border crossing east of Puerto Natales. It had finally stopped raining. There were whitecaps offshore when we had lunch at the small hotel, and a freighter sailed past slowly, working to its moorings at the big *frigorifico* just north of town. It was raining again when we left, and the big mountains were still hidden in storms and squalls.

Our route led north into the brushy foothills of the Sierra Dolores, skirting close along the Argentine border for sixty-odd miles. We stopped for fuel at Tres Pasos. Strong winds buffeted the empty bottoms at Cerro Castillo, rattling small stones against the windshield. The road beyond its famous *estancia* grew steadily worse. Big stones had been pushed to the surface by frost heaves and cattle trucks. It was badly rutted and dried in a series of wet-season rights of way. Torrents of rain concealed the mountains at Lago del Toro. Other squalls hung in the treeless headwaters of the Rio Baguales and the Rio de las Vizcachas. We forded the Rio de las Chinas several times, gearing down and churning across its rocky shallows, until we started climbing toward Laguna Amarga. It was filled with ducks and geese. The Torres themselves were quite close, but it was still too stormy to see them.

The road climbed more steeply now. We circled into the grassy foothills above Lago Sarmiento until the switchbacks grew narrow, filled with big stones and outcroppings. There were a few trees struggling to grow in the sheltered hollows, scrubby copper beeches and snags. The gearbox groaned and whined until we reached the summit of a barren ridge. Angry clouds rolled just overhead, but there was strangely no wind. The stillness was eerily unsettling. It was getting dark when the switchbacks dropped down and started climbing again, and we startled a small flock of *guanacos* in a grassy draw. The driver suddenly stopped dead in the road.

My God! I gasped.

We sat there helplessly in the truck. The clouds stopped rolling over-head and grew patchy, and we were struck dumb at the immense mountain wall that filled the entire twilight sky. Cirques and broken spires seemed to explode from immense buttresses and pilasters of dark chocolate talus and pale scree. Talk seemed silly under such huge turrets. It seemed foolish to chatter noisily in this empty windswept cathedral. Such mountains were almost frightening, towering five-thousand-foot battlements and pinnacles like a petrified apparition, patchy with snowfields and gloomy scraps of cloud.

We were both completely stunned. I was filled with a puzzling mixture of joy and wild melancholy and awe. These huge turrets were both beautiful and threatening. It was like finding the sheer rock-face walls of Yosemite, rising like a theater backdrop from the prairies of western Kansas.

Torres del Paine! I thought.

The Torres are spectacular, and the entire Cordillera del Paine rises abruptly from its sculptured foothills, still surrounded by big icefields and milky lakes and rivers. Glaciers were the catalysts that shaped their volcanic world, carving a series of brackish fjords and big foothill lakes. The icefields have ebbed and slowed steadily for thousands and thousands of years, finally shrinking back into the Ventisquero Dickson. The silty chalk-colored rivers that drain them rise in iceberg lakes, almost completely circling the entire Cordillera del Paine, spilling down miles of travertine ledges. The towers themselves are huge, their broken turrets are layered in dark but-terscotch and chocolate, steeply crenellated and carved. The chocolate strata are volcanic, slumped across the older bedrock and sharply eroded. There are three giant primary spires. The western summit is like a giant butte, with sheer walls rising from its talus slides. The northern peak is a broken butte, its dark strata slumped and sliding off toward the Rio del Paine and eroded into a shattered lava dike. Pale volcanic plugs rise like organ pipes from a series of fissures in the escarpment, where the milky Paine spills over a lacework of shallow hot-spring terraces toward the windy Lago Nordenskjold.

The lake was named after the Baron Nils Otto Nordenskjold, a pioneer Swedish geologist who explored the Torres del Paine country in 1904. The Nordenskjold glacier in the icefields behind Lago Argentino was also christened on that expedition, and the glacial rivers surrounding the Torres del Paine are too silty to support fish.

The principal tower of the Cordillera del Paine rises 6,710 feet above Lago Nordenskjold, its pinnacle sharply carved into a broken snaglike molar. It is a startling parapet, with sheer cliff faces rising thousands of feet above the lake. Lago Nordenskjold serves as a settling basin, precipitating out the glacial milkiness until the Rio del Paine itself is almost clear when it spills into Lago Pehoe.

Pehoe is a beautiful lake, perhaps a mile of sapphire-blue water with a brushy little island in its center. It is reached by a floating footbridge. There is a simple *hosteria* on the island, with big windows overlooking the lake, and small cottages in the boulders and scrub cypresses above. Rocky cliffs and ledge rock surround the lake, and the immense Torres del Paine fill the sky.

The skies cleared completely before supper. The night grew crisp and absolutely still, and the stars glittered fiercely. The full moon rose while I stood staring at the Southern Cross, thinking that Pehoe was perhaps the most achingly beautiful place in the world. Finally I went inside and ordered a sour. *The Torres del Paine are impossible fairy-tale mountains*, I sighed happily. *They're so beautiful I don't even care about the fishing.*

We'll see, the inkeeper laughed.

The sea trout had arrived early that season, running up the milky Rio Serrano from the fjord called the Ultima Esperanza. The chalky flow of the Rio de Grey, which drains a series of big glaciers behind the Torres, mixes with the Serrano a few miles below its outlet at Lago del Toro. The Serrano is a large river with a smooth, surprisingly strong current. Its flow is broken by several sheep bridges, their skeletal pilings and planking weathered black and thickly coated with moss. The Estancia del Paine stands surrounded in windbreaks of poplars, between the ferry-crossing on the Rio del Paine and the grassy Llanuras del Paine, where the Rio Serrano loops back south against the foothills. These beautiful river meadows lie less than a hundred feet above tide water, which make their prospect of the Torres del Paine quite spectacular, and there are flocks of Darwin's rhea along the Serrano.

Ostriches! I flushed several from a copse of copper beeches and cypresses near the bridge. *I didn't expect to find ostriches!*

I took a few good sea-run browns on the Serrano, particularly working near its junction with the Grey, and took another at the waterfall below Lago Pehoe. The fish had sea-lice and ran eight to twelve pounds. Our fieldwork included surveying the entire Torres region for its wildlife, and I willingly agreed to explore its fisheries. Our funding for the project was sparse. There was neither time nor budget for extensive fisheries work. The watershed holds only brown trout, both riverine and migratory sea-run stocks, but each genetic strain has distinct habits and spotting patterns. Sea trout still hold unmistakable cross-shaped markings, even after they are washed with tea color and starting to spawn. We planned to fish every drainage, exploring each primary tributary, and the major river *bocas* too. The spotting patterns on any fish caught could tell us whether they were riverine or migratory trout and quickly help us understand how the sea-run fish penetrate the entire watershed. The good flying weather held a week. The Chilean military provided a helicopter to facilitate our fieldwork, and I eagerly hopscotched along the Rio de las Chinas and its tributaries, taking good fish everywhere we stopped. There were migratory fish in the Chinas itself, and in the lower Baguales and Vizcachas. Such fish had entered the Serrano from the salt, passed through the twelve-mile length of Lago del Toro, and were ascending beyond the big lake to spawn.

There was some intriguing water that we explored later in the week, particularly the flowages that join Lago Porteño with Lago del Toro. Their weedy currents were like a British chalk stream, and I left their fishing reluctantly, wishing I had more time to explore. We flew farther upstream in the helicopter, where a sheepherder had reported fish jumping to ascend the falls into Lago Porteño.

It was getting late when I waded out to fish the gathering currents at the outlet, testing the bottom cautiously, and I hooked a good fish on the first cast. It quickly became obvious that I had found a migrating shoal of big sea trout. I had twelve strikes in as many casts, missing two and losing a strong fish that bolted deep into the lake. The nine fish we released were mostly sea-run browns running six to ten pounds. The helicopter pilots finally grew worried about flying time, and we flew back to Cerro Castillo in the twilight.

Mucha suerte! the pilots said.

Good fishing, I agreed happily. *Wish we had more time*.

But the fishing seems less memorable than the Cordillera del Paine, with its immense turrets and spires rising in the moonlight. We drove back to Punta Arenas in surprisingly good weather, stopping at Puerto Natales for lunch. There was a copy of *Mercurio* in the dining room, and it is always startling to read that the United States is axle-deep in winter blizzards—on the opposite side of the earth, only a few hours away on a big four-engine jet.

Such memories of Patagonia still fill my thoughts.

There are wonderful echoes and images of those expeditions. It is difficult to forget the shuttered room at the old Hotel Oceania at Bahia Blanca, with its palm trees and cool marble floors and ceiling fans, and the old women walking to church before breakfast. The heat grew intolerable farther west, until the brushy *mogotes* shimmered in the blinding February sun, and I bought beer and sandwiches in a dark bead-curtained café at Rio Colorado. There was the large party of Argentines riding with their horses in a big truck that stopped when I broke down and stood ankle-deep in gritty dust. The men drew lots to decide who would go for help, quickly built a big bonfire in the middle of the dusty road, found several big wicker-wrapped bottles of Argentine *tinto* in the truck, started roasting a freshly killed lamb, sang and played the guitar and danced scraps of a Chilean *cueca*, and started a party that lasted until daylight.

Such things were a happy introduction to Patagonia, when I drove across the entire continent from Buenos Aires, but there are fishing echoes too. The fishing is curiously exotic. It is difficult to imagine trout with parakeets chattering noisily in the trees, the metallic pot-banging cries of *bandurrias*, and great flocks of pink flamingos in the milky saltpeter lagoons. There was the startling beauty of the hotel gardens at Tunquelen, with its strange Japanese-looking trees and the deep blue of Lago Nahuel-Huapi. There was an afternoon sipping cherry-pit *kirsch* with Gustavo Schwed at his pretty cottage above the lake, with its rolling surf pounding on the rocks below. There were *siesta* hours spent under the trees with Guy Dawson on the Collon Cura, and his introduction to the beautiful Marquesa Pool on the Rio Chimehuin. There was a leisurely picnic at the Pozo de las Manzanas, on the big sheep station called Casa de Lata, with Richard Santa Marina and Douglas Reid. We gathered at evening cook fires below the Boca Chimehuin, grilling succulent cuts of beef and drinking wine and sharing *mate* from a silver-rimmed gourd, with José de Anchorena and Prince Charles Radziwill. Both men are famous Argentine anglers, and Anchorena once held the world fly-record for brown trout with a fish of twenty-four and a half. There was a float trip down the Collon Cura with Sascha Turbanoff, who told stories of the Russian Imperial Guard before the revolution in 1917. Our trip was measured in eighty-odd miles of floating, hundreds of big trout and hours of lusty songs, and two wicker-basket *botellas grandes* of wine. It is impossible to forget those *asado* afternoons thirty years ago, when old Pim Lariviere was still alive, and I first fished with his sons, Maurice and Philip, at the old La Primavera on the Traful. There were tiny lambs and *cabritos* roasting on open wrought-iron spits, and fresh *michay* berries and cream, with the wine chilling in the Campamento Pool.

There were nights at Grisu and the Tres Reyes in San Carlos de Bariloche, and a wintry night at Esquel, with an early storm filling its April streets with snow. We stayed one afternoon on the Rio Corcovado in a simple *puesto*, when a horseman who had never seen us before generously offered us his house, although he was leaving for Jaramillo. The last morning at Cerro Castillo, I counted almost fifty condors circling the lava battlements at Lago del Toro. The last night I stayed at Calafate, the huge ice dam blocking the outlet of Lago Argentino suddenly purged itself, its rumbling and cracking explosions sounding like a sullen barrage of artillery fire.

But there was also a stormy night at San Carlos de Bariloche, with fresh snow falling on the Cerro Catedral and rain drumming hard on the windows. We were sitting high above Nahuel-Huapi in the little bar of the Hotel Cristal, listening to the soft music of Spanish conversations and drinking Rincon Famoso. It was getting quite late, and the folk singer had stopped playing to join us at the bar, when the young doctor arrived for a nightcap. The doctor looked tired, and when he finished his drink, he bought another round for everyone.

I lost an old patient tonight, he explained quietly, *and she was a wonderful old woman—let's drink to her!*

The rain was changing to snow, hitting the big windows wetly, and the lamps glowed softly in the streets. The bartender filled our glasses. The doctor stood and proposed the toast to his dead patient. It was snowing softly, filling the streets and falling across the sepulchral waters of the lake. We stood looking out into the April storm and raised our glasses to the handsome old *estanciera* that I believe was actually Etta Place.

Letort Soliloquy

Its world was filled with peace and plenty. The hot winds eddied across the valley, and fat dairy cattle drowsed in its tidy pastures. Springheads bubbled up from faults in its limestone outcroppings, chill seepages choked with watercress.

The pastoral landscapes were well tended, with neatly whitewashed fences surrounding stone farmhouses and outbuildings and barns. The barns themselves were huge, beautifully framed with big hand-shaped timbers skillfully morticed and tightly fitted with pegs of hickory and ash. Hex marks were set into their stonework or meticulously painted on their wooden gables.

Ledge-rock cellars and pantries bulged with potatoes and fruit jars and jams. Tiny stone buildings enclosed springheads outside the farmhouse kitchens, chilling big cans of fresh milk and cream. Wooden churns waited too, where the icy springs welled up through the pebbles and stones. The cornfields and orchards stood in tidy rows. The trees were heavy with fruit, and the empty slat-walled granaries would steadily fill with corn. The sense of quiet husbandry was obvious in these valleys.

The fields were tilled with horses, and the cows were milked by hand. Crows swarmed noisily in their woodlot rookeries. Sailing the hot thermals along Blue Mountain, a single red-tailed hawk rode the sky in lazy circles, watching the patchwork fields. The barns were filled with a chorus of sparrows and scuttling pigeons. It was a world to itself, its measured pace like the steady hoof clatter of its Amish carts on the Gettysburg pike.

It has been thirty-five years.

The sleepy college town in Pennsylvania has changed, like small towns everywhere today. The stone farmhouse just north of town was a charming place to stay in those summers. Big elms sheltered the lane that reached down from the county pike. Still larger trees surrounded the old masonrywork house, and a hot wind whispered in the leaves. There were chalky outcroppings in the pastures. Pheasants cackled from the ripening corn, and across the fertile bottoms of the Cumberland Valley, the mountains were smoky blue.

It was the world of Letort Spring Run.

During my first pilgrimage there, I had been fishing lazily across central Pennsylvania, exploring the rivers found in the books of Charles Wetzel and John Alden Knight.

The mountain country beyond Williamsport was thickly forested, in the remote counties of its Allegheny tier, and still held few people. Its small towns had atrophied steadily after the big trees were cut. The trout streams were seldom crowded. Eagles circled in the August heat, riding the afternoon winds. I had fished lazily through these mountains, following a rough map John Alden Knight had drawn in his study. It took several days to explore the Kettle, First Fork of the Sinnemahoning, Bald Eagle, Lycoming, Loyalsock, Big Fishing Creek, and Slate Run. It was a wonderful time.

Wetzel was still alive that summer too, and I carried a letter of introduction to his farm on Penns Creek. I found him on the screened porch, dressing big lacquer-bodied ants. Six big flies were hooked neatly into the millwork sill while their lacquer dried. His book *Practical Fly Fishing* was in the car, and he signed it later that day, after we fished together through the afternoon at the springhead below the Iron Bridge.

My duffle also held a first printing of *A Modern Dry Fly Code*, and I drove south along the Susquehanna to explore the famous spring creeks at Carlisle. The book was a cornucopia of fresh thinking, and I hoped to meet Vincent Marinaro, although both Knight and Wetzel had warned me that few people knew him well.

He still likes to fish Big Spring, they said.

Big Spring itself intrigued me, because its upper millpond had surrendered the biggest brown trout in Pennsylvania history. It still held a surprisingly selective population of wild brook trout. Brown trout held sway in the marshy reaches toward Newville. The springhead at its source spills full blown from a limestone wall. Its pond had the empty ruin of a huge gristmill. Both the stonework mill and its emerald millpond, its fountain-moss channel almost glowing with color, are gone. It was a stone-mill ruin worthy of Andrew Wyeth, but it was destroyed to build an asphalt parking lot.

I drove slowly downstream from the mill, passing several fishermen. Their behavior was puzzling. Most were watching the water instead of casting, behavior seldom seen on our streams but typically found on the rivers of Europe.

Below the farmhouses, the spring creek wound quietly under a stand of big delicately leafed willows. The marshy flats downstream were filled with cattle egrets. It did not look much like trout water. Fish were rising across the road from the farmhouses, not splashy or showy rises, but tiny dimples that scarcely disturbed the current. Some of the fishermen were casting now, changing flies surprisingly often, but few trout were actually hooked. It was getting dark when I turned around at Newville and drove back slowly.

The men fished skillfully. One angler stood like a heron in a half-crouch along the county road. The man had a bulky metal fly-box strapped to his chest. He wore a khaki long-billed cap and was fishing a pale five-strip rod. When I stopped the car, the old man stood up and grinned, spilling an expert stream of tobacco juice into the road. I got out to talk, and he reeled up his line, extending a calloused hand warmly.

Ross Trimmer, he said.

Trimmer was a retired police officer, and he was surprisingly generous with his knowledge and time. The trout he had been fishing continued to rise, dimpling tight against the elodea. He described the local fly hatches in great detail, and showed me the unique imitations they tied and fished in the Letort country. When I suggested that he try his fish again, he expelled another stream of tobacco juice and grinned.

He's thumbing his nose, Trimmer cackled. *He's just too spoiled rotten and smart—like all these limestone-country fish!*

It was getting dark. Trimmer suggested that I fish Letort Spring Run in the morning, and that I take a room at the Molly Pitcher in Carlisle.

I'd enjoy fishing it, I said.

I'll meet you.

Trimmer made a rough diagram of the route to the Turnaround Meadow, on the farm where Charles Fox lived, and we agreed to meet at ten o'clock. When I suggested an earlier hour, he explained that the limestone creeks were too cold until the morning sun warmed them. *It's getting pretty dark*, he added offhandedly, *but you should still find Marinaro upstream.*

Vincent Marinaro! I gasped.

That's right.

He's fishing Big Spring tonight?

See those big willows? Trimmer cut himself some fresh tobacco. *You should find him at those willows—smoking a big cigar!*

And I did.

Trimmer was waiting at ten o'clock the next morning, exactly where his map suggested, and Charles Fox was waiting too. Both men were knowledgeable and friendly. We walked down through the meadow to the bench where the Letort regulars gathered, and the old war-surplus hut where Marinaro had first tied his famous junglecock Jassid. The hut is gone today, and the little river there is dwarfed by the bridges of the interstate highway that completely erased both the hut and the grassy bends where his Jassid was born. Few fish were working. We walked the Letort that morning, from the photographer's blind where Marinaro had shot his rising-trout pictures for *The Ring of the Rise* to its Barnyard Water.

Fox and Trimmer pointed out the holding-lies of particular fish and captured grasshoppers and Japanese beetles to chum each trout, clearly proving it existed. The rises were soft and shy, sipping and bulging tight against the grass. The biggest fish barely disturbed the smooth currents, and it was difficult to guess their size. Every fish lay exactly where they pointed, and every fish seemed to have a proper name. Sometimes their size was betrayed by the quiet waves that gently swelled behind their dimples and ebbed against the grassy banks. It was obvious that both men had watched and caught most of these fish many times, and knew their size and feeding habits in surprising detail. It was a remarkable morning.

It was a contemplative school of fishing, typical of the British style evolved on the gentle chalk streams of Hampshire and Wiltshire. It was wonderfully fresh and new, utterly different from my boyhood fishing in Michigan and Colorado. The fishing on Letort Spring Run had overtones of liturgy and ritual.

Our fish are like old friends, Trimmer cackled and spit. *We try to give them pretty good names—like the Trout-without-a-Mouth!*

Trout-without-a-Mouth?

Lives under the willow below the Barnyard, Trimmer explained. *He inspects everything you throw, pushes his nose right against the fly, and rejects everything we try—and nobody has ever hooked him yet.*

That's why, Fox interrupted.

Why what? I asked.

Why we to call him the Trout-without-a-Mouth.

I followed them back through the Barnyard, and Trimmer threw several Japanese beetles into the current. Nothing happened until five or six beetles drifted past the big willow, and a shadow seemed to follow. Trimmer threw another handful of beetles. The Trout-without-a-Mouth took a single beetle, but it took nothing carelessly. It inspected everything, even

the live beetles, drifting back under them cautiously. It rejected several
live beetles too.

He's always picky, Trimmer said.

But he's rejecting the real beetles! It was difficult to believe. *Rejecting
live beetles!*

Waiting for the legs to kick, Fox smiled.

Chess player, I said.

The fish frustrated all of us that summer, and it was the Trout-without-
a-Mouth that ultimately led me to the Letort Beetle. Its history is mixed,
but its roots are verified in *This Wonderful World of Trout*, which Fox first
published in 1963. Fox played a role in the pattern's birth. His cellar held
a big cannister of hybrid pheasant skins, birds that were almost completely
black except for a glossy dark-green cast. Fox gave me several pieces.
Trimmer and I were sitting in my car with a fly vise clamped to the glove
compartment, experimenting with beetle imitations. Trimmer was sitting
behind the wheel, sorting through my feathers, when a small piece of
black pheasant plumage fell under the brake.

Look! I pointed.

What are you pointing at?

Look at the color of those throat hackles! I said excitedly. *Just like the
color of the beetles!*

It helps to be crazy, Trimmer said.

We quickly tried several techniques of working these pheasant throat
hackles. It was obvious that a Marinaro-style pattern might work. His prin-
ciples were unique. With his Jassid prototypes, Marinaro concluded that
with small flies lying in the surface film, silhouette and light pattern were
the most critical factors. His first Jassids and junglecock beetles were tied
to float flush, offering an opaque silhouette. The junglecock beetles were
elongated, although the actual Japanese beetles are round. It seemed logical that the dark pheasant-throat hackles offered an oval silhouette like
the beetles themselves, but our first attempts made it obvious that a single
feather did not offer enough opacity. We tried two feathers together, tied
flat with their glossy sides out, but those flies were quite fragile. Still using
the basic Marinaro concept, I finally tried saturating two ebony pheasant
hackles together with lacquer, trimming them into oval shapes to match
the Japanese beetles closely. It lost the glossy sheen of the feathers, but it
offered a perfect silhouette, size, and opacity. Our flies were completed
like a Jassid pattern. The hackles were trimmed to receive the wings laid
flat and to ride flush in the film. The wings were seated in a flexible cement
and tied off. Our imitations had no thickness, but their oval silhouettes
were exciting.

We had steadily improved our patterns to evolve the Letort Beetle. *It looks pretty good*, Trimmer admitted grudgingly. *But it's the fish that still get to vote.*

Our Letort Beetle worked from the first day in 1956, taking fish consistently from the Buttonwood bench to Otto's Meadow. The Beetles were still a little fragile, but they really worked. It was Ross Trimmer who first christened our little pheasant-throat patterns, but withheld his full blessing until its second week in the Barnyard, when our Beetle took the Trout-without-a-Mouth.

Pretty good test! he cackled.

Ross Trimmer also played a role in the original Letort Hopper. Grasshoppers were particularly thick that summer thirty years ago, but they hatched late and were relatively small. Most grasshopper patterns were too large. Fish consistently refused the popular commercial dressings. Since I had sometimes taken a grasshopper-feeding trout on a small Muddler, it seemed logical to tie a small grasshopper imitation Muddler-style. The synthetic yellow yarn we used helped to float the flies, and the clipped deer-hair suggested the bulky silhouette of a grasshopper's head. The early grasshoppers were too small, and it was difficult to add the mottled turkey wings. We decided to forget them. Our first patterns were simple bodies with flaired deer-hair wings, no turkey-quill sections, and carefully trimmed butts to suggest the bulky heads. The flies worked.

Trimmer was also fishing with me at the Turnaround Meadow in 1956 when our first prototype was tied. It was so effective that Charles Fox joined us the second afternoon we fished them. Fox also tells the story of the Letort Hopper in his book *This Wonderful World of Trout* and how well it fished that first Appalachian summer.

Its fledgling grasshoppers grew quickly. It was obvious that our imitations needed wings when the grasshoppers grew larger, and Fox proposed knotted pheasant-tail fibers to suggest their rear legs. Our first attempts were pretty clumsy, but I was staying at the old Greystone Manor when only its farmhouse offered rooms, on the night the Letort Hopper was finally born.

Charles Fox was so excited about the fly that he took me north to visit his friend Clyde Carpenter on a small spring creek near Williamsport. We carried a box of the early turkey-wing prototypes. Their impact on the big limestone browns is also described in *This Wonderful World of Trout*, and it was an unforgettable day's fishing. The creek rises in a pair of big limestone sinks, with a suspension bridge leading to a fishing cottage in the trees. Downstream it was more open, with a weedy flat just above the county road bridge. Big trees sheltered the opposite bank, and just beyond the twin-rut tractor lane, the fields rose steadily toward the south. It was almost harvest season. The fields were crawling with grasshoppers, and a hot wind was blowing. Its gusts flushed coveys of grasshoppers, and the wind caught them quickly, carrying them helplessly into the creek. The hapless grasshoppers fell awkwardly into the flat, and its big browns stalked them without mercy. We caught big trout and released them gently, while others were lost or broke off. Carpenter came down to see how our fishing had worked out, found us both into big brightly colored browns, and asked to borrow our last grasshopper. It was promptly lost in a heavy fish.

We finally quit fishing when we had no more flies. Some were left in fish, and some were lost in the brush. Wings were shredded and the deer hair grew brittle, and quickly they came apart when their heads and bodies unraveled. It had been an explosive baptism. The simple fly with its yellow body, mottled turkey wings, deer-hair collar, and tightly clipped grasshopper head still lacked a name until Trimmer and I took a big brown with it at Otto's Meadow.

It really works, he laughed. *Let's call it the Letort Hopper!*

It was a fish they had called the Bolter. It got its name because every time it was hooked, the fish had bolted upstream under a brush pile and broken off. It took the Letort Hopper freely.

Those were wonderful years, and I fish them again often in my thoughts. The little river flowed smoothly through its watercress and elodea, its bottom scoured clean of silty marl to its pea-gravel in the channels. It was still crystalline and beautiful. Hatches were still prolific, particularly the pale little *Ephemerellas* called Sulphurs in the Letort country. Its weeds still teemed with scuds and sow bugs. The fishing was most challenging, its rhythms governed by friendships and fiercely held codes, and the summer always ended with a picnic supper.

The things I was taught by the little Letort Spring Run and its disciples have passed the test of thirty-five years of difficult fish throughout the world, and I cannot measure the depth of my debt.

Both celebration and sadness fill my memories of those Letort summers. The rock quarry and the watercress farms and urban growth have left the little river choked with weeds and silt. Several old friends have died. Others no longer fish, and the watercress farms that expanded production until their fertilizers choked the Letort were finally guilty of a massive fish-kill triggered by their pesticides. The fly life was decimated too. I stopped briefly to look at the stream last year.

It's gone, I thought.

It flowed under the big interstate bridges through a linear riprapped channel, milky looking and sad. It was like stopping at a mortuary. The big highway structures that scar the meadows below the Barnyard dwarf the countryside, and its quiet summers are lost forever to the powerful threnody of Peterbilts and Kenworths swiftly carrying freight across Pennsylvania.

The little river and its ghosts are lost in a cacophony of traffic, and the scent of lilacs in the dooryards of old stone farmhouses is overwhelmed by diesel fumes. Letort Spring Run lies crippled, its solitude and sport swifty atrophied to rituals, because something subtle and splendid has been lost.

A Morning on the Gaula

Sverrehølen is a beautiful salmon pool on the Gaula, a river that rises high in central Norway, in the mountains of Dovrefjell. It is a full-blown river that can demand deep wading and hundred-foot casts. Its ghillies frown on fishing single-handed rods, because there are giants in the river.

The pool is classic water.

It lies under a mile of swift, broken rapids with big rocks showing in the tumbling flume. The steep mountains are thickly timbered. Old farms have been cut from these forests over the past century. The wooden farmhouses are painted white, with Victorian scrollwork eaves and porches, and facades as spare as a Shaker sideboard. The stout barns are bright scarlet, a color originally derived from a primitive mixture of iron oxide and milk that protected their pine siding. Older outbuildings are often built of logs. There are small plots of barley and cauliflowers and potatoes, since the growing season is short just south of Trondheim. The polar circle lies only 250 miles away.

The pastures along the river are still thickly grown in early summer, bright with cotton grass and arctic harebells and buttercups. Trout lilies grow in the seepages. Later in the summer, when the hayfields are cut into windrows of grass, the pole hay-fences are constructed in the fields to cure it for storage. Life is still simple on these country farms, filled with gentle echoes and images, like a serving girl holding a goblet high to check its polish in the light flooding through lacy dining-room curtains.

Just above the pool, there is a large boulder in the river, breaking its flow. Running fish sometimes hold there briefly, splashing and catching the light, but it is difficult to wade the swift cobble-bottom currents.

The pool itself shelves off under the alders and birches across the river. It is fished from the shallows off a rocky beach. The throat of the pool is swift. Its dark chute is quite deep, and during the spate season, its back eddies scour out a backwater too deep to wade. The middle of the pool is fully two hundred yards of smoothly flowing current, slightly more than a hundred-foot cast across to the big alders. The ghillies insist that its entire length can surrender a fish anywhere. The tail of the pool forms an immense slick, gathering silken and smooth where a skeletal goatherd's hut still stands under a large birch. The current is much stronger than it seems, bulging slightly where there are big stones hiding, until it slides and breaks back toward the cobblestone bar.

Sverrehølen is almost five hundred yards of optimal salmon water. It seems to fish at almost any level other than a milky cloudburst, and I hooked a salmon there almost every time I fished it through. Its character usually seemed friendly, in spite of the casts required to cover it completely, and I always fished the Sverrehølen with optimism.

My last morning on the pool was crisp and bright. Big cumulus clouds hopscotched past the steep mountains, and the river glittered in the early summer sun. Roland Holmberg was my ghillie that week, and we drove upstream from Støren to the Sverrehølen after breakfast.

It seems alive, he said pensively.

What's that? I asked.

The river, he replied. *It seems alive this morning.*

Holmberg is a young Swedish soldier garrisoned on Cyprus, serving with the Royal Swedish Brigade stationed there by the United Nations. His military leaves in recent summers have been spent as a salmon ghillie on the Gaula. His flies are workmanlike and effective, particularly the big tube flies his colleagues tie for the river, and Holmberg is big and strong. His pale eyes and hair are unmistakably from Stockholm, and his companionship is welcome. His knowledge of the Gaula is welcome too, and we fished happily together.

We took a twenty-three pound henfish at Sverrehølen the first time I fished it. The salmon was lying in the strong currents just below the throat of the pool, and when I worked the big 1/0 Black Sheep through in concentric swings, its broken currents seemed to bulge. The false rise was so imperceptible that I doubted it had actually happened, but I backed upstream patiently to fish it through again. The second time I made the same cast, mended quickly to get the big Sheep down and fishing, and mended twice again. There was a small splash when the fish left its holding-lie, and there was a heavy strike. The big henfish never jumped. It fought stubbornly after two long runs that half-emptied my backing, and I steadily coaxed it back. We waited patiently while it bulldogged back and forth, cutting its sullen half-circles on the bottom, until it finally surrendered to Holmberg's net.

It's a henfish, he grinned and shook hands. *Perhaps ten kilos.*

It's a beautiful pool, I said.

The second morning that we drew the Sverrehølen, I hooked another fish that made a strong run into the heaviest water upstream and held there effortlessly until the fly pulled out. Both mornings we fished out the entire pool without moving another salmon, but it was a reach of river that always seemed restlessly alive, willing to share its secrets. Our last morning, the Sverrehølen surprised us both when I fished its throat twice without any luck. *It is nothing*, Holmberg said. *I believe the tail of the pool is usually best.*

We've caught nothing there, I said.

We will, the ghillie smiled.

Another fisherman had taken a fine cockfish of almost thirty pounds from the belly of the pool that week. It had been holding about sixty feet above the goatherd's hut, just at the bottom of the alders and big stones. I fished past its lie with a quietly growing excitement, but nothing happened. My sense of anticipation ebbed slightly. I fished through to the goatherd's hut with no sign of a salmon. Six more casts and I was past the big tree. My next cast would work teasingly above the sunken boulder at the tail, its bulk faintly visible in the bulging currents.

It's a good lie, the ghillie shouted from his seat on the cobble beach. *Storlaks plass—keep fishing!*

Ja, takk for hjelpe! I yelled.

The first cast fell badly, but I fished it through, well short of the lie. The second rolled out and settled in the rocky shallows, with the backing knot hanging in the guides and my fly-boxes slightly awash.

Hard work, I thought.

I mended twice to get the big Sheep fishing well, and it bellied smoothly into a long, teasing swing. The tail shallows were glassy smooth. Their sliding currents erupted in a heart-stopping boil, its loose circle spreading and ebbing, and the fish bulged again. I did not strike at either rolling swirl, waiting to feel the salmon's weight, and the line bellied tight.

Fish! I shouted. *Fish on!*

The fish simply held stubbornly for five minutes, almost ignoring my pressure. Its simple weight was startling. Nothing happened quickly, and it swam powerfully upstream and stopped again. It held there along the bottom, and I could not budge its strength. The salmon felt incredibly strong, and I had no sense of controlling the fight. Perhaps it was foul-hooked. It was a terrible thought, and when the fish started to shake its head, I was both awestruck and relieved. Head-shaking that echoes so strongly into the rod is impossible in a foul-hooked fish, and I felt better. But the cadences and strength of this head-shaking were a little frightening. Small fish shake their heads quickly. My fish shook its head at a sullen pace, like a big fighter working out patiently, driving strong body punches into the heavy bag.

Storlaks, Holmberg said quietly. *Storlaks.*

Ja, I agreed. *Storlaks!*

The fish worked slowly upstream into the wild throat of the pool, holding effortlessly in the spume. It hung there almost ten minutes. It shook its head angrily and stopped. Head-shaking is worrisome, and I exhaled happily when it stopped, completely surprised that I was holding my breath. The salmon had been holding above us most of its fight, struggling against both the river and the rod, and it still felt uncontrollable.

But I think we can beat him, I thought.

It was wishful thinking. The great salmon drifted back several feet, turned slowly deep in the pool, and started downstream. It was not an explosive run, but simply took line with a quietly frightening power, and its strength was troubling. The fish stopped at the big stone where it was first hooked. It held there briefly and moved back upstream, repeating the entire performance. Twice I thought I moved it slightly.

I think he's getting tired, Holmberg said.

Not yet, I shook my head.

The fish started downstream again, stripping great lengths of line and gathering speed. It seemed completely unstoppable. Its first long run had stopped in the tail shallows, and we thought it would stay in the pool. It was a serious tactical mistake. The fish had suddenly exploded, escaping the pool easily, and we had started running too late. The big Saint John was empty now. It was difficult to follow down the rocky cobblestones, and we were both running clumsily. The steep riffle seemed like a mile, but it was probably two hundred yards. The big fish stopped without warning, holding behind a big stone while I wildly tried to recover some lost backing.

Can you see the fish? I yelled.

Holmberg shook his head worriedly. The fish slowly drifted back into the spreading shallows. The entire river was a shallow riffle almost a hundred yards across, spreading toward the steep, impassable rapids another three hundred yards downstream. The immense shingle also drained toward our bank, spilling abruptly into a deep flood-scour tight against the jetty-sized boulders there. The fish had seemingly stopped. It had given me time to recover all my backing and get closer, and we circled to get a better playing angle.

You see him yet? I asked.

No, he said.

What's your guess? I was getting worried.

Twenty, he said, *maybe more.*

Pounds? I asked.

Kilos!

The fish drifted back into the flood-scour, wallowing momentarily where the stones shelved off into its dark channel. The deep water was almost a hundred yards long, and the ghillie had me circle downstream in the shallows.

I don't like it, I said.

Why not? Holmberg asked. *We've got the perfect angle to play him.*

What if he starts another run?

You can't stop him now? he seemed surprised.

I don't know, I confessed.

The fish was only an immense shadow just upstream, and I tried to test its remaining strength. It almost seemed possible to bully it off balance. It still felt immensely strong. I laid the rod on its side and leaned into the fish. Suddenly it rolled on the bottom, turned downstream, and erupted past us into the rapids. I tried to stop it and burned my fingers on the backing. It was impossible to follow and stay dry. The big reel was emptying fast.

We'll have to swim! I yelled. *You take the camera—let's go!*

My old Leica was wrapped in a sandwich bag and tucked into my waders, and I handed it to Holmberg. We locked arms across our shoulders and plunged in. The flood channel was surprisingly deep, but we windmilled our legs, touching enough boulders to push off and keep our heads up. The ghillie stumbled and nearly went under, still holding my camera above his head. I crossed and floundered ashore. The only dry things left were my hat, shooting glasses, and straining rod. The reel was empty again. We were running over the big rocks, past a gallery of startled Norwegians, our bodies dripping like otters. The fish was gone.

The young ghillie waded out again to untangle my line from the rocky chutes downstream, and we were both surprised to find it had not broken off. My fly had finally pulled out.

We were completely soaked, walking back through the wildflowers and hayfields to the car. The fight had carried us almost a mile. The young ghillie was leading the way, tired and dripping, his clothing and pale hair plastered to his body. The hot sun was welcome. I felt chilled and beaten in spite of its heat. Water was running everywhere in rivulets, working past my wading belt to creep under my wet trousers. Holmberg stopped and came back, grinning in spite of everything, and shook himself like a big sheepdog.

You all right? he asked.

Yes, I said.

You know, there was a strangely happy wildness in his eyes. *It was a wonderful thing—and we were almost heroes!*

Kiwi Country

The helicopter was coming.

Its sharp rotor chatter came faintly on the wind. The shrill turbine whine identified it unmistakably. It was the brightly painted Hughes 500D that had dropped us into the headwaters of the Greenstone just after breakfast. We had hiked slowly upstream from the Rat's Nest, the empty sheepherder's hut lying on a big moraine south of the river.

It had been a perfect day's fishing.

The upper Greenstone winds lazily back and forth across the floor of its steeply walled valley. *Manuka* and copper beech thickets cover its mountain walls, mixed with *karo* and ribbonwood. The bottoms are chest deep in pampas grass and wildflowers. Waterfalls spill lacily from parapets and ravines. There are no sheep and the valley is lush. Mount Christina rises beyond the glacial tarn in its headwaters, across the Hollyford country. Christina is a beautiful mountain, its broken summits like a giant armchair, with big glaciers spilling across its seat like icy antimacassars.

The river is utter poetry too.

Just downstream from the sheepherder's hut, its bright jade currents plunge into a tiny postpile gorge, gathering and boiling in swift pools that flow deep and swimming-pool green. The Greenstone is incredibly clear. Its shallow flats are a sharply etched mosaic of pebbles and cobblestones and jade. The river lies tight against the mountain, where immense slides of broken talus and scree have tumbled boulders into several pools. Other rocky pools lie upstream, lying in the shade of exotic-looking trees and spilling down a series of stairstep flats. It is a fine reach of water.

The last pool under the mountain is like a fairy-tale pool, too perfect to seem anything less than a fisherman's dream.

It is difficult to picture such a beautiful pool. It is simply too beautiful, its gravelly bottom clearly visible in a circling amphitheater of sheltering trees. Each fish is clearly visible too. It seems almost suspended in light and air, spotlighted in the sun. The throat of the pool is a swift chute of icy water, shelving off deep into jade-colored spume. Its primary current tongues circle and slide, glassy smooth in the shade, losing themselves deep under the trees. It is futile to wade. It is almost impossible to cast over such skittish trout, since false casting can frighten them, particularly in its sweeping tail downstream. It is a pool best fished on hands and knees. The gravelly shallows upstream can hold surprisingly large trout if no one has fished them yet, usually big rainbows facing a riffling spring-hole current. Sedges often hatch there in the morning sun. The fish drift into the gravelly shallows to intercept the fluttering sedges, feeding with quiet dimples.

It is poetry itself.

The first time I stumbled across the pool, I was stunned when I saw a big trout rising in the spring-hole shallows. I quickly dropped to my knees on the gravel bar and changed to a dry fly.

Kneeling in a carpet of *Geums* and silverleaf *Celmisias* and eyebrights, I hooked the fish on the first cast. It simply exploded into the sun. It cartwheeled full-length from the pool so many times that I stopped playing it with a sense of awe and was not unhappy when the line went slack. It easily went eight pounds. Few rainbows on the upper Greenstone are that large. Most run between two and three pounds, and they take a dry fly eagerly. It often fills my thoughts across ten thousand miles.

The helicopter chattered past swiftly. Its pilot finally spotted us, pulling back into a tight turn and side-slipping across the valley floor. We had covered about six miles. The afternoon sun gleamed on its Plexiglas cockpit as the helicopter flared gracefully and settled. Its rotor throttled back, idling and windmilling lazily. The pilot sat grinning and lobbed me a cold Steinlager from the ice bucket beside the console.

Hello mate! he yelled. *How's fishing?*

We gave him a thumbs-up signal, and he clambered down to stow our tackle in the compartment behind the rotor mast. We climbed aboard and buckled in. The engine whine gathered into a shrill scream, and we lifted off almost magically, turning to gather speed hanging nose down as we crossed the river. Our shadow hopscotched along the valley floor until we passed the Rat's Nest and started into a steep climb.

Working the thermals skillfully, the pilot rose past the steep mountain wall. Waterfalls plunged past before we reached the summit. Spray beaded across the Plexiglas canopy. We leapfrogged past Mount Mavora, with the upper Mararoa a thousand feet below. Stark crags and turrets passed close enough to touch. The Wyndon Burn tumbles from its windy, treeless valley where Shirker's Wood clings thickly to the shoulder of the mountain. It got its name from a family that hid there to escape conscription throughout the First World War.

Thick clouds hung threateningly beyond the Wyndon Burn, billowing up to spill across the broken ridges of the Livingston Mountains. We chattered up steeply again, attempting to cross the chocolate-colored crags and use the Upukeroa, flying its winding channels back to Te Anau.

Heavy weather had been building all day along the Tasman Sea, from the Pyke and Hollyford to Doubtful Sound. The pilot had encountered its front while deer hunting just after daylight in the coastal fjords. Its clouds had pushed steadily into the mountains until it filled the entire Te Anau Basin. Our helicopter soared past a staircase of glacial cirques and tarns, glittering with a strange emerald fire. Clouds billowed among the barren peaks, catching the evening light. The Upukeroa valley was completely filled with clouds, and our route to Te Anau was no longer possible.

We circled back across the Mavora Lakes, searching for a tiny opening in the overcast. It was somber and gloomy. Our probing tried every possible pass across the Livingston Range, its shattered battlements and crags like the serrations in some gargantuan saw.

The pilot soared high and hovered, studying canyon after canyon, searching and turning back. Our helicopter was surrounded by towering cliffs and swirling scraps of clouds, billowing in thickly rolling mists that grew pink and bright gold and alabaster. Huge spinnakers of cloud flashed past the cockpit like brightly colored silks, until we finally slipped under the overcast at Mount Snowden, chattering home in the rain.

Bob Kahn rummaged through his fishing vest and found his silver flask of Remy Martin. *It's incredible*! He passed the cognac back. *I'd come all the way to New Zealand just for the flying.*

Almost twenty years ago, while working on a large construction project in Australia, I stopped off at Auckland to sample the trout fishing. Such plans seldom prove workable. The countryside of the North Island was beautiful, well tended, and almost British in some places, but the fishing was not exceptional. It was the wrong place at the wrong time of year. With only a few days to fish, it was naive to expect great fishing on rivers accessible from Wellington and Palmerston and Auckland by highway, but many visitors have made the same mistake. I caught some fish on the pastoral north-country rivers, but it was not fishing worth the tiring ten thousand mile flight from New York.

But I met several people who knew the entire country well, understood its seasons and fly-hatches, and had fished with the best outfitters and guides from Auckland to Invercargill.

Later I traveled back to New Zealand as a guest of the government, fishing with such outstanding anglers as Rex Forrester, Geoffrey Thomas, Murray Knowles, Geoffrey MacDonald, and the late Fred Gill, who was considered the dean of fishing guides in New Zealand. There was good sport at some accessible locations, but there were also two helicopter flights into the bush, and the backcountry was a revelation. The backcountry fisheries were spectacular. I took a thirty-inch brown on a dry fly, fishing a remote mountain river with Fred Gill. Geoffrey Thomas chartered a helicopter into the Rangeitiki Gorge east of Taupo, where I took six rainbows between six and twelve pounds, fishing nymphs in big cliff-faced pools that held still larger trout. These fish were taken with six-weight tackle and relatively small flies, and we stalked them visually. The helicopter flew us back through the twilight to Turangi.

Pretty good work, mate! Thomas yelled. *We caught some crocodiles!*

It's unbelievable, I sighed.

There have been several other trips to New Zealand since, fishing with guides such as Lloyd Knowles, William Stewart, Dick Fraser, Tony Hayes, Peter Church, and the colorful Hugh MacDowell. Geoffrey Thomas worked with me later on a film for the government, fishing the big rainbows on the Rangeitiki. Although there have been more than a dozen trips now, I have written little about trout fishing in the Antipodes.

It takes time to sort and digest such a diet of riches, and I am still thinking. Kiwi country is such a tapestry of images and echoes over the past twenty years that I fish it often in my thoughts. Both its people and its places are remarkable.

During one early trip, there were fine days with Charles Waterman and the colorful Fred Gill, fishing the Eglinton and upper Mararoa. We took several dry-fly browns better than four pounds. The fish were skittish and spooked easily. It took a few failures to start stalking them properly, and when I found Waterman beaching a big fish in a muddy shallows, I stopped to watch.

You make that water muddy just to blindfold that brown? I asked.

You bet, Waterman worked the fly free carefully.

Think it's ethical? I teased.

I've spooked so many, he grinned, *I'll resort to anything.*

Later I was playing a huge trout, a hook-jawed fish that arm-wrestled me down a rocky shallows, when Waterman arrived on a grassy bluff and stood there cheerleading and joking.

You match its hatch? Waterman asked.

Not exactly, I said.

What did he take? he pressed his advantage ruthlessly.

Royal Wulff.

It's nice to know, Waterman observed drily, *you're not too proud to admit such a terrible thing.*

There are many echoes of the fjord country at Te Anau over the years. We fished the little Iris Burn with Murray Knowles, stopping often to brew a billy-pot of tea. There were rainy afternoons on the Spey, and the still-flowing Grebe, where Ralf Stinson took a ten-pound rainbow on a dry fly. We stopped after a stormy, fishless day on the lower Mararoa to fish a beautiful meadow pool on the Oreti, and Lloyd Knowles led me to a twenty-nine-inch brown that salvaged the trip. Bill Stewart led us on a trek along the lower Worsley, where we stopped to admire a fat weka bird that followed us curiously, flightless and twitching its tail like a friendly puppy. We caught so many fish that I finally stopped fishing and just sat on the grassy bank, happily studying a cactuslike colony of woolly-leaf *Haastia*.

Too tired of catching fish to cast, I sighed.

Another year I trekked into the Castle with Lloyd Knowles, exploring its pools along a mountain valley that is breathtakingly beautiful, its waterfalls plunging into rainy thickets of *toi* and fat cabbage trees and tree ferns. There were horsetails and scaly-stalked whipcords and *Dracophyllum*, looking like wildflowers in a diorama of the Coal Age. *Tui* birds and rock wrens were everywhere, and the thickets were alive with wren-sized riflemen that filled the morning with their nervous *zip-zip* cries. The Castle almost vanishes under a thickly laced canopy of trees, interlocking branches as graceful as the nave of a Gothic cathedral, darkly hung with moss and flickering with shafts of sunlight.

Geoffrey MacDonald was our guide at Queenstown, where we took a number of good fish on small dead-drift nymphs, fishing the weedy chalk stream called the Diamond Burn. It is a fertile little spring creek that reminded me of several favorites in Montana, particularly spring creeks near Chico Hot Springs on the Yellowstone.

Charles Waterman and I shared a bright wine-aired day with Mac-Donald on the lower Greenstone too, crossing Lake Wakatipu in his motor launch to hike the forest trail upstream. Waterman caught a huge brown in a deep jade-green flat, and we were hiking high above the river when we spotted a second large trout. It was surface feeding in the swift rock-walled throat of the flat, porpoising and clearly visible. It was clearly a big rainbow.

Your fish, Waterman pointed.

I picked my way carefully down a steep, rocky scree thick with eye-brights and fringe-leaf buttercups and azure *Coprosma*, grateful that New Zealand has no snakes. There was a big eel, lazily browsing the backwater downstream, and Waterman jokingly warned me to watch my step.

It's pretty big, he shouted. *Big enough to eat a bugologist!*

I'll watch my step, I laughed.

I picked my way across the rocky shallows, skirting the deep backwater, and tightroped slowly for footholds behind a huge boulder. The fish was still working. Crouching low, I clambered quietly into casting position and waited behind a big rock. Wildflowers were sprouting from its fissures.

The cast fell luckily, cocking the fly, and I mended twice to extend its drift, hiding behind the stones. The big rainbow tilted up slowly and took the fly. I tightened and it pole-vaulted wildly, tumbling laterally across the current. It was a spectacular trapezelike explosion, and I struggled to control its surprising strength, gasping and stunned.

You see that jump? I shouted.

Missed it completely, Waterman grinned. *Too busy watching the eel.*

What eel? I asked.

Eel at your feet, he laughed. *Wondering if you're edible!*

Two big stones flushed the eel. It disappeared furtively among the rocks. I parried two long reel-wearing runs, working the fish patiently back to the net. We live-weighed it in the meshes, estimating its weight quickly at eight pounds, and released the fish. The big eel came back while I revived the fish, and the guide routed it with another barrage of well-placed missiles.

Some fish, MacDonald said.

The hell with the fish! Waterman stood laughing on the trail. *What about these trophy eels?*

They don't take flies, we both said.

The flamboyant Dick Fraser is the best-known outfitter on the South Island today. His charming Cedar Lodge stands on the Makarora River, forty miles north of Wanaka. His beautiful country includes the Mount Aspiring watersheds, a straight-flush hand of great dry-fly rivers.

There are many seasons of happy memories at Fraser's little camp. Robert Buckmaster shared a wonderful day on the Dingle Burn, flying into a grassy airstrip high in the mountains above the big sheep station at Dingle Peak. The burn is scarcely more than twenty feet across, its pretty little pools like bathtubs and billy-pot pockets and lavatories, but every tiny lie seems to hold a surprisingly good fish.

I don't understand it, Buckmaster shook his head at lunch. *It doesn't have enough water to have so many fish.*

But it has them! I grinned.

There is a huge cliff-sheltered pool on the Wilkin, its big pale-olive rainbows rising like ghosts through its milky blue depths. Its cliffs are thick with beeches and *manuka* trees and fuchsia. The thickets swarm with yellowheads and *miro-miro* birds and wrybills. *Myrsine* and pineapple scrub and *Gaultheria* are found there too, and the meadows across the river are bright with harebells and white gentians and daisies. It is a gorgeous pool I have shared with many friends over the years. It has so captured my heart that I have never reached the Siberia Burn, our real trekking destination after the helicopter dropped us off. Some day I should ignore the Blue Cliff Pool on the Wilkin and continue walking upstream, because the beautiful Siberia has a superb reputation.

The Newland Burn is a surprise. It lies under a bridal-veil cataract that spills from cliffs thickly grown with swordlike *toi* and tree ferns and *tarata*. Tooth-leafed *koromika* and scaly whipcord thrive in the spray. Wildflowers cling to fissures and crevices in its high cliffs. The little burn flows less than two hundred yards, tumbling steeply to the Wilkin through a labyrinth of mossy stones and cottage-sized boulders calved off from the mountain wall. Its wild flume changes the little burn each spring, in torrents of snow-melt in the Mount Aspiring country. There is a single cauldron-shaped pool under the falls, and a staircase flume of small pools and pockets is tucked among the boulders. The first time I fished it, I was still shaking out line to cast to a promising hole and laid the fly down briefly on a stony shallow just above the fast chute that spilled into the Wilkin. I missed a big fish clumsily.

Big fish! Fraser hissed.

I wasn't fishing yet, I protested sheepishly. *I didn't expect a fish in that shallow water!*

Bloody hell! he said. *Pay attention!*

The Young has several big dry-fly flats in its alpine-walled valley, its grassy bottoms alive with gentians and *Celmisia* daisies, and big colonies of Wahlenberg's harebells. Moss hangs thickly from the trees, and there are thickets of *manatu* and tree ferns and grass-tree *inakas*. The rainbows in the Young are just as eager to take dry flies as their cousins on the Wilkin, but they are slightly larger, with six- to eight-pound fish entirely possible. The last time I fished the Young, I shared it with Ernest Day, an old friend who has a small fishing camp on Silver Creek in Idaho. We took nine dry-fly rainbows between us, fish running from three to eight pounds. We lost fish too, including a big rainbow that I hooked in a shallow flat, a fish that easily emptied a Hardy Princess.

Douglas Preussing and I fished the Makarora on a day we could not fly, and we also fished the Hunter together, a remote glacier-melt river so good that it was chosen as a fishing site for the Prince of Wales.

Its fishing is quixotic. Sometimes I have fished it, catching as many as thirty coin-bright rainbows in a single day's sport. Other times it has surrendered only dark, sparsely mottled brown trout. It seems likely that the Hunter receives several runs of fish each summer, discrete schools ascending almost like salmon from Lake Hawea. The Hunter fish are surprisingly susceptible to dry flies, like the big trout of its sister rivers. Dick Fraser has been our guide every time I fished it, and Fraser has a genius for spotting its big trout. His tactics lie between the drill sergeant and a stork-legged clown. His stamina and fish-hunting skills and excitement are contagious.

He's coming up! he shouted from a high bank. *He's coming*! The fish was hooked and stripped line noisily from the reel.

Big fish? I yelled back.

Big enough! Fraser shouted happily. *Good on you, mate!*

Geoffrey Thomas and Hugh MacDowell have often been my guides on the North Island, along with Tony Hayes and Peter Church on the Tongariro and its sister rivers. Some fishermen who have traveled to New Zealand and have never helicoptered into its gentle forest-covered mountains, will argue that North Island fisheries have declined. The late-fall steelhead runs from Lake Taupo and spring-spawning rainbows at Rotorua and Tarawera are still as prolific as ever. But there are big urban populations on the North Island, and these fisheries are accessible by highways. The rivers feeding the big lakes are quite popular. When the rainbows are running, there are local anglers fishing armpit-to-armpit off rivers like the Waitahanui, and the famous pools on the Tongariro are crowded too. The fishing is still good in spite of the crowds. But the North Island fisheries should not be judged in such terms, and these rivers are deceptive, because there are remote rivers that are still magic.

Some fisheries there have become famous, perhaps too famous to survive, since their big trout grow slowly and are relatively few. The fisheries on both islands are already more fragile than most local biologists seem to understand, perhaps because they have largely focused their studies on the incredibly fertile ecosystems at Taupo and Tarawera. There are no shallow volcanic lakes or drowned calderas providing lake-run hordes on bush-country rivers like the Ngaruroro or Rangeitiki, and their wonderful fish need help.

Their world is remarkable.

Early mist still fills their forest watersheds when the helicopter lifts off after breakfast, its rotor chattering and hanging low, swiftly circling and crossing the Tongariro Lodge. The neatly cultivated tree farms at Turangi quickly drop behind, leaving Taupo and its volcanic islands to fill the horizon, still and shimmering and pale in the haze. Ngauruhoe stands smoking between its volcanic sisters, and the empty bush-country valleys of the Kaimaniwa Mountains pass quickly under our canopy in only minutes. The headwaters of the river lie ahead, hidden in early-morning mist or already glittering in the sun. Its swift riffles explode as they catch the early light. Tributaries spill steeply through forest ravines, swelling the wild river until its cliff pools eddy deep and turquoise against the *manuka* and cabbage-tree cliffs. We crossed the last brush-covered ridge, scattering *miro-miros* and bellbirds in our wake, and the Rangeitiki lay ahead.

That's it! Geoffrey Thomas pointed.

Thomas has been my guide on almost every trip into the Rangeitiki over many years. It holds immense rainbows in its middle pools, ghostlike shadows the size of salmon. Such fish remain stubbornly in my thoughts. It has surrendered a dozen fish better than ten pounds on those trips, fish that we stalked visually and fished with patient nymphing, and I have never taken a fish between the Taihape and the deer-hunter's camp that went less than five. Our party of five helicopter anglers once released seventeen big rainbows there. Frank Bertaina took the best trout, a fat-bellied henfish that we estimated at fourteen pounds.

My best fish was caught above the deer-hunter's camp and measured thirty-one inches. Its capture was witnessed by Fred Losch, who had elected to fish the tail-shallows of a hundred-yard flat, while I circled through the trees to prospect the chute at its throat. Three immense shadows were ghosting restlessly back and forth among the submerged ledges there. It was unthinkable that such huge shadows were actually trout. But I fished them an hour without luck, giving up when they finally drifted deep under a lava outcropping.

Eels, I thought apologetically.

Rangeitiki fish are large, but they are seldom gullible, and these restless shadows were probably trout. Excuses were only a half-serious ploy. The tumbling throat of the pool lay just ahead, with a deep smooth-flowing slot in its white flume, and I waded upstream to try it.

The big rainbow took the first drift through the slot and jackknifed high into the sun, wildly throwing spray. It exploded mindlessly again. It bolted downstream and jumped, showering my sunglasses with spray, and nearly dry-docked itself on the stones. It flopped there wildly, threshing and writhing to regain the water. It succeeded and bolted downstream, and emptied the Princess right to its spindle, cartwheeling six times. The silvery henfish jumped six more times, almost stripping the reel again before it surrendered. It circled stubbornly in the shallows for several minutes, and I finally worked it gently to the stones.

It's just like a steelhead, Losch said.

It was one of the biggest river-bred rainbows I have caught. It had no trace of its rainbow stripes and gill covers, only its sword-bright length faintly washed with lavender. Its back was indigo, and it looked like a summer steelhead fresh from the salt. The fish recovered quickly and bolted, showering us with roostertails of spray.

Strong fish! I sighed.

Hugh MacDowell is a justly famous guide from Rotorua. His birthplace was Belfast, a strife-torn city with little need of guides and fly dressers in recent years, and MacDowell is a wry storyteller too. His energy and good humor are legendary, perhaps matched only by a fierce capacity for whisky, taken neat in a water glass. Belfast is a city desperately in need of laughter, but lacking its climate these days, and MacDowell wisely emigrated to New Zealand.

He's a bloody wonder! Geoffrey Thomas jokingly explained. *He's the only wild, bloody Irishman to sail Down Under voluntarily—without wearing leg-irons and bloody chains!*

My glass is empty, MacDowell said drily.

MacDowell took us into the Ngaruroro last season, where its pampas-grass headwaters wind into a steep-walled gorge. Its walls are thickly grown with brushy *manuka* and black-trunked tree ferns and palmettolike growths. The river's headwaters lie in the Kaweka Hills, beyond the conifer farms at Tauranga-Taupo. It is not large, winding through high serpentine walls in a series of swift chutes and cliff-face pools. There are mosses and flowering vines and horsetails wetly clinging to the cliffs, and we stopped for lunch on a grassy gravel-bar island, in a tapestry of buttercups and *Ourisias*.

The gorge looks and sounds almost tropical. Its junglelike character includes the bird life too, with shrill parakeets and the flutelike trilling of bellbirds. Sometimes its stillness is broken by the piercing cries of long-tailed cuckoos and nervous flocks of *tui* birds.

Bloody beautiful, MacDowell said happily.

The first time I fished it, we had planned to helicopter into the Rangeitiki but found it still murky from an early-morning storm. The Ngaruroro is smaller, and I thought it held smaller fish. It was a mistake.

Geoffrey Thomas had the pilot fly the river slowly, just high enough to avoid spooking the fish too much. We sat stunned in our seats. The little river held some really large fish. We put down on a big gravelly shoal and started patiently upstream. I landed four good rainbows that day. The best was a hook-jawed cockfish that went ten pounds and forced me to follow it past the swinging bridge in a fight that carried us a quarter mile. The smallest fish of the day went only three pounds, but I spent almost two hours working a brace of immense trout lying deep in a pumice-cliff pool. I hooked one on a nymph fished dead-drift, tight against the mossy wall. Its fight was mercifully brief, its length flashing silver in the greeny depths of the pool before the fish wrenched free.

The day's fishing changed my mind about the little Ngaruroro, but it was another full year before Ralf Stinson and I buckled into Toby Clark's brightly lacquered 500C at Turangi. Hugh MacDowell finished stowing our equipment and clambered quickly into the back.

I'm excited, I confessed.

It's a bloody good river, MacDowell shook his head and grinned. *I'm excited about fishing it too!*

Stinson took a twenty-nine-inch brown trout that afternoon, stalking it with MacDowell in the tail-shallows of a deep cliff-walled pool. It fought stubbornly, boring deep under the cliffs and trailing vines, and I caught up with them as they finally beached it.

Stinson stared at the big fish in disbelief. *How big is that fish?* Stinson gasped. *It's huge!*

Ten pounds, MacDowell stood grinning.

They nursed it patiently until its big gill plates were working again, and MacDowell held it facing the current. Its eyes studied us while it gathered strength, until it simply left with a kind of solemn dignity.

That's the biggest trout I've ever seen! Stinson stammered as it disappeared. *It was a monster, and we—we just let it go!*

I took the biggest stream-bred brown trout I have ever caught that same afternoon. It was holding deep in a two-hundred-yard pool. Steep cliffs plunge directly into its jade-colored springheads. Big ledges and outcroppings lie along one cliff. The other wall is impassable, and the entire pool is too deep to wade. Its bottom pebbles are sharply defined in fifteen feet of water, and we worked cautiously along the steep cliffs.

MacDowell was leading the party, searching out footholds in the mossy ledge rock, clawing at the thick vines and branches. The plants were strongly rooted and I followed haltingly, with Stinson twenty feet behind, refusing to look down. The water was at least six or seven feet deep.

I can't believe we're doing this, he said.

I can't either, I laughed.

How are you holding your rod?

With my teeth, I joked weakly. *I'm holding on with everything else.*

Like Errol Flynn's saber?

Exactly like Errol Flynn's saber, I said. **The Crimson Pirate.**

Captain Blood, Stinson corrected.

We had almost reached the big ledges halfway up the pool, and MacDowell had nearly disappeared in the matted vines and thickets ahead. We could hear him wrestling with the brush and muttering when his brogues triggered a tiny scattering of stones into the quiet pool.

Sweet Jesus! he hissed.

What's wrong?

Big fish, he said quietly. *Climb out on the ledges and stay back in the shade—it's a really big brown!*

We followed his instructions carefully. I studied the sunny throat of the pool, and Stinson sat down on a big stone. The entire bottom of the pool was clearly lighted, and I worked higher to study it from a better angle, carefully avoiding the bright sun.

Don't see anything yet, I shaded my eyes. *Except the big stone.*

It's not a stone, MacDowell chuckled.

You're joking! I said.

Watch it carefully, he insisted. *I can see it clearly from here—it's a fish and it's moving!*

But it's huge! I protested weakly.

It's a fish, he said.

My heart almost stopped when the big chocolate-colored shape drifted a few inches to the right, paused briefly, and drifted back.

It took something, MacDowell called. *I'll stay up here on the cliff—it'll take a weighted nymph and a sinking line to get that deep.*

Let's wait a few minutes, I said.

Why wait? Stinson asked.

Let's wait until the whole ledge is in the shade, I explained. *I'll have to stand out there to reach that fish—and I want to stay hidden.*

The trout was lying just above the bottom, ranging back and forth majestically, sixty feet below the ledge. I switched reels to rig a sinking line and a fresh six-pound leader. The fly was a black nymph with darkly mottled ptarmigan legs and tails, and a body ribbed with gold wire on a size ten sproat hook. The cast had to fall well beyond the fish to get its drift and sink rate right. Such clear water makes depth difficult to judge. It took several long casts, studying the sink rate and drift, before I was getting the nymph down to the fish.

It looks good! MacDowell hissed from his observation post high in the *manuka* brush. *He's drifting to the right—and he took something!*

The drift stopped and tightened.

Feels like I'm snagged.

You're not snagged! MacDowell came tightroping back along the cliff in a shower of twigs and stones, *You've got him!*

You're right! my voice broke.

The fight took ninety minutes. The big trout lazily explored the entire pool at will. Several strong runs threatened to reach the rapids, and once it attempted to foul the leader in the big rocks lying deep at its throat. Its struggling finally ebbed into a dreamlike series of figure-eight circuits past our ledge. Several times it fought to probe under the ledges where we stood, its spade-sized tail working slowly.

Finally I could control its fight, worked the big fish closer and closer, and netted it with a quick sweep. Its huge tail writhed angrily above the rim. Its big head wrenched and thrashed deep in the meshes, and the net bag tore slightly. It was butter-fat and measured thirty-two inches, a perfectly shaped henfish we estimated at twelve pounds. MacDowell and I both photographed the trophy brown and revived it, until it drifted deep into the pool, an amber specter that held briefly over the cobblestone bottom and vanished.

Thank you for sharing that, I said weakly.

There are many such memories of those latitudes, thoughts of people and places mixed with daydreams of anticipation too. Sometimes it is snowing outside in the chill weeks just before Christmas, but my thoughts are filled with images thousands of miles across the South Pacific.

It is late summer in New Zealand. We are camped with Geoffrey Thomas at the deer-hunter's camp on the Rangeitiki, and our Maori cook is passing another compulsory round of almost undrinkable black rum. Rex Forrester sits grinning in the helicopter, hovering just above a gravelly beach. Hugh MacDowell is standing awestruck in a clear pumice-gorge river, stunned at the size of the fish he has just flushed from its ledges. Peter Church is scrabbling to keep his perch in a spotting tree when I hooked a huge fish we had worked for almost an hour. Crown rack of lamb at the Tongariro Lodge, with several bottles of Wynne's Coonawarra Cabernet, and a sunny morning with Tony Hayes on the beautiful Tongariro itself. Dick Fraser and his forced quick-step marches along the upper Hunter, his uncanny skills at spotting fish, and his bubbling good humor. The lobster-and-champagne picnic on the Greenstone with Dick Deaker, the storied helicopter pilot from Te Anau. Bill Stewart and a pretty day's trekking on the Worsley. Geoffrey MacDonald and the weedy little Diamond Burn, like a British chalk stream in the Southern Alps. Lloyd Knowles on the Castle and Oreti, and Murray Knowles tending his billy-pot fire on the Iris Burn. The late Fred Gill, chain-smoking as he shields his eyes on a grassy, looping bend below Shirker's Wood on the upper Mararoa, expertly spotting its big browns at great distances.

Just another hundred yards. Gill's pale eyes were twinkling with mischief between rivulets of sweat. *Always a good fish in the next bend—and I might bring you a cold Steinlager from the lorry, mate.*

These people are unique, like their tiny country at the bottom of the world. It is impossible to forget either, and I particularly remember a morning in the Hermitage at Mount Cook. It was just after daylight, and I was awakened by the brash chattering of kea parrots just off my balcony. It seemed unusually bright outside, and I pulled the drapes. Light exploded into the room. The sun was barely above the horizon, but the summits of Mount Cook were glowing and afire, with snow plumes billowing beyond eleven thousand feet. But the fierce light came from Mount Sefton, its sheer icefields looming directly over the hotel, catching the early morning sun. There is a Maori poem that captures my feeling about these people and their beautiful little country in the Antipodes:

> Here in our ancestral *marae*
> Wast thou buried
> Under the steep-walled Maunga-Roa
> Thy spirit returns to this dark and secret place
> Among the thick *toi* and tree-ferns, hovering
> Hidden in the cabbage trees
> And wild rocks.
>
> Loved now, only by spirits and shadows.
> Such was my dream.

The Spider at Buttonwood Pool

Yesterday I walked down the brushy path below the Buttonwood, its pale stones brightly exposed in the early sun, and stopped to watch a trout smutting in the shallows. It was a morning that I decided to fish the Slide Pool, still deep in shadows just after breakfast, where its tumbling throat spills under a thicket of rhododendron.

Both pools have fine early-morning hatches of olive-bodied *Ephemerella* flies in late spring. The little river spills through boulders at the tail of the Buttonwood, and a riffling chute reaches all the way to Slide. It was a beautiful morning. Flycatchers were waiting nervously for the mayflies to hatch, and the music of the river filled my head. The brushy path ahead was blocked by a big spider busily spinning its web.

Good morning! I thought.

Its industry had already partially spanned the path, with the tensile grace of spiders, and the growing symmetry of its work told me things about the morning. Spiders seldom work so busily when they sense a threat of rain. It was crisp and dry. The morning clearly held the promise of fine weather, and the delicate spiderweb told me that no other fishermen had passed.

The textbook precision of the spider's work caused me to stop. Its silken geometry was wonderful, glowing brightly in the sun. Since I was grateful to the spider for its judgment about the weather, and that no one else had fished the pool, I circled cautiously past its web.

The flies had started hatching. Two phoebes were darting out from the alders to catch them. Their acrobatics were worth watching, capturing the freshly hatched flies in midflight, fluttering to make their rapier-quick thrusts. Wheeling back to their perches, the phoebes held the mayflies firmly whiskered in their bills.

Slide shelves off with a heavy current that scours deep along the rocks. It eddies back under the alders downstream, and several boulders break the flow at the tail of the pool. The steep shingle below the pool holds a few fish in its pockets before it tumbles into the Barrel.

The Slide has a history of big fish. It has often been usurped by hook-billed brown trout that drive lesser fish away. Several times I have hunted such trout, hoping to free the pool for smaller fish that rise better to fly-hatches. Once I attempted to extract a large brown by fishing a big silver-bodied marabou at Slide, stalking it infantry-style through the shallows downstream. Using a big rod and throwing most of the line from my knees, I fished through the entire pool without actually entering its shallows. It required stripping the fly back fast, with a quick full-arm pull along the bottom. There was nothing until I threw the big fly to the throat of the pool, and there was a wrenching strike that easily sheared the Ox tippet.

Crocodile! I thought wildly.

We never caught that big fish. It is impossible to fish the pool even fifteen years later without remembering its strike. Once I took a brace of sixteen-inch browns at Slide, fishing a small nymph upstream into its tail shallows. There have been many times when Slide has surrendered a decent fish or two during a good fly-hatch, but I took the best fish there a few years ago when the little Brodheads was in spate.

It was murky and faintly chocolate. Its currents rose until it sucked almost angrily at tree roots and boulders. The pool looked almost hopeless, and it was still raining hard, but I decided to fish it anyway. Usually I fish the pool from below, although most fishermen simply work it wet-fly style from its throat, where they stand easily seen by its fish. It looked so roily and discolored that it seemed easier to jettison my usual stealth, since I was masked by dirty water, and fish it downstream like the others.

The river had started to rise while I was fishing, and it was time to change reels. I worked quickly to string a sinking line and add a fresh leader in the rain. There was another big marabou in my fly-boxes, its white stork feathers dressed with a topping of olive and turquoise hackles and

• THE SPIDER AT BUTTONWOOD POOL •

herl over a body of silver mylar piping. It was feathery and almost four inches long and looked like a fat *Notropis* shiner.

It was unnecessary to cast, and I simply stripped off line into the fast chute above the pool and shook the rod to layer it out into the current. When the line settled deep and bellied taut, I stripped the fly back with the rod held low. It had traveled a dozen quick pulls when a fish lunged up from the bottom and took it hard. The fish was surprisingly strong. Its run bored deep along the bottom, carrying it the full length of the pool, and when I coaxed it back there was a second run almost as stubborn. It finally came grudgingly to the net. It measured twenty-two inches, and it did not bolt back when I released it. The fish was tired and held quietly at my feet, using my ankles to break the flow.

Good fish, I thought happily, *but it's not like the fish that broke me— that fish was a shark.*

The memories ebbed when I circled downstream on the spiderweb morning to study the pool. It seemed wise to wait until the hatching flies had started the fish. The pool is fished often, and its trout are usually skittish and shy.

Almost an hour passed before a single fish fitfully started to work, but I still waited, thinking more flies might come. My patience was wasted. Our hatches of Blue-Winged Olives seldom last an hour, and after thirty minutes, the flies still were so sparse that only one other fish was visible. I slipped into the shallows, working stealthily on my knees, and prepared to cast. The tiny dry fly darted out, settled across the water, and cocked perfectly on the smooth current. It disappeared in a quiet dimple. The trout bolted upstream until I coaxed it away from the other fish that was rising. It was not large, perhaps ten inches at most, but it had the ruby mottlings of a wild trout.

It darted back when I released it. The second fish was slightly larger, but it took the fly with the splashy rise of a stocked trout. It seemed healthy enough, bulldogging along the bottom until it was finally netted, but it fought clumsily and its colors were dour. I fished the entire pool without moving another trout and saw no other rises. It was getting almost hot and I was thirsty. It seemed like a good time to quit for lunch at Buttonwood.

Bird in the hand, I waded out contentedly. *Maybe we'll still see a hatch of sulphurs this evening.*

I had completely forgotten the spiderweb across the path, and I stopped to study it when I walked back. It was shining and perfect in the sun. The spider had completed its silky geometries, and I studied its craftsmanship with a grudging envy.

Well, I told the spider, *there wasn't much hatching this morning, but it doesn't really matter.*

The spiderweb shuddered slightly as the spider shifted its weight. It paid no attention. It was greedily devouring a mayfly freshly trapped in its delicate traceries, and most spiders have better things to do than waste a morning's work in idle talk about fishing.

Song of the Stillaguamish

The beautiful Olympic Hotel is old and richly detailed, suggesting that its city has a sense of history, in spite of the faceless glass-sheathed office towers that surround its Renaissance splendor. It has the character of Florentine palaces, with large stones set in ashlar masonrywork, rusticated and streaked with rain. Its cornices and entablatures are intricately worked, in a counterpoint of metopes and triglyphs. Its doorways and windows are beautifully framed in pilasters and sills, capped with architraves and arches, and acanthus leaves and volutes. The lobby is a Florentine *cortile*, its ceiling coffers mixed with dentil ornament and egg-and-dart work, with loggias and staircases leading from the street. Big mirrors are framed in lavabos. Both columns and pilasters are fluted, and the building has echoes of Michelozzo and Brunelleschi and Sangallo.

The city itself stands on a gentle range of coastal hills. Its busy ferryboats work steadily between the big ferry slips and its island suburbs and the Olympic Peninsula. Steep streets and buildings rise between Lake Washington and the kelp-smelling tides of Puget Sound.

Seattle and its old Olympic Hotel lie in steelhead country. Its coasts are a countinghouse of famous rivers, draining the beautiful snow-covered Cascades that rise behind the city. Their names are magic among fishermen. The Snoqualmie lies just outside the city, with its famous falls, but is no longer a great fishery. The Skykomish rises in the mountains farther north and has given its name to a famous steelhead fly-pattern, the Skykomish

Sunrise. The Skagit is perhaps the most productive steelhead river left in northern Washington, rising among the snowfields and glaciers at the threshold of British Columbia. It is famous for both its winter-run fish and its bald eagles. But the steelhead fishery with perhaps the richest history and tradition is the lovely Stillaguamish.

It has been celebrated by writers such as Zane Grey and the late Roderick Haig-Brown, who took his first steelhead on its principal tributary. Its poet laureate today is a young Seattle writer, Steve Raymond, and in his lyric book *The Year of the Angler* he writes lovingly of the Stillaguamish. Several years ago, finding myself scheduled to lecture in Seattle, I contacted a few old friends in search of some steelhead fishing. Their replies were not encouraging. It was still early summer, and only a few scattered fish might have entered their favorite rivers.

It's too early, the tournament caster Jim Green told me. *We might try to find a fish or two on the Bogachiel—but don't hold your breath, and call Ralph Wahl in Bellingham*.

Wahl was an old friend and knew the fisheries above Seattle. His photographs of those rivers are found in *Come Wade the River*, a portfolio with quotations taken from the books of Roderick Haig-Brown.

Our summer fish are not really running yet, Wahl confirmed Green's judgments. *We might find some fish in the Olympic rivers*.

Bogachiel? I asked.

It's possible, Wahl agreed. *It gets some early fish*.

But I've always wanted to fish the Stillaguamish, I suggested excitedly. *Could we just see it?*

I'll call Wes Drain, he said.

Drain is among the best steelhead fishermen in the world. The beautiful rivers surrounding Seattle have spawned an entire generation of great anglers, including the late Ken McLeod, who was a popular fishing writer at the *Seattle Post-Intelligencer* before the Second World War. Ken McLeod developed the Skykomish Sunrise, and Enos Bradner first tied the pattern still called Brad's Brat. It was a Stillaguamish steelhead fly. Enos Bradner wrote for the *Seattle Times,* had a little fishing cabin at Oso, and was still fishing the river at eighty-three.

Wahl also had a little place at Oso, near the cabin owned by Frank Headrick, another famous steelhead pioneer. Lew Bell had his place on the Hell Hole and served as president of the prestigious Federation of Flyfishers before his untimely death. The list of steelhead pioneers devoted to the Stillaguamish includes Letcher Lambuth, Don Ives, Lee Richardson, Rick Miller, Dub Price, Walter Johnson, and Al Knudsen—whose bright-feathered flies are in the collection of the Museum of American Fly Fishing.

Seattle was shrouded in misting rain at daylight, when Ralph Wahl met me at the Olympic. *You can see why we eventually rust*, Wahl laughed. *It should clear a little before lunch.*

Let's hope so, I said.

The parkways that loop through the city past its skyscrapers were almost empty. Sea fog was layered thickly along the sound and held along the lower Skykomish. The big mountains and their snowfields were still hidden in the overcast. It was a pastoral countryside of tidy farms and dense windbreaks of pines and cedars. It was still raining when we stopped for breakfast, and when we started north again, the wipers beat a steady rhythm in the rain.

I'm starting to rust, I said.

Wes Drain was waiting outside the store at Oso, where Deer Creek joins the river. The creek was a famous steelhead fishery itself before it was completely lumbered off, and restoration efforts are being coordinated by my old friend Alec Jackson. The stream was once the primary spawning tributary of the entire Stillaguamish, the source of its legendary summer-run stocks. Mindless timber cutting had already begun when Haig-Brown surveyed its stands in 1926, and its privately held tracts were extensively stripped at midcentury. Its steelhead runs atrophied swiftly. The headwaters were still relatively pristine until twenty years ago, when an aggressive policy of timber sales was started on public lands managed by the United States Forest Service. Their widespread policy of clear-cutting triggered a series of big slides, including an immense slump of hundreds of acres along De Forest Creek. Silts quickly smothered both spawning beds and aquatic fly life. Such impacts are still eroding the entire watershed today, and public opposition finally got the Forest Service to accept a moratorium in timber sales on upper Deer Creek and its tributaries. But the Scott Paper Company ignored the fishermen who loved the river and coldly stripped a tract lying just above the Stillaguamish itself. The future of the Stillaguamish and its steelhead is cloudy, in spite of its obvious beauty and a host of friends.

Wes Drain is among its most devoted pilgrims and is widely acknowledged as the fisherman who understood its moods best. *Not many fish in the river yet,* Drain told us. *Might find a fish at Skier's or the Fortson Hole.*

Which should we try first? Wahl asked.

Skier's Hole, Drain said.

The history of the Stillaguamish and its coastal valley is surprisingly old. The waters off its mouth were first sailed by Juan de Fuca in 1592, and his name still graces the strait connecting Puget Sound with the Pacific.

Juan de Fuca was a Spanish navigator. The first British vessel to chart this strait was commanded by Charles William Barkley in 1787. Captain George Vancouver explored these coastal seas meticulously, including the wooded islands and channels off the Stillaguamish, five years later. Puget Sound is named for his first officer, Lieutenant Peter Puget.

Vancouver was a widely experienced officer, having served aboard the HMS *Resolution* with Captain James Cook, in his second circumnavigation of the world. Vancouver sailed with Cook again in 1776, on Cook's third world voyage, when the famous explorer was killed by natives in the Hawaiian Islands.

The expedition that took Vancouver into the Strait of Juan de Fuca lasted almost five years. Since Cook had sailed these waters earlier, Vancouver already knew something of these wild coasts, and his mission was twofold. Royal hydrographers and chartmakers were to survey the complex coasts and archipelagoes between Puget Sound and the Queen Charlotte Islands, and Vancouver was to take control of tribal lands recently ceded to the British Crown. The Vancouver expedition circled Vancouver Island and thoroughly charted its Discovery Passage and the Strait of Georgia. The expedition was an immense success. The Captain finally returned to England in 1795 and immediately began work on the three-volume account of his expedition. Vancouver died just before the work was completed, and it was finished by Lieutenant Puget. The three-volume edition was titled *A Voyage of Discovery to the North Pacific Ocean and Around the World* and was published with a comprehensive atlas in 1798.

Several trading posts were established in the region after Captain Robert Gray explored the lower Columbia in 1792. Gray admired the snowcapped symmetry of Mount Saint Helens, which Vancouver had christened after a minor British diplomat earlier that year. Gray named the river after his ship HMS *Columbia*. Thirteen years later, Meriwether Lewis and William Clark reached its mouth and built a winter stockade. Their primitive sanctuary and none of the British trading posts survived, although Clark tells us in the elkskin journals of the Lewis and Clark Expedition that he was deeply moved by the beauty of Mount Saint Helens.

Wilson Price Hunt established the fur-trading post called Astoria at the Columbia's mouth in 1811. It was controlled by John Jacob Astor and his Pacific Fur Company. Robert Stuart joined the Hunt party at Astoria, having brought the gaff-rigged schooner *Tonquin* around Cape Horn with another company of Astor's men. Both Hunt and Stuart crossed the continent, becoming the first to travel the overland routes that later evolved into the storied Oregon Trail.

Astor sold his outpost on the Columbia to the British North West

Company in 1813. The British firm had started at Montreal twenty years earlier, but explorers had pushed into the Pacific territories after 1787. The British fur trader David Thompson played a considerable role in the expansion of the North West Company. Thompson had no formal training, yet evolved into a self-taught cartographer who displayed great skills at making geodetic and celestial observations. His painstaking work fixed many important geographic features across Canada, and satellite cartography has largely confirmed Thompson's astonishing precision. Thompson crossed freely into United States territory to chart the headwaters of the Missouri and Mississippi before 1798, and traveled the entire length of the Columbia thirteen years later. His party also circled east into the Montana territory, carefully charting the American headwaters of the Columbia and ascending such tributaries as the Blackfoot, Bitterroot, and Clark's Fork in 1807. Hostile war parties blocked Thompson's possible routes across the Howse and Kicking Horse passes in 1810, so his party circled north across Yellowhead Pass in the Athabasca country. Thompson traveled south into United States territory again and reached the mouth of the Columbia to find Hunt's men had built a stockade at Astoria, a few miles above the site where Lewis and Clark had wintered earlier at Fort Clatsop.

David Thompson was not given his proper place among formally trained geographers for more than a century, although he returned to Montreal in 1812 and prepared large, richly detailed maps of western Canada and the upper United States that are still the wellsprings of our cartography today. His maps contributed to the subsequent success of British trading companies in Idaho, Montana, and the Oregon territories. Thompson also filled many uncharted places in our frontier maps of British Columbia, and his name still graces the great steelhead fishery that drains the Kamloops country.

John Jacob Astor surrendered his Pacific outpost when his relations with British traders soured during the War of 1812. Astor took control of Astoria again five years later, and missionaries soon followed.

Francois Blanchet founded his mission on the Cowlitz in 1839, and Marcus Whitman built his ill-fated mission at Wailatpu the following year. Whitman played a considerable role in raising American interest in the Oregon Territory before his death. Cayuse warriors attacked the Whitman mission in 1847, killing Whitman and his entire family. The massacre strongly influenced the United States Congress in establishing the Oregon Territory the following year.

Cayuse war parties briefly slowed the tides of immigration along the Oregon Trail, which had already reached Tumwater in 1843, only sixty-odd miles south of Seattle.

Washington was separated from the Oregon Territory ten years later, and Isaac Stevens was appointed its territorial governor. Settlers had already founded Seattle and were aggressively cutting timber in the forests between Lake Washington and Puget Sound. The steep ravine the lumberjacks used to skid giant logs to the mills and wharves on Puget Sound became thickly lined with honkytonks and saloons and passed into the frontier language as Skid Row. Seattle remained rowdy and relatively small until late in the century, when the Northern Pacific crossed the Cascades through Snoqualmie Pass and the Yakima Valley.

The Washington Territory was extensively settled before the Civil War, but its Indian tribes still bitterly resisted. War parties of Yakima and Cayuse ravaged backcountry settlements in 1859, and older towns along Puget Sound feared that the raids might spill west through the mountains. The United States Army knew its response to such war parties would be too cumbersome to prove effective. It dispatched military engineers to build a primitive road connecting Fort Steilacoom, on the tidal narrows a few miles south of Tacoma, with the virgin forests beyond the Stillaguamish country.

The military road was never used during the tribal uprisings of 1859, but it offered access to a growing flood of trappers, land speculators, farmers, highwaymen, and traders. The Stillaguamish watershed was split between Skagit and Snohomish counties by the territorial legislature in 1867. Snohomish County had a total of thirty-six frontiersmen in its first census. The only settlement lay in Skykomish County, some forty miles farther south, until Henry Marshall cleared his homestead on the lower Stillaguamish in 1864.

Marshall started a modest emigration into the country north of Seattle. Such pioneers were only a trickle during the Civil War years, but when a trader named James Perkins bought the Marshall farmstead in 1869, his enterprise quickly helped the Stillaguamish country to prosper. Trade with the Stillaguamish tribe steadily grew, and other settlers arrived to populate the freshly cleared forests with cattle and small plots of grain and orchards. Perkins was perhaps the first to cut the giant cedars and firs along the lower river. His profits soon evolved into a small country hotel and saloon, and a series of logging camps throughout the lower valley in 1875. Perkins had perfect timing, since timber prices skyrocketed to ten dollars per thousand board feet, and the cathedral-dark forests were stripped and sold as quickly as the lumberjacks could fell them. The drumfire rhythms of axes were mixed with the shrill whine of the big saws. Steam engines drove the sawmills, small trains carried loads of giant logs, and smoke hung across the valley from its fires of sawdust and slash.

Although few settlers understood, the rapacity of ringing axes and falling trees was a threat to the Stillaguamish itself. Our rapacity still threatens its fishery.

Other settlers quickly followed the logging camps. Such pioneers were mostly farmers who worked terrible hours, pulling stumps and loading stoneboats with cobbles and glacial till, and draining bogs and salt marshes and sloughs. The uncontrolled logging triggered huge slides and spates, collapsing banks and threatening the settlers downstream. The pristine river had become silty and dour. The landowners downstream were losing precious soil to the floods. Dikes and timber barrages and weirs were built to protect their river-bottom farms from flooding. The spates came steadily now, not just during the spring thawing, because the forests were swiftly disappearing upstream. The farmers stubbornly fought to protect their lands, tilled the rich alluvial soils, and planted fruit trees and crops.

Land speculators followed the clear-cutting like carrion birds, pushing a wagon trace upstream in the summer of 1884. Gullible settlers bought freshly timbered tracts, and some actually started orchards and farms. The best landowners survived, selling their crops and livestock to the lumber camps. The timber markets thrived, and the farmers prospered. Settlements along the watershed were thriving, and they had few rivals north of Seattle, including much older towns nearby. The Stillaguamish settlements were prosperous in 1889.

Washington achieved its statehood that year, and emigration continued to swell. Settlement had reached almost explosive proportions after 1879, and the completion of the railroad to Seattle accelerated its growth.

The Stillaguamish watershed itself was no exception. Arlington lies at the junction of its principal forks, and it had less than fifty citizens when Washington was granted statehood, but it grew to more than two thousand people early in our century. There were farmsteads as far upstream as Darrington, where the river flows glacier cold from the icefields on Whitechuck and Snow King and Spire. The timber crews had pushed well beyond Fortson and Darrington, ruthlessly cutting trees and hauling logs with oxteams to the river, where rafts were floated to the sawmills.

The railroad reached Darrington in 1901, and other small towns were thriving in the timber boom. Arlington and Florence were full-fledged towns with tent camps at their periphery, and tiny settlements like Fortson and Oso were growing too. Oso stood where Deer Creek joins the Stillaguamish, and it was not long before it had its own country store and post office.

Yet everything was threatened by such explosive change. The forests had been ruthlessly cut, felling primeval stands of cedars and sugar pines and firs. The great trees had fallen heavily, crushing their understory of seedlings and brushy thickets and small trees, shaking the earth with their thunder. Small locomotives rumbled through the stillness now, puffing and hissing steam and scattering wildlife with their shrill whistles. Small tributaries lay choked with sawdust and freshly scaled bark and slash. Entire hillsides had slipped, spilling their raw clay into the river and its feeders, choking them with silt. Sawdust and slash collected in the deep holes and backwaters, settling and rotting slowly, with steady bubbles of methane rising. The rotting sawdust and slash leached tannic acids into the river, slowly killing its fertility.

The Stillaguamish tribe had been ruthlessly exploited too. They had originally called themselves the Stoluc-wha-nish people, and even their tribal name had been corrupted by the lumberjacks and settlers. The coastal wilderness lay in tatters. With its death, the poetry of the valley was gone, a casualty of the brutally alien culture that had forced itself on their primitive world.

The cut-over acreages were cleared of their stumps and brushy thickets, and in some river bottoms, they became a rich patchwork of crops and hayfields and fruit trees. Steep hillsides and barren tracts grew back quickly, their great conifers replaced by maples and quaking aspens and alders. Deer and small birds and grouse all prospered after the loggers had passed. Dogwoods and laurel grew swiftly, thickly mixed with trilliums and serviceberry. White snowberry and scarlet rosettes of bunchberry thrived, along with bear grass and hillsides of fireweed. Grassy clearings were bright with lupine and shooting stars and three-leaf *Oxalis*, and the sunny hillside pastures were filled with white bistort and farewell-to-spring and scarlet paintbrush. Penstemons and globe mallow and avalanche lilies grew higher in the grassy balds, mixed with bird's eyes and phlox. The entire valley had been changed forever.

But the prosperity of the farms and fruit growers and stores was short-lived. The lumber camps that sustained them had flowered briefly, like saw-mill towns and mining camps throughout our western mountains, and had faded again swiftly into ghost towns and ramshackle obscurity. The immense forests that had shrouded the valley and its beautiful river, forests of red cedar mixed with spruce and Douglas fir and hemlock, were largely cut before the Stillaguamish became famous for its steelhead.

The Stillaguamish had magnificent runs of these bright sea-run rainbows, unique genetic strains of summer fish. Most steelhead penetrate their parent rivers in the late fall and winter, when the streams are swollen with rain. It is the coin-bright fish of summer that are prized by fishermen, and the Stillaguamish was among the finest summer steelhead fisheries in the world.

The river had sustained magnificent runs of steelhead before the timber-cutting years, when few had time to mine its riches, and its fishery was still pristine. The summer steelhead started to come in increasing numbers after early June, and most of the run usually arrived in July. The fishing usually ebbed gradually into August, and any late summer storm could pull most of the fish into Deer Creek. Its headwater riffles spawned most of the original summer-run population in the entire watershed. The fishing dropped off swiftly once an August spate had flushed its summer steelhead upstream, and there was not much sport until the October rains pulled the first winter-run fish from the Pacific. The autumn fish were always bright.

Like freshly minted dollars! Wes Drain explained while we drove upriver. *Those winter fish were unmistakable—you could spot them a quarter-mile away when you saw somebody else carrying one.*

The winter fish that arrive after Thanksgiving are erratic, perhaps too heavily cropped over the years by tribal netting, and few bright fish arrive until late winter. Indian steelhead netting is still a serious issue on rivers like the Stillaguamish. *The courts sustained their fishing rights*, Ralph Wahl said quietly, *although it's really stretching things to talk about anything like a Stillaguamish tribe on the river today*.

All six of them, Drain said drily.

February fishing is typically spare, but it picks up again in March and has historically been closed in spawning time. Hatchery programs have changed these ambient migratory patterns. Earlier runs come before June, hatchery stocks mixed with mended kelts and a few winter fish that failed to spawn successfully. The hard rains in late September sometimes triggered October runs of big pewter-grey hatchery fish. Summer-run smolts are also stocked in the Stillaguamish itself at the Fortson Hole, and these hatchery fish bypass Deer Creek today, returning to the Fortson from the sea. The principal spawning grounds of wild stocks are still reported in Little Deer Creek, in spite of the logging that decimated the entire watershed. It is puzzling that any fish survived.

Amen, Drain nodded.

The Stillaguamish also boasted a fine run of giant chinook salmon in the early fall. Such fish apparently entered the river in a seasonal niche between the discrete runs of summer and late-fall steelhead. Bright sea-run char and heavily spotted cutthroat arrived with the harvest moon. Chum salmon were historically sparse. Pink salmon arrived in great hordes during alternate years, spawning mostly in the lower river, and some coho also gathered to spawn there. Since sockeye fry spend considerable time in lakes before smolting into the Pacific and there are no suitable lakes in the Stillaguamish drainage, only sockeye strays are found in the watershed.

Summers in the Stillaguamish country are relatively warm and wet. Its winters are surprisingly mild. The steelhead is the secret, silvery wealth of the river, and its summer-run steelhead are unique. The steelhead on most rivers is still winter's child.

We've got both, Ralph Wahl explained happily.

We drove steadily upstream in the rain, past Oso and Deer Creek, with skeins of mist still drifting like catkins in the trees. Both men were watching the river now, judging its clarity and depth, and talking about its history.

It started with Zane Grey, Wahl said.

When did Grey fish it? I asked. *Why did he pick the Stillaguamish?*

It was an accident, Drain replied.

Accident? I asked.

Grey was fascinated with bigger game when he started fishing, Wahl explained, *and he first went to Campbell River.*

British Columbia?

Tyee Club, he continued. *Grey was trolling at the Tyee Club for big chinooks—he fished where Haig-Brown later worked as a guide.*

Grey heard about steelhead there?

That's right, Drain said.

Grey heard more than steelhead talk at the Tyee Club, Wahl continued. *Grey heard talk about the Stillaguamish.*

And Deer Creek too, Drain added.

Grey came to Seattle, Wahl explained, *and he asked around until he found men who knew the Stillaguamish.*

Enos Bradner? I asked.

Grey died in 1939, Wahl replied, *but he fished the Stillaguamish about twenty years earlier.*

Too early for Brad, Drain guessed. *Too early.*

Brad came in 1929, Wahl nodded.

Grey traveled north from Seattle to Arlington in late summer and was advised to try the North Fork. The steelhead runs had been quite good. Several local fishermen recommended the big junction pool at the mouth of Deer Creek, telling Grey that it was literally filled with steelhead.

But when they came up the Stilly, Drain said, *it had rained heavily.*

The fish went straight up the creek, Wahl said.

It's good to know old things don't change, I laughed. *They told Grey he should've come last week!*

You're right! Drain chuckled.

Zane Grey found the Stillaguamish quite beautiful, gathering itself to slide into glittering half-mile riffles between its famous pools. His guides were skilled bait fishermen who used split-cane bait rods and braided lines, with short gut leaders and sufficient lead shot to work a fine-mesh sac of fresh roe along the bottom. Some fished fly rods with enameled lines, shooting surprising casts across the river with a contraption Grey found intriguing. It was apparently first developed on the Stillaguamish and consisted of a wire or canvas basket strapped to a fisherman's belt. Several loops of fly line were layered in the basket before casting, and these loops shot out easily when a cast was made. Grey's book *Tales of Fresh-Water Fishing* described his discovery of these primitive stripping baskets on the Stillaguamish in 1918.

Did they catch anything? I asked.

Nothing, Wahl replied. *They decided to follow the fish*.

The party traveled north to a lumber camp at Lake McMurray, having recruited a local fisherman who knew the headwaters of Deer Creek to guide them. The trip quickly became a minor odyssey. The narrow-gauge logging train that carried them was primitive, rumbling along poorly buttressed and maintained trackage. The timber trestles groaned and sagged as they passed. Grey tells us in *Tales of Fresh-Water Fishing* that their engine actually left its tracks before they reached their destination. The party spent the entire night on a rough half-seen trail through the dense forests.

Exhausted and hungry, Grey finally saw the headwaters of Deer Creek at daylight. It flowed swiftly through its giant cedars, sparkling in tumbling chutes among the boulders, eddying deep and jade colored in its pools. It lay in a steep-walled canyon, topography too difficult to lumber off, and Grey wrote that it was crystalline and icy cold.

Grey caught nothing the first day, but he thought he saw steelhead hovering and flashing in its clear jade-green riffles and pools.

The second morning, he hooked his first summer steelhead. It exploded in spray and raced swiftly into the tail shallows, wildly stripping line from his shrill reel. It rolled and flashed, catching the sunlight on its polished armor, and jumped in a high pirouette that left Grey gasping. Its fight was savage and wild, yet strangely filled with beauty and grace. It was a fitting prelude to Grey's later passion for steelhead fishing, and his lifelong fascination with other rivers happily graced with summer-run fish—rivers like the Rogue and Umpqua.

Grey became a steelhead addict right here on Deer Creek, Ralph Wahl said. *Haig-Brown hooked his first steelhead here too!*

It is curious that both writers discovered a passion for summer-run steelhead in the Stillaguamish country. Roderick Haig-Brown had just arrived on the Pacific Coast, half exiled from a British family that had rigorously planned his life in terms of reading history and politics at Cambridge and a subsequent career in the British Colonial Service. Haig-Brown was working as a timber surveyor along the Stillaguamish in 1927, nine years after Grey's first steelhead trip. Haig-Brown became fascinated with the fishing talk around the lumber camps and sawmills, and the steelhead was obviously held in something like awe among the crews. His first attempts at fishing them ended in failure.

His poetic anthology *A River Never Sleeps* describes those abortive beginnings and a subsequent trek into the headwaters of Deer Creek. The chapter describing his early experiences with steelhead has these observations:

> I cannot remember now what I expected of steelhead before I ever saw one. The name almost certainly gave me a mental picture of a fish whose back was a polished blue-gray like steel and whose strength was all that steel implies. One could do a lot worse than that.

The lumber-camp myths and stories about steelhead did not lack drama, and even the wildest exaggerations still held the ring of truth. One friend told Haig-Brown that he had hooked a big steelhead that had simply taken his telescopic bait-rod, its casting reel, and its entire spool of Cuttyhunk line.

Another lumberjack described clearing a logjam, leapfrogging back and forth across its giant jackstraw puzzle, and stopping transfixed. Through a roughly framed opening in the tangled logs, he could see a dozen steelhead better than thirty inches almost suspended in its watery shadows, a pewter school of giant fish working lazily in the depths.

Haig-Brown got another chance at steelhead. His timber-cruising party was sent into the Deer Creek drainage, and Haig-Brown hiked still farther to fish it on the weekends. Those minor expeditions into these towering woods were another world to a young exile from the United Kingdom, and Haig-Brown described them with the perceptions of a young architect staring up into the soaring vaults and traceries of cathedrals like Winchester and Salisbury and Wells.

Haig-Brown was also finding bear-sign while fishing, and grizzlies were unsettling to a young angler whose Sussex chalk downs and Dorsetshire moors were limited to foxes and hares. Deer Creek was almost poetry itself.

During his first hike there, he found a fine pool above a tangled logjam.

The tributary was large enough to qualify as a river in England, fully as large as the Frome of his boyhood. Haig-Brown found a gravelly bar upstream, with room for his casting, and shelving off into smooth depths over a cobblestone bottom. He was excited and hurried to rig his tackle, but let these fragments from *A River Never Sleeps* tell his story:

> I was standing on a wide gravel bar which gave me every chance to cast and fish as I wished, and my heart beat hard and my fingers trembled as I dumped my pack and began to put my rod up—they do that even today when I come to the bank of a river I have not fished before, and find its reality better than anything I had dared to hope.

Haig-Brown was better equipped than most of his lumberjack friends. His tackle included a nine-foot rod fitted with a Hardy Silex reel, and his lure kit included a fistful of salmon spoons and plugs and Devons.

The chute above the pool flowed swift and strong into its throat, and he fished it first, casting well across and letting his Devon minnow settle before fishing it slow and deep. There were no strikes. But when the current began to still itself in the emerald belly of the pool, he began to sense and expect fish. His Devon lure was working deep, ticking sometimes against the stones and grating across the gravelly bottom in its drift. It swung past some sheltering logs, flashing coppery in the sun, and there was a heavy strike.

Haig-Brown tightened into a good fish. It made a strong run back under its logs, and he deftly turned the fish before it fouled the line. It made a second strong run the full length of the pool.

Haig-Brown expected the fish to jump in the wild, explosive struggle of the steelhead stories he had heard, but this fight was puzzling. The fish was stubborn and strong. It bulldogged deep and rolled itself in the line, and finally it surrendered. Haig-Brown beached it easily. It was perhaps four pounds, silvery grey with pale lemon spots and orange fins. He did not think it was a steelhead and hoped it was not, clinging happily to the wild lumberjack stories.

It was a scrappy sea-run char. Deer Creek was apparently filled with these feisty Dolly Vardens, and he caught several more before nightfall. Haig-Brown dressed his catch of bright-finned char and cached them in a cool springhead below his campsite along the creek.

Supper was finished quickly, and he scoured his dishes. It was getting cold, and he happily wrapped himself in his heavy bedroll. Strange noises awakened him at daylight, and he later found a bear had stolen his fish. Its unmistakable tracks were everywhere, a fact Haig-Brown clearly found sobering.

Knowing his crew would never believe his story and merely laugh at his poor fishing luck, Haig-Brown worked feverishly that morning. He killed three big char and finally stopped to enjoy the sun on a broad, gravelly shingle. When he started fishing again, he chose to work back through the pool he had just covered. It looked like it must hold fish. He caught and released several more char, and *A River Never Sleeps* tells us what happened:

> I came to a pool near the foot of the round mountain just as the sun was going down. It was a good pool, with the deep water on my side and a long sloping beach of pale gravel on the far bank. I had worked about halfway down it when a fish took, well out in midstream, right on the swing of the Devon. There was no question of striking. He was away before I had the rod point up, taking line with a speed that made the ratchet of my reel echo into the timber. Then the fish jumped three times, going away, and the sunset was gold on his sides. He turned after the third jump and started back across the pool, and suddenly I knew I was reeling in a slack line with only a Devon at its end.

Like Zane Grey with his first steelhead, Haig-Brown found his fishing transformed and spent the rest of his life in search of these sea-bright rainbows. Steelhead still haunted Haig-Brown's thoughts when he briefly returned to England, and he ultimately stayed in steelhead country.

He arrived back in Vancouver during the Great Depression, with the lumber camps and purse-seine fleets and sawmills shut down. But Haig-Brown was willing to work at almost anything to stay, and the British Columbia officials grudgingly admitted him. He found jobs surveying timber, working on fishing boats, bounty hunting for cougars, trapping, guiding salmon fishermen, gyppo-logging, and salvaging stray logs on the beaches of the Discovery Passage.

Haig-Brown had already written two books before he finally settled in British Columbia, and after he married a girl from Seattle, he bought a small farm at Campbell River. He lived beside his beloved Campbell throughout the rest of his life and died there in 1976.

We'll always miss him, Wahl said.

We drove slowly upstream to the Fortson Hole, where the railroad passed during the logging boom, and found several anglers already fishing. Wahl stopped the camper and sighed. *Pretty crowded these days*, Drain said. *It's where the hatchery smolts are stocked, and it's where most of them come back.*

It's where the fishermen come too.

That's right, Drain chuckled. *Too much of a good thing at the Fortson.*

It's not like the old days, Wahl said.

How's that? I asked.

The frontier steelhead populations were different, Drain explained. *Most of our summer steelhead were spawned up Deer Creek—and few wild fish came into the upper river in those days.*

The history of the watershed has been troubled since its frontier times, and the rapacity of its logging has steadily threatened both the Stillaguamish and its fishery. *When you think how these forests were stripped*, Wahl said bitterly, *it's a wonder anything is left!*

It was Brad! Drain interrupted. *Brad saved us!*

Enos Bradner? I asked.

That's right.

That the steelhead fishery survived in spite of the mindless logging practices is not merely a tribute to the strength and resilience of these hardy trout. It has also survived because of people like the late Enos Bradner. The North Fork is still fly-only, the first steelhead river in the world to receive such protection. Its surprisingly early fly-only status had its beginnings in Bradner's arrival at Seattle in 1929.

Bradner had come to operate a bookshop. Since the threshold of the Great Depression proved a poor time to launch a business of any kind, the young bookseller sold few books. Bradner had plenty of time for fishing. Topographic maps of the region were fascinating, and he studied them religiously. Bradner occupied a growing surplus of free time exploring rivers found on the government maps, and his curiosity finally led him to the Stillaguamish.

The bookshop refugee quickly found himself in love with the river and played a strong role in proposing that both Deer Creek and the mile of river below its mouth be made fly-fishing only. It did not prove a widely popular issue. Fly-only regulations were first publicly proposed through the Snohomish County Sportsman's Association in 1934. The Stillaguamish regulars were happily stunned when state officials at Olympia agreed. But the strident chorus of protest that soon followed was too much for the fish commissioners, and they quickly reversed themselves. The willful decimation of the river continued, but Bradner refused to accept defeat.

Brad was stubborn, Drain grinned.

Support for the fly-only regulations on the Stillaguamish continued to germinate and grow. Fly-only had a small strong-minded band of believers. Bradner took the fight to the Seattle Trout Club and precipitated a virtual civil war. The Seattle Trout Club quarreled bitterly, with a majority of its membership ultimately refusing to support fly-only on the Stillaguamish.

The fly-fishing minority quickly bolted the Seattle Trout Club and met to create a new organization that has evolved into the prestigious Washington Fly-Fishing Club. It was started in the winter of 1939, and its founding president was Enos Bradner. He soon proved himself a dynamo, and subsequently became the fishing writer for the *Seattle Times*, where he spent twenty years.

Bradner and his colleagues still fought for fly-only regulations to protect the unique summer-run steelhead in the North Fork of the Stillaguamish. Bradner himself wrote tirelessly about the fly-only issue. The proposal gained surprisingly wide support in the Seattle region, although many rural sportsmen's groups remained angrily opposed. Bradner's band of partisans finally won when fly-only rules on the Stillaguamish were approved in hearings at Olympia in 1941.

But it wasn't over, Wahl continued. *Bitter opposition erupted throughout the state—and there were several petitions circulating widely.*

It was a fight, Drain nodded.

Bradner rallied his troops again. His popular colleague Ken McLeod, from the *Seattle Post-Intelligencer*, also offered his help. Together with Letcher Lambuth, a richly inventive Seattle fisherman who tied exquisite flies and collected aquatic insects and planed his own split-cane rods, the two fishing writers toured the state for several weeks. The three experts lectured and lobbied and begged for help. They patiently outlined the impacts of logging and agricultural land use on the Stillaguamish and described the steady decline of its steelhead. They explained that fly-only regulations were designed to protect the unique summer-run stocks and their fragile spawning grounds in Deer Creek.

The debate grew protracted and quarrelsome, dividing the state's anglers into sharply hostile factions. The ultimate vote found a slim majority favoring fly-only management on the Stillaguamish. Bradner's partisans breathed a collective sigh of relief.

It saved our summer-run fishing, Wahl said gratefully, *and the North Fork had the first fly-only steelhead water anywhere.*

The remarkably farsighted regulations were not the only contribution of the Washington Fly-Fishing Club. Its members wanted to restore the Deer Creek steelhead and create a summer-run population in the upper Stillaguamish itself, between Oso and the Fortson Hole. They believed that wild fish were the catalyst in their plan and proposed the trapping of wild fish in Deer Creek. Their plan involved holding the trapped fish at a hatchery until they ripened and could be stripped of their eggs and sperm. Such a program had never been attempted, and the biologists from Olympia were still wary.

Some state officials argued strongly against the proposal, believing it was scientifically unsound. It had simply not been tried before.

The Washington Game Commission grudgingly agreed to attempt a wild-fish hatchery program with live-trapped parent stocks from Deer Creek. The biologists were still doubtful. The fish culture experts at the hatchery had doubts too, but a field party helped build a steelhead trap in 1945.

It worked! Drain interrupted excitedly. *We got seventy-five wild brood fish that summer—and it worked!*

Deer Creek fish! Wahl added.

The seventy-five steelhead were quickly transferred to holding ponds at the hatchery, where they ripened patiently through the winter. But these were wild fish tempered in the salt, and they proved quite skittish in captivity. The wild steelhead refused hatchery food, and some withered, until only 40 percent survived the winter. But those precious few supplied thirty-five thousand pale orange ova, and the biologists stripping the fish washed them patiently in milky sperm. The eyed ova were hatched in bubbling oxygen-filled chambers, and their freshly hatched alevins were placed in shallow trays. The tiny fish were wild, shrinking warily from the light and scattering when people entered their shed. Subsequent experience with fry derived from such wild stocks has taught us that their trays must sometimes be covered and opened only slightly during feeding times. Special finely ground foods work best on such wild fry. But the remarkable thing about such tiny fish lies in their hair-trigger wariness, behavior utterly unlike relatively tame hatchery stocks, when they are still less than an inch in length. Recent experience with wild stocks has consistently taught us how precious wildness is, and our conceptual debt to the Stillaguamish project is large.

The fry were held in rearing ponds for two years until they reached smolting size. The smolts finally turned silvery, were gently loaded aboard hatchery trucks, and taken upstream to the Fortson Hole. The smolts were planted at Fortson in the spring. Drifting downstream steadily, they mixed swiftly with a silvery flood of wild baby steelhead, traveling the milky snow-melt currents quickly toward the sea.

Everybody thought we'd failed, Drain said excitedly, *but two years later our fish started coming back.*

Where did they come? I asked.

Fortson Hole! Drain grinned. *Right where we planted them!*

Why did you pick the Fortson?

Bradner and the others thought we could get more fishing mileage over summer-run fish that way, Wahl explained. *Pull the old Deer Creek stocks past its mouth at Oso—pull them all the way to the Fortson Hole.*

It worked! Drain laughed.

The unique Stillaguamish program had clearly worked, and it stimulated some fresh thinking. Bradner and his colleagues had unwittingly become pioneers in fisheries management with their bold, intuitive theories for transplanting wild steelhead smolts. It was clearly possible to restore and protect summer-run steelhead, and the returning summer-run fish in the Fortson Hole suggested that summer-run populations might be started where they had not existed before.

The implications of their success remain exciting more than forty years later. Watersheds that have lost their summer-run populations to pesticides and lethal temperatures and silts triggered by clear-cutting might be restored with smolts derived from wild parents. Threatened populations might be supplemented with such smolts too, and some transplanting has clearly worked. Other rivers that lacked summer-run steelhead in the past are blessed with such fish today. Old-timers still argue that these partially wild steelhead are not as lithe and beautiful as their fully wild cousins. Such men are right. Hatchery-reared steelhead clearly lack the river-tempered strength of fully wild populations. Yet most surviving runs of summer steelhead are partially or totally based on such hatchery-reared smolts. It is possible that few summer steelhead populations would survive today without such help.

They're not completely wild, Ralph Wahl admitted, *but we're grateful.*

It's our Deer Creek miracle, Drain said.

Deer Creek itself was less fortunate than the Stillaguamish its fish helped to restore. The logging precipitated its steady decimation and decline, and the tragedy of Deer Creek has left the Stillaguamish largely dependent on hatchery technology today. Although its entire watershed was finally closed to fishing, both to protect its valuable brood stocks and its future runs of wild summer fish, Deer Creek still declined swiftly.

Its fate is a classic example of the futility of fisheries programs that manage only the river itself, without meaningful jurisdiction over land use throughout its entire watershed. Stream fertility depends as much on its timber and plant communities and soils chemistry as it does on its aquatic character. Topography and geology are critical too. Although the critical acreages might lie miles from the streambed itself, such impacts as erosion and extensive timber cutting and agriculture can still have potentially lethal effects many miles downstream.

But you closed Deer Creek to fishing, I said. *How could it collapse so completely and so soon?*

It died quickly, Drain said.

The big timber companies were not barred from ruthlessly cutting the forests along Deer Creek, where Zane Grey and Haig-Brown had hooked their first steelhead, although fishing itself was stopped. The trees were clear-cut on steep slopes, and their switchbacking haul roads quickly eroded into raw impassable gullies. The volcanic glacier-polished soils calved off the mountains in huge slumps and slides. Along the creek itself, the big trees were stripped right down to the water until the forest was gone. Its life-giving shade was gone too, and the big conifers no longer held the steady winter rains in their root systems. Shade-loving mosses and lichens withered quickly in the sun, and the soft spongelike carpet of needles was lost too, permitting the rain to run off quickly. The springheads flowed warmer and the big pools grew tepid. Erosion soon filled its spawning riffles with silt. Sawdust and brushy slash and bark choked its tributaries, and the debris was ruthlessly bulldozed into the creek itself. The soaked debris gradually sank to the bottom and collected in thigh-deep shoals, rotting sourly and slowly, bubbling with methane and tannic acid. Herbicides were wantonly sprayed to suppress the thorny brambles and alders that grew explosively once the loggers had departed. Pesticides were sprayed to protect the dwindling forest tracts that remained. Such poisons were swiftly leached into the creek, killing aquatic fly-hatches and baby steelhead alike. Deer Creek was dying too.

Its sweet-flowing headwaters, whose clarity and ice-cold currents were legend in the Stillaguamish Valley, grew tepid and sour. The tumbling chutes were milky with silts. Pure oxygen-rich water no longer trickled through the pea-gravel riffles where steelhead eggs lay ticking in their redds. The watershed lay almost entirely naked, stripped of its dark cathedral of trees, and spates churned toward the Stillaguamish in coffee-colored torrents.

It didn't flood like that before the loggers stripped it clean, Wahl said grimly. *It floods constantly today.*

Our problem is still big floods, Drain shook his head. *We just get things cleaned up and cooking—and a flood scours everything out.*

Floods every time it rains, Wahl said.

Although the lessons of history are unmistakable along the Stillaguamish, little has really changed in timber policy. The Scott Paper Company recently stripped a tract on lower Deer Creek, less than a mile above Oso, cutting trees right to the water to satisfy our society's need for kitchen towels and toilet paper. Slides triggered on public lands through timber sales by the United States Forest Service are still growing, gaping wounds that display few symptoms of healing after ten to fifteen years. Forest Service officials have grudgingly agreed to suspend timber sales on Deer Creek itself. Timber cutting on private tracts and the widespread spraying of herbicides and pesticides are still permitted. Wild steelhead return as stragglers and refugees to the tributary that once spawned most of the summer-run fish in the entire river. The few remaining fish are remarkably stubborn and hardy. Deer Creek has steadily withered to a skeletal trickle in its dry stones, silty and flowing ten degrees warmer than the main Stillaguamish itself. Steve Raymond wrote eloquently of this tragedy in his wonderful book *The Year of the Angler*:

> Even if the senseless destruction of the watershed is checked, it will take generations before the Deer Creek of Zane Grey and Roderick Haig-Brown returns to its former pristine glory, if ever. In the meantime, the hatchery fish compose the bulk of the steelhead run, swimming past the mouth of Deer Creek almost as far as Darrington, and each pleasant summer day draws hordes of fly-fishermen to the North Fork.

Ralph Wahl drove back downstream from the Fortson Hole, where the trainmen had stopped to watch a lucky angler play a jumping silvery fish, and turned into a brushy road toward the river. We left his camper at a railroad crossing, rigged our tackle, and walked to the first pool. It was a beautiful reach of water. Its throat shelved off against a brushy bank, flowing strong and smooth under a tangled copse of mossy trees that reached almost entirely across the belly of the pool, and a branch hung throbbing in the current. Below the trees, the current stilled just above its tail shallows into a silky, transparent window. It was a beautiful pool, spoiled only by the corroding skeletons of derelict cars that hung in the current at its swift throat.

Does it have a name? I asked.

Not really, Drain said. *But it should have fish just below the trees.*

Maybe it's the Junkyard Hole, I said.

They're pretty ugly, he admitted. *They hung the cars along the bank to help stop the erosion.*

Did it work? I asked.

It helped some, Drain replied.

I don't know, I said. *When stream improvements are ugly, I think they're a failure—even when they really work.*

Although a steelhead flashed several times in the weak sunlight and another porpoised lazily back under the branches, I failed to move a fish at the ugly Junkyard Hole.

Let's try Blue Slough, Wahl suggested.

We hiked upstream through the grassy shallows to the Blue Slough, and worked slowly along the thick sedge-grass bank. The river came down a long cobblestone riffle and dropped off along a grassy tree-hung bank. It was obviously chest-deep along the deeper bank, flowing turquoise and smooth. The bottom was good, grating easily under my brogues, and I started fishing at its riffling throat.

Where do they lie? I asked.

They're all the way through, Drain replied. *Just lay the fly tight against the bank and keep mending it through until it swings.*

What fly?

I'd fish the Blue Charm, Wahl said.

But that's an Atlantic salmon pattern, I protested. *What about something with brighter feathers?*

Try the Charm, Drain insisted.

We're using it these days, Wahl nodded. *It's taking steelhead too.*

Blue Slough is a beautiful pool. I fished it through patiently with Drain at my elbow, both watching the fly-swing like ospreys. We covered it with a tight pattern of concentric drifts. The pool deepens quickly below the shallows at its throat, and its smooth flow pulled heavily through our legs. It was deep enough to wet my wading-vest pockets. Blue Slough looked like steelhead water, and its currents worked teasingly at the fly, but we fished through to its shallows. Our luck stayed sour.

Not many fish coming yet, Drain said. *We're still too early.*

You're singing the old song, I joked.

Let's try the Skier's Hole.

We drove back upriver and crossed the trusswork bridge on the country road below Fortson, passing cottages and small farms and orchards. The sun was breaking through the overcast, and it was warmer walking down to cross below the Skier's Hole. The current below the Skier's is broad and swift, flowing down a rocky reach of water and disappearing among the hardwoods and alders downstream. The river itself flows steeply below the bridge, past a fallen maple that lies across the shelving throat of the pool, and turns sharply against a high bank. It is a classic elbow pool. Its deep currents well up strong and smooth, swirling and bulging, echoing big stones and boulders lurking in its depths. The primary current tongues lengthen smoothly into a surprisingly long tail over river-polished cobbles.

It's the best pool yet, I said.

It's a favorite of mine, Drain nodded happily.

The tumbling currents sweeping off the big deadfall were deceptively strong. The tree has probably swept downstream since, purged by a winter spate. I fought to hold my footing and keep my backcast free, dropping the fly across the current. It was only a sixty-foot cast, angling its stroke high to clear the branches of the fallen tree and changing its forward cast thirty degrees.

It's easier downstream, Drain grinned.

Farther down the pool, the throat dropped off into a ninety-degree chute against the steep bank, working back in a big, glassy smooth eddy. Reaching a steelhead there demanded honest eighty-foot casts to place the fly against the rocks, and a series of intricate mends to compensate for its reversing flows. The current below the eddy seemed like fine holding water. I fished more carefully there. I dropped each cast more closely, spacing them about a foot apart. Mending and mending again quickly after each cast, with a rolling stroke of my wrist I worked the fly deep and let the sinking line-belly fish teasingly through.

When I had fished patiently into the tail shallows without moving anything, I reeled up the Blue Charm and waded back quietly.

They don't seem to want this fly, I said.

Fish through again, Drain said.

What fly? I asked.

Give them something they haven't seen, Wahl shouted.

It's been fished today, Drain mused thoughtfully. *They've been looking at things like the Skykomish and Thor before—you pick the fly!*

Something bright, I thought.

My fishing vest still held a fly book of Atlantic salmon patterns, and tucked into its sheepskin were several General Practitioners dressed on size six double hooks. I had tied them on the Midfjardará in Iceland. They were dressed with scarlet seal's fur bodies, ribbed with oval silver, and tightly palmered with bright orange saddle hackle. Their slender tails were almost two inches long, fibers taken from the rusty scarlet saddle of a golden pheasant. Unlike most salmon flies, with their wing materials dressed conventionally, the Practitioner layers its wing flat. It alternates rusty golden pheasant saddles with darkly barred tippet feathers from a golden pheasant's cape, layering them flat to suggest the shell-and-carapace silhouette of shrimps and prawns.

What's that? Drain asked.

It's a British salmon fly, I said. *It's tied to suggest a crustacean—and it works pretty well on bright fish that have just arrived.*

It's pretty early in the year, Drain laughed. *Except for mending kelts, we don't have anything else.*

It's a good fly, I said.

I've never seen it before, Drain studied the pattern. *What's it called?*

General Practitioner, I explained.

It's British? he asked.

It's a salmon pattern from the Derwent, I continued. *It was developed by a retired British officer named Esmond Drury—a pretty colorful character.*

Colorful? Drain grinned.

Drury's pretty colorful, I laughed. *I've fished with people who fought with him in Africa.*

He fought against Rommel?

Western Desert Force, I nodded. *Intelligence patrols behind German lines—and he took his fly-tying materials along!*

Behind German lines?

Playing tag with Rommel, I continued, *and carrying enough to tie fully dressed Victorian patterns in the desert at night—working under his blankets in blacked-out tents.*

Jock Scotts? he asked.

Drury carried enough feathers for everything!

Carried a lot of feathers, Drain laughed.

The throat of the pool was fishless. I worked past the circling eddy, into the swift belly of the pool itself, and the smooth current along the stones. The smooth run lasted almost fifty yards before spreading into its glassy fan-shaped shallows.

Fish it slowly, Drain called.

The sun came out and changed everything. The lower pool seemed alive, its currents swelling smooth and transparent over its stony bottom of boulders and cobbles. I covered it patiently. It was throwing long now, most of the eight-weight line, and steadily mending its drift. Each cast dropped beyond the channel, a few inches from the stones, and I fished it back. Once a cast had fished through, I took a half-step downstream and repeated its swing. The pool was getting shallow, but it still looked good.

You can quit pretty soon, Drain said. *You've about covered it.*

Just a few more casts! I protested.

You've fished it, Drain grinned. *You guys always want a few more casts!*

But it still looks good.

Might hold a fish, he admitted. *Fish through.*

We'll see, I said.

I fished through several more casts, mending the brightly feathered Practitioner deep along the bottom. I could feel the sinking line slide across the stones, and I was ready to quit when there was a strong pull.

Fish! I yelled. *Fish!*

The steelhead shook itself fiercely. It flashed silver as it sliced upstream along the bottom, twisting and writhing. The bellying line ripped audibly against the swift current. The fish flashed again and again. It held effortlessly in the heaviest flow, deep in the swelling throat of the pool, and the line hummed like a guitar string.

The fish turned suddenly and exploded into the tail shallows, wildly stripping line until it threatened to escape the pool. It faltered briefly and I turned it back. It threshed weakly at the surface without jumping and bolted upstream again. It finally leapfrogged into a clumsy jump, falling on its back and drifting, momentarily stunned. It threw another halfhearted jump, scattering spray wildly across the current. It came grudgingly into the shallows, circling in roostertails and splashings, spending itself stubbornly. I finally dropped to my knees in the shallows, and when the fish lay gasping, I took it gently across its gill covers.

Good fish! Drain said happily.

The eight-pound henfish lay quietly, and I held it up for Ralph Wahl. He waved from the cutbank, and I cradled it gently in my hands, carrying it into deeper water. Its lavender gill covers were steady and strong. It suddenly fought free with a wild splash. The henfish darted back into the pool, flashing as it turned, and it was gone.

We gathered later at Frank Headrick's cabin along the Stillaguamish at Oso, with grilled steaks and several bottles of California cabernet. We had caught the only steelhead taken that day, and we both told and retold our story willingly. There was fishing talk from the old days too, and some of the river's steelhead giants were there. The gathering included Enos Bradner, Ken McLeod, Walt Johnson, Charles Cole, and Ted Rogowski too. The fire was welcome, particularly when the chill wind rose gently in the big cedars outside, and fog drifted in thickly from the stormy Strait of Juan de Fuca.

Well, I winked at Wes Drain, *I had the best guide on the Stillaguamish today, and your faith in the Skier's Hole paid off.*

It helps to know the river, Drain admitted, *but it helps to have guys who can actually fish too!*

Well, I said. *We did it!*

Blind luck didn't hurt! Wahl said drily.

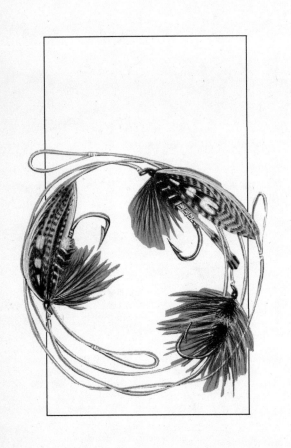

The Ring of Kerry

Richard Oldfield stood waiting in the cobblestone dooryard of the Old Ground Hotel at Ennis, as thin and stiffly correct in his dark suit as a Dublin undertaker. It was raining and the narrow streets were wet. There was a small fire burning in the sitting-room grate.

We've been expecting you. We shook hands while the porters struggled with my luggage and fishing gear. *Good flight?*

It's always a good flight with a shamrock painted on the tail, I stood rubbing my hands at the fire.

And our pretty colleens, Oldfield warmed to his subject and smiled. *Wearing the green—serving sweet whisky and smiles!*

Plenty of Irish coffee too!

It was raining harder, drumming across the dark slate roofs and chimney pots of the stonework houses. We sat down in the high-ceilinged dining salon to a lunch of smoked trout and freshly poached salmon and tiny potatoes. The brief shower soon passed. Weak spring sunlight filtered in through the filmy curtains. Family portraits watched us solemnly from the walls, and the lilting music of good Irish talk filled the room.

Our talk ranged freely, from fishing to the ring-forts of Irish prehistory and colorful outlaws on the American frontier. Oldfield spoke knowledgeably of the colors and calligraphy found in the ancient Book of Kells, and ruined monasteries like Killone and Tintern Abbey and Kilcooley. We talked of poets and playwrights too, particularly Sean O'Casey and John Millington Synge, and the string of fishing images in the poetry of William Butler Yeats.

Oldfield was intrigued with stories of the American frontier, and his

137

wit bubbled with anecdotes about our explorers and buffalo hunters and trappers. Outlaws fascinated him too, especially the colorful Butch Cassidy, and he was disappointed to discover that Cassidy was merely the *nom de pistol* chosen by a wayward Mormon named Robert Leroy Parker.

The American film director, John Huston, lived just north of Ennis at Loughrea, Oldfield finally changed the subject. *Bought a country manor called Saint Clerans and became master of foxhounds with the Galway Blazers.*

Fox hunting? I asked. *Huston?*

Irish fox hunting is not quite as stuffy as the British hunts. Oldfield studied his pastry cart. *Our hunts sometimes get a bit boisterous.*

Galway Blazers? I interrupted. *How did they get their name?*

It had nothing to do with their coats, Oldfield chuckled. *Most hunt balls find that smashing champagne glasses in the fireplace is fitting enough— but they drank all night and wanted more.*

Wanted more?

Their revelry refused to ebb at daylight, he explained. *With all the champagne gone, and all the crystal smashed—the Galway fox hunters torched and burned the house!*

And became the Galway Blazers?

Exactly, he said.

Your hotel also has a curious name, I pointed to the strawberries too. *Why is it called the Old Ground?*

It involved one of your countrymen, he said.

It involved an American?

He was actually an Irish boy gone off to your New World. Oldfield stopped to savor his last strawberry. *Later he received a letter from a family solicitor in Dublin, telling him he was the beneficiary of a rather large estate at Ennis.*

It was the hotel?

That's correct, Oldfield nodded and sipped his tea. *When he returned to Ennis, the old hotel porter remembered him from childhood—and welcomed him back to the Old Ground.*

When I stopped later that week for breakfast at Adare, the street was filled with fox hunters. Their hounds surrounded the horses in a milling, yelping pack. The horses glistened in the rain. Their brightwork and polished saddles and tack gleamed in the dull morning light. The horses looked supple and strong. Limerick horses are bred to clamber and scrabble across ancient earthworks and hedgerows, and seldom get to jump walls and fences in the classic sense. The townsfolk stood watching or peering from the windows of their thatch-roofed cottages and shops. The hounds were still barking and yelping, and shaking themselves in the rain. The street was a tapestry of color, and after a stirrup cup at the dooryard of the Dunraven Arms, the horses of the Limerick Hunt clattered off noisily through the cobblestone streets.

The fertile countryside beyond Adare, with its improbably green fields and old Georgian manor houses and hedgerows, is part of a fertile patchwork of beauty that reaches into the hills of Killarney and Tipperary.

The country is less fertile farther south, but it becomes still more beautiful and half-wild. Its harsh coasts between Donegal and Bantry Bay are a sparsely populated world of cliffs and surprisingly high mountains. The prosperous landscapes at Limerick are finally displaced by barren foothills and hillocks thickly overgrown with bracken and bright-yellow gorse, and solitary stone farmhouses lie whitewashed and plain in their jigsaw puzzles of stone walls and fields. The country grows still more wild at Abbeyfeale, where the narrow turnpike circles the Glanaruddery Hills. There are fishing villages like Ballylongford and Ballyduff. It is a world steeped in the past.

Stone ring-forts are found in the barren hills beyond Tralee, and many of these sites date to the Bronze Age. Ghosts still walk these ring-fort sites. Their stratigraphy tells us that some were occupied for centuries. The Epic of Rathangan ring-fort dates to the eighth century, its verses filled with the Irish character and a somber sense of time passing:

> The fort opposite the oak wood
>   Once it was Bruidg's and Cathal's
> It was Aed's and it was Ailill's
>   It was Comaing's, it was Cuiline's
> And it was Maelduil's—and the fort
>   Remains, with each coming in his turn
> And its kings asleep in the ground.

Castlemaine sits on the cobblestone high road that follows the coasts of Dingle, its stern peninsula of rocky beaches and beehive abbeys and kelp shallows rising from a leaden sea. The earth is stony and poor. Its farmers gather kelp from its tidal flats to fertilize their fields. Dark mountains shape its brooding spine and its people. Its coasts are a world of storms and treeless moors and hill-country passes between Castlegregory and Dingle, empty landscapes that have been the setting for films like the brooding *Ryan's Daughter*.

It has spate rivers that sustain minor runs of salmon and sea trout. The little Maine rises in the Scartaglen Hills and winds to Dingle Bay. The

Laune rises among the Lakes of Killarney, circling like a watery necklace through a collage of gorse and rich pastures and farms. It finally reaches the sea at Killorglin. The dour streets of Killorglin are the threshold of the spectacular highway called the Ring of Kerry.

Its circling route holds some of the finest fly-fishing water in Europe. The Ring of Kerry measures about a hundred miles, tracing the rocky shores of Dingle and Ballinskelligs and Kenmare, and it circles the highest mountains in Ireland. Cahirciveen lies along the tidal shallows above Knight's Town, where the highway climbs beyond the village into the mountains and moors at Ballinskelligs toward the fishing village called Waterville.

Ballinskelligs hides several drowned escarpments on its horizons. Storms often shroud them until they appear again like ghost ships on the horizon, broken pyramids rising more than seven hundred feet from the Atlantic. These pyramids conceal strange ruins. The sawtoothed ridges of Great Skellig hide stone sheepfolds, and the beehive huts and oratories of an ancient monastery. Some historians believe that its clerics were driven from the mainland by the Viking raids, since the monastery dates to the eighth century.

The charming old Butler Arms stands above the cobblestone beaches at Waterville. Storms rattle across its breakfast room windows, and fishing boats patiently work the bay. Gulls scream above its narrow streets, dipping and wheeling above the chimney pots, and cattle graze in fieldstone pastures that were cleared a thousand years ago.

It was raining the first morning, and I left my tackle in the hotel foyer. *We've got something of a problem*, Noel Huggard looked crestfallen and embarrassed. *We've made an error in the fishing beats.*

What's the problem? I asked.

We've booked somebody else into your morning salmon-beat, he said.

What do you suggest?

Our other angler is leaving for Edinburgh after lunch, he explained unhappily. *We hope you'll agree to letting him take the salmon beat—we've already engaged a boatman for you on the lake.*

That's fine, I said.

The narrow road climbs steeply above the lake, winding between lilacs and orchards and fieldstone walls. The fruit trees were starting to bloom in the sheltered places. Bright yellow gorse hung across the walls. The lake itself is beautiful, surrounded by its amphitheater of mountains. It lies well below the road, past the dense plantation of conifers just above the village. Oystercatchers and terns work its rocky shores and skerries. The outcroppings and alders of its largest island hide the stone ruins of a tenth-century church. There are ruins lying under the lake too, often visible when its waters are still, perhaps drowned during some half-forgotten catastrophe. Lough Currane is considered the finest sea trout fishery in Ireland.

Paddy Donnelly sat waiting below his orchard, playing with his cats in the dooryard of his ghillie's cottage. *Good morning, sir*! he pulled off his houndstooth fishing cap. *'Tis a beautiful morning for the fishing!*

It might rain, I thought doubtfully.

I have preferred fishing streams since boyhood, intrigued with the obvious poetry of their steadily changing moods, but I was curious about the tactics employed on the Irish loughs. Clare de Bergh had described the lough-fishing flies and techniques during a long weekend at Oughterard, when the village and its inns literally bulged with anglers.

Lough Currane lay perfectly still again. The ghillie walked ahead, setting a brisk pace in spite of my tackle bag and his boat net. The bright blue oars were shouldered like an Enfield rifle. He was already bailing out the boat when I caught up. His face was deeply weathered. Its nose was parrot-shaped and strong, and the blue eyes were almost fiercely bright. His smile was startling, with its gleaming gold tooth, and it seemed as welcome as the fitful Irish sun.

The weather changed and changed again. Black clouds drifted across the mountains. The lake became a dark mirror, sepulchral and dour as a lead-sheathed coffin, until the wind stirred again. The ghillie secured our equipment in his boat and pushed off from the stone jetty.

'Tis a fine sweet morning, he said.

But it's raining hard in the hills! I protested. *It's going to rain and blow—and it's starting to rain at Waterville already!*

'Tis correct, sir, Donnelly nodded agreeably. *But we're fishing and we're alive—and considering the alternatives!*

The wind was rising sharply. Cold rain rattled across our boat, and the ghillie turned into the squall, pulling hard at the oars. The rain shrouded the mountain until we could not see the ghillie's cottage.

Why don't we just go back?

'Tis perfect this morning, Donnelly shook his head. *'Tis a soft morning of rain we'll be finding from time to time, with lots of flies coming on the lough to start the fish looking up—and a proper crust on the water!*

Crust on the water? I asked.

'Tis perfect for fishing the lough, sir. He was still pulling hard into the troughs. *'Tis a bold crust we need to make our fish less shy.*

Wind riffle! I finally understood.

The ghillie settled into a steady stroke. The cumbersome oars groaned and rattled in their pegs, and he was surprisingly strong. The wind ebbed slightly and the blue boat came grudgingly to life. The waves lapped past its lapstrake hull, until its bow plunged sharply into the swells. It finally seemed to gather itself quartering into the wind.

Where do we fish?

We'll be starting to fish just along the Church Island, Donnelly pointed across the water toward the ruins. *We may not see them, but we'll fish the shoals and skerries there—drifting and fishing with the wind.*

I've rigged a three-fly cast, I said. *What flies should I fish?*

The ghillie searched my fly books and quickly selected three flies. *Fish whatever flies you please*, he suggested gently, *but on the Currane we like to fish something pea-fowl gaudy like the Watson's Fancy—and the dour little Bibio and Connemara Black on the droppers!*

You have Bibio flies? I asked.

Some years they're everywhere, he nodded. *Like black snowflakes.*

We call them March flies, I continued. *Several years ago, they were like a plague on our streams—in our shirts and picnic baskets and hair.*

Did the fish like them?

Loved them for a week or two, I said. *Stuffed themselves like sausages.*

What happened after a week or two? he asked.

Stopped taking them, I said.

Donnelly studied the hillsides, searching the rain-shrouded face of the mountain for its secret benchmarks, and turned back to study the island. There was a quiet confidence about his work, with little of the poetic exaggeration sometimes found in Irish ghillies, and I trusted his judgment.

Shall I start? I asked.

Wait, sir! he said quietly. *Wait a just bit more—just a few feet more and we're over the fish!*

You're pinpointing shoals? I guessed.

That's right, sir.

We were drifting with an ebbing wind. The ghillie rested briefly at his oars, quietly aligning his private landmarks on both shores to locate the shallows. Sometimes his mouth worked wordlessly, and sometimes he sat mumbling to himself. He finally used a few deft strokes to position our boat, its hull and leather oarlocks creaking.

Start the fishing, sir! he said. *Start now!*

The lake obviously concealed secrets behind its blind face. We drifted about fifty yards. Gulls and oystercatchers protested our fishing. The ghillie watched each cast and retrieve like a kingfisher, obviously convinced that we were actually covering trout, and I began to concentrate too.

Patience, I thought.

Lake fishing is a mixture of geometry and discipline, but patience is critical too. Each cast was dropped in a clockwise pattern ahead of our drifting boat. The rod was held high, and the flies were stripped back steadily against the riffling surface in a subtly teasing wake. The ghillie rowed to hold us against the wind, timing his rate of drift to the length and timing of each cast. Our rhythms had dovetailed now. My casts rolled out tightly, settled briefly under the surface, and I stripped them back. There was a sudden splash.

Fish! I grunted.

There was another wild splash. The reel surrendered fifty yards of line, and a big fish cartwheeled twice. I had been expecting two-pound trout. The fish I had hooked was much larger, and I was stunned.

'Tis a fine bright fish you have, sir! the ghillie said eagerly. *'Tis about four pounds—'tis a fine fish!*

It's pretty strong, I agreed.

The reel was singing shrilly. The big fish jumped several times before I finally turned it, and coaxed it back toward the boat. It bolted out again, but I pumped and reeled until it circled deep under the gunwales. The ghillie reached for his net and waited. The fish came back grudgingly, and he netted it with a deft heron-quick stroke. It writhed and twisted in the meshes.

'Tis a fine bright thing we've caught! the ghillie said proudly. *Coin-bright and strong!*

It is a fine trout, I agreed.

Our fish was silvery, its shoulders the color of a peat-darkened spade, and delicate little cross-markings covered its flanks. It had taken the Connemara Black. The ghillie unhooked the fly and preened its feathers. I was getting excited now. Stripping out line, I started a series of lengthening false casts, and the ghillie turned us skillfully to bring his skiff around. He rested briefly at his oars, pinpointing our line of drift.

Wait, sir! he said. *'Tis still too deep.*

The ghillie pulled briefly to align the boat, studied the church ruins across the water, and turned toward his farm. *Start fishing, sir!* he said. *'Tis a fine reach starting here!*

You're the captain, I said.

It took less than a dozen casts before there was a wrenching strike. The line exploded from my fingers, and the big reel was a shrill soprano. It was a run that stripped about sixty yards of backing. The fish did not actually jump. It hoarded its strength like a miser, spending it in a series of reel-wearing runs. It still felt strong. The fight finally became a sullen struggle just under the boat, and we did not see the trout until it was netted.

Eight pounds! I guessed happily.

'Tis a grand fish, sir! Donnelly was obviously excited too. *'Tis our best sea trout of the season!*

See many this large? I asked. *It's a beautiful fish.*

Not many, he replied.

Our sport lasted less than two hours. Sporadic hatches of dark *Leptophlebia* flies came drifting and hopscotching with the wind. The big trout had erased any thoughts of losing my salmon beat. The ghillie worked his lines of drift patiently, and we fished carefully from shallow to shallow. We took a third fish we estimated at six pounds, working along a rocky island guarded by nesting swans. The birds circled us aggressively when we drifted too close to their nesting grounds, and the fish finally stopped taking.

We started happily toward home, and when we finally reached the stone jetty below his farm, I searched the duffle for my silver flask. *It's time to celebrate*, I suggested. *We fished well this morning!*

'Tis a welcome dram, sir!

Paddy! I lifted the flask in salute. *We should drink to you and your sea trout—and to your beautiful Lough Currane!*

The ghillie lowered his eyes modestly.

It's been a wonderful day, I continued. *I've never seen a better job of fishing—it all looks alike out there, but there were fish lying exactly where you told me to fish.*

Donnelly drained the silver cup.

It was raining softly when I finally left the Butler Arms. Squalls drummed lightly across the still expanse of Lough Currane. Faint rainbows blossomed and dissolved. The high road circled beyond Waterville, where the cliffs rise steeply from the water. Ballinskelligs was shiny and still, dappled with fleeting patches of sun, and the plunging tides had briefly ebbed at Lamb's Head.

The road climbs steeply from the dark-walled estuary at Ballynacallagh, and winds east into Killarney. The morning was filled with strange moods. Dark mists spilled from the treeless moors at Molly's Gap, gathering in the dour MacGillicuddy Reeks, where the Ring of Kerry finally escapes the sea.

The Orchard and the River

Seattle was a somber February city, with dark tatters of overcast drifting across its waterfront. Gulls huddled together at the ferry slips and jetties, and the big loading cranes stood birdlike and skeletal in the bitter chill off Puget Sound. There was no trace of Mount Rainier, and even the coastal mountains were almost lost in weather. It was starting to rain as we left the city, and the road reached north into the afternoon.

Dan Callaghan reached for the windshield wipers again after we crossed the Skykomish, rolling through coastal farm country, and we pushed steadily north in the winter rain toward Vancouver. Our route took us across the winter-swollen Stillaguamish and Skagit. Both are great steelhead rivers. The lights of Bellingham dropped behind, and it was still raining when we crossed the border. It was a trip we had talked about before, but it had become a pilgrimage.

We've known him for years, Callaghan suggested over a streamside lunch in the Yellowstone country. *We should spend a few days with Haig-Brown and get him talking, about his life.*

Somebody should, I agreed.

But we postponed the trip many times. I had met Haig-Brown several times during his intermittent trips to meet with publishers in New York, and I remember a small dinner party that friends gave for him many years ago, with a covey of other writers at the table. Our paths crossed again at conferences in Aspen and Sun Valley.

147

When I was scheduled to lecture at Portland, I called Callaghan in Oregon a few weeks earlier. *We've been talking about driving up to visit Haig-Brown for years, and it's time to stop all the talking*, I said. *Can you get away from your law practice for a few days?*

Sure, he said, *I'll meet your plane.*

When I called the farm at Campbell River, I found that Haig-Brown was in Newfoundland, gathering material for a book commissioned by the Canadian government. I finally telephoned him at a small hotel in Saint John's.

I'll be back in Campbell River, Haig-Brown said. *I'm glad you're coming.*

We'll be there, I promised. *We're excited too.*

It had stopped raining when we reached Vancouver, and the lights of the city glowed in the thick overcast. It was almost midnight. We drove slowly through the city, admiring its strikingly modern office towers, and stopped for the night above the ferry slips at Horsehead's Bay.

Callaghan shook me awake just before daylight, and fine sleet rattled on the windows while I shaved. The big car-ferry to Nanaimo was waiting in the darkness. Its cavernous hold was already filling with cars when we found a place in the gathering lines. Crew members were signaling with lighted batons. The ferry glittered like a Christmas tree, with its illuminated car decks and passenger salons and navigation lights. We finally drove aboard and felt the gentle rolling swells. Callaghan locked his car and asked a car-deck attendant about breakfast in the dining salon.

Callaghan, I teased, *you're always starving.*

I'm hungry, he admitted.

The big dining salon was almost empty. We settled on a table as the ferry's engines stirred to life, churning in the darkness as it backed out from its berth. Its screws shuddered and worked and throbbed powerfully. Gulls screamed outside the dining salon, and the morning seemed brighter, smelling of the sea. The Strait of Georgia lay silvery and still.

Callaghan ordered a gargantuan omelet stuffed with onions and sliced peppers and tomatoes. I sipped my coffee and watched the gulls with a growing sense of *déjà vu*, the curious feeling that I had been aboard the ferry before.

It's strange, I shook my head in puzzled disbelief. *I think I've been on this ship someplace.*

The waiter arrived with breakfast. *Just steal some of my omelette*, Callaghan suggested. *You'll feel better.*

I'm serious, I called the waiter back. *Was the ship built here?*

No, the waiter refilled my cup. *She was originally built in Germany and first sailed in Scandinavia.*

Copenhagen to Malmö? I gasped.

How did you know?

It seems almost impossible, I explained, *but I've been aboard the ferry before—crossing the straits between Denmark and Sweden.*

That is strange, Callaghan said.

The darkly mountainous spine of Vancouver Island lay ahead in the grimy morning light, its forests the color of wood smoke in the distance. Sea birds rested in huge rafts. Great fields of kelp lay rolling with the quiet swells. Breakfast was finished long before the ferry reached Nanaimo, and we quickly started north along the coast to Campbell River, where Haig-Brown busily lived out the closing years of his life.

Callaghan has a large collection of his books, and we drove the coastal highway talking about his work. Callaghan likes *Silver*, the story of an Atlantic salmon that Haig-Brown wrote in London after leaving school, and *The Western Angler* in its wonderful Derrydale edition. I particularly like the little-known *Measure of the Year*, a lovingly thoughtful collection of essays about books, tools, fishing, bird life, courtrooms, and the rhythms of family life at a small farm along the Campbell just outside town. Callaghan talked of the tragic beauty in *Return to the River*, which tells the life story of a chinook salmon, and I have always been fascinated with Haig-Brown's descriptions of Argentina and Chile in *Fisherman's Winter*. We are both strong admirers of *A River Never Sleeps*, which is perhaps his finest book on fishing.

It's a great title, I said. *It's a title so good you always wish you'd thought of it first.*

We passed through Qualicum Beach and stopped briefly to look at the river. *It's the village where a famous steelheader lived*, I said. *General Noel Money.*

Wasn't Money in **The Western Angler***?*

That's right, I nodded. *Haig-Brown dedicated the book to Money, and the fishing they shared on the Stamp.*

We had both known Haig-Brown over several years. Callaghan had shared some fishing with the writer at Sun Valley and Jackson Hole, and had visited him with Jack Hemingway at Campbell River. My first meeting with Haig-Brown had been over a publisher's lunch in New York, but the most memorable meeting was over dinner with Ed Zern, with fine potstill whisky like Glenmorangie and Laphroaig, and classical Spanish guitar music, surrounded by Zern's collection of richly ornamental primitive art from New Guinea and Africa.

There was another memorable meeting at Aspen, during a series of meetings at the Aspen Institute, where we were participating in round-table discussions on fisheries and demographic change and ecology. We fished together briefly, on my boyhood Frying Pan above Seven Castles, and again at Sun Valley. Haig-Brown was having serious spinal troubles in those years. The institute sessions and the fishing overtired him, until he was finally in traction at the Aspen Clinic, and we later carried him aboard a classic DC-3 belonging to my friend Hugh Chatham.

The farmstead lies a short distance above Campbell River, its gravelly lane leading through fruit trees and gardens. It is a relatively simple house typical of the coastal province, except for its big studio library. Few farmhouses are so filled with books on our continent. There are grape arbors and apple-tree orchards and a rolling lawn reaching to the river. The farm has been dedicated a historical site by the Canadian government, honoring the life's work of its owner, and will ultimately belong to British Columbia.

Roderick Haig-Brown was waiting on the porch steps when we arrived. *It's been a long time*, he said warmly.

Ten years, I said. *Maybe twelve.*

Has it really been that long? he smiled. *Well it's past and no matter.*

How is your wife? Callaghan asked.

Anne's pretty busy studying Renaissance Art and Italian, he replied. *She should be back from her Italian lesson soon.*

It'll be nice to see her.

Haig-Brown was surprisingly tall, much taller than I remembered, and carried himself with a watchfully detached, almost somber manner. Some people found him dour. They were obviously mistaken, but such people had never seen beyond the dignity and shyness, had been denied the privilege of his laughter. He seemed a little thin. It was surprising in a man of his years, with only a slight thickening at his waist to betray the sedentary hours spent thinking and writing at the desk under the big library windows.

He moved easily, with a faint trace of aging or awkwardness in his gangling frame. It was possible to think he had been a fine athlete in his schoolboy days. His character suggested the clean strides and mental disciplines of a solitary long-distance runner, or a long-legged soccer goalie waiting to strike with the startling grace of a heron.

Haig-Brown could seem deceptively ordinary at times, with his softly halting speech, until you studied his slightly aquiline face and found the osprey's look in his eyes. Our first afternoon, he wore an old pair of brown

Cheviot trousers, rumpled and baggy at the knees with the timeless quality of old tweeds, and an old cardigan with a pair of scuffed brown English brogues. It was possible to think that the principal character in *Return to the River* had been merely a prelude to the writer himself, thirty-odd years in the future:

> On the bank of the pool, leaning forward over a fir stump, an old man watched her. He was a lean, tall old man, and everything about him—arms, legs, nose, jaw, eyebrows, even his coat—seemed long.
>   Almost everything about him seemed also gray or brown: gray hair, brown face, gray clothes, brown hands, gray stockings, brown shoes: only his eyes were strongly blue in all the grayness and brownness.

Haig-Brown led us back through the house to the half-stair that led down to his library. It has a high ceiling, perhaps a full story and a half. Excepting the fireplace, and the high French doors where the Labrador retriever was scratching, its walls are completely lined with books. There was a fire in the grate. It was a welcome antidote to the chill and spitting snow outside, like the coffee maker gurgling merrily behind his work table.

So this is where you write, I said.

Yes, Haig-Brown poured three mugs of coffee. *I've done pretty much all of the writing since the Second World War right here.*

It's a beautiful room, Callaghan said. *Beautiful.*

It's been a pleasant place to sit and work, he admitted and leaned back in his big squeaky chair. *But Anne tells me there are too many distractions here—between the orchard and the river.*

Anne might be right, I said.

Well, Haig-Brown continued wryly, *writers spend a lot of time with their feet up—just thinking what they're going to write next.*

I've got a room filled with books too, I said. *It's wonderful to work surrounded by books—it's like having walls of friends.*

Good insulation too, he smiled.

What do people think of so many books?

Well, Haig-Brown sipped his coffee, *some people wonder if I've read all these books, and they're disappointed when I tell them that I've not—but I know pretty much what's in them.*

It's a lot of books.

Others think I've written them all, he continued, *and they're always disappointed to find I've only written these two shelves.*

Haig-Brown refused to describe himself as a fishing writer. He considered himself a serious writer who sometimes chose to write about fishing. There were twenty-five books published while Haig-Brown was still alive, but less than half were about his favorite sport. Several fishing collections have been issued since his death. Several Haig-Brown titles were actually intended for children, and were his most successful in terms of royalties. Others like *The Living Land* were concerned with ecology at a regional scale, and some were fiction, stories set in the timber country and fishing villages of British Columbia.

Haig-Brown was born at Lancing, along the south coast of England on February 21, 1908, where his father was a teacher.

His father published three books during a tragically brief life. The books included a collection on the field sports called *My Game Book*, a history of British military units like his Middlesex Regiment at the threshold of the First World War, and a book of poetry written at Cambridge. His father was also a famous athlete, reputedly skilled enough to play regularly as an amateur with professional soccer clubs like the Corinthians and Tottenham Hotspur. The older Haig-Brown also wrote for British periodicals about soccer and the field sports, and such writing helped to double his teacher's salary. He had been a strident pacifist throughout his college years at Cambridge, but the older Haig-Brown found himself increasingly preoccupied with rumblings of war heard from Berlin and the Balkans, and he subsequently accepted a commission in the British Army.

My father survived all the awful bloodletting of the Somme with only minor wounds, Haig-Brown stared down through the orchard to the river, *and was killed later commanding his Middlesex Regiment in 1918.*

Almost the end of the war.

It was at Cateau, Haig-Brown nodded. *The last big German push.*

My father was with the 26th Infantry, I said, *and relieved the American marines at Belleau Wood.*

The famous Yankee Division, he said.

That's right, I shook my head. *They crossed the Marne and took Chateau Thierry—and from his stories of the artillery barrages and machine guns, it's remarkable that anyone survived such terrible battles.*

You're right, he agreed.

Although his books display a remarkable calm and quiet poetry and force, Haig-Brown had a stormily troubled boyhood. He lived with his mother at 15 Banbury Road in Oxford after his father was killed, but after his grandmother died, the family decided that his mother should look after his grandfather. Haig-Brown and his mother moved to the country. His mother's father had almost three thousand acres in Dorsetshire, including ten miles of the beautiful Frome. His paternal grandfather was the headmaster at Charterhouse, where Haig-Brown later attended school.

Didn't he know Thomas Hardy? I said.

That was my mother's father, he replied. *He took me to visit Hardy often in Dorsetshire.*

Did others write? Callaghan asked.

Others?

Others in your family, I said.

Yes, Haig-Brown explained, *but it was not a literary family in the sense of people like the Sitwells or Lambs—people in the family wrote and expected to be paid for their work.*

Did they write often? I asked.

Yes, the writer nodded. *Writing was going on a lot—it was an everyday thing in the family.*

That can help a young writer, I said.

How's that? Callaghan asked.

It means a lot when you want to write, I explained, *to have a family that writes—or accepts writing as work.*

It matters that nobody laughs when you're writing a book.

And what about too much fame?

Too much fame in the family can hurt a young writer with aspirations, Haig-Brown observed sadly. *My father was good at everything he tried, but to have a father killed when you're still only ten—you've got no way to test yourself against such a formidable ghost.*

Wasn't there a joke about your name?

Family joke, Haig-Brown chuckled. *When I was christened Roderick, my father suggested that his second boy could be called Gunnar or Gundry—and he could call us Rod and Gun.*

Your mother didn't think it was funny?

Not really, he laughed.

His schoolboy years were filled with strife, in spite of the paternal help that Haig-Brown received from his uncles. His surrogate father was probably Major H. M. Greenhill, an old Cambridge classmate and soldier who later served with Haig-Brown's father in Flanders.

Greenhill was apparently a superb wing-shot and a skilled fly fisherman. The retired officer often fished with George Selwyn Marryat on the Frome and Coln. Marryat was the best-known trout fisherman of his time, more skilled than men like Francis and Halford, and could reputedly drop a fly on a half-crown at fifty feet. Both men fished well and tied beautiful flies, and Haig-Brown devoted an entire chapter of *A River Never Sleeps* to Greenhill. It is clear that Haig-Brown's deep love of nature evolved under Green-hill, roving the hills of Dorsetshire and fishing his grandfather's water on the Frome.

His schooling was fitful and troubled. Haig-Brown had already been dismissed from several prestigious schools before he was sent to Charterhouse, where his grandfather was still in charge. The family expected him to read history at Cambridge, following his father's example, and subsequently enter the British Colonial Service. But the family was unprepared when Haig-Brown was dismissed from Charterhouse too, spent a difficult time with tutors, and finally accepted an officer's appointment in the territorial regiment. Those were troubled years.

What happened? I asked.

It's not easy to get sent down from a preparatory school where your grandfather's in charge, Haig-Brown observed wryly, *but I managed it pretty well.*

What did you do? Callaghan asked.

Pretty much everything, Haig-Brown laughed. *We were sneaking out from Charterhouse and heading for the nightclubs in London—I got caught red-handed at the old Forty-Three Club.*

Anything worth doing, I said drily, *is worth doing to excess.*

You're right, he smiled.

Haig-Brown finally went to interview with the British Colonial Service at London and also thought briefly of Cambridge. The university did not view his disciplinary record with much happiness, but his scores were relatively good, and its officials grudgingly decided to admit Haig-Brown because his father and grandfather had both distinguished themselves there. Cambridge was unyielding in its insistence that a single breach of its discipline would terminate his college years, no matter where he tried to study in the entire United Kingdom.

It was sobering knowledge, and an uncle in the United States had also offered work in the logging camps north of Seattle. The offer held the promise of adventure, while schooling threatened to cage his spirits.

I didn't know that schooling is filled with adventure too, Haig-Brown admitted. *Still had a pretty wild streak in those days.*

His wife came down the half-stairs into the big library with some sandwiches. *You should have known him before all the books*, she laughed. *He was tall and good-looking and British—but it was the wildness that I liked.*

Anne always exaggerates, he said affectionately.

No, she said. *I don't.*

The British Colonial Office suggested that practical logging experience in the United States and Canada might prove as important to a career in the colonies as Cambridge. Such advice tipped the scales. Haig-Brown quickly accepted his uncle's offer and left for Seattle in 1926, promising his mother that he would return to England in a few months. It was a long sea voyage through the Panama Canal to Seattle. His first work was scaling timber at a sawmill, but later he began surveying stands in the valley of the Stillaguamish. His status in the United States was precarious, since he had entered the country on a student visa. Fearing that he might be deported, Haig-Brown took another job his uncle offered in British Columbia, along the Nimpkish on Vancouver Island in 1927.

Was that your first trip to Campbell River?

No, Haig-Brown explained, *I went up on the coastal steamer and sailed past it in the night.*

But you saw it? Callaghan interrupted.

No, he said. *It was a pretty stormy night.*

Didn't you catch your first steelhead during your lumberjack days on the Stillaguamish? I asked.

That's right, he said. *But it wasn't caught on the Stilly itself—it was caught on Deer Creek.*

Was it exciting?

The boys in the sawmills and lumber camps were always talking about steelhead, he nodded. *Hooking one was always exciting—the mystique of the steelhead was really something.*

What was the talk about? I asked.

Pretty much the same thing, he explained. *You could hook a steelhead easily enough—but you could never land it.*

Why not? Callaghan said.

Cash was pretty scarce, Haig-Brown replied. *People were fishing telescopic rods and cheap reels.*

No line capacity or anything? I asked.

No! Haig-Brown laughed. *It would take a pretty skillful fisherman to land a summer-run steelhead on such equipment.*

Lucky too, Callaghan said.

Haig-Brown first traveled to Campbell River in 1928, when he quit the Nimpkish country to take a job with Delafield & Welsh. He left again that year, with no inkling that it might become his home throughout most of his life. Keeping his promise to his mother, he sailed home to England later that year, fully intending to enter service in the British colonies.

I found the same official who had encouraged me to take a job in Se-

attle, Haig-Brown seemed wary of the fickle winds of government. *He apologized for giving such poor counsel—and told me he could only accept university men.*

Another curious twist of fate had ended the family's dream of training Haig-Brown for the British Colonial Office, and he was almost getting too old to enter Cambridge. He was bitter and disillusioned. The family had established a small trust to provide for his Cambridge education after his father was killed in France, and one of his uncles had served as principal trustee of that account. It proved difficult to touch that money, because the family remained stubborn. Finally he talked his uncle into a small weekly stipend to take a tiny London flat and to accept his dream of writing.

Haig-Brown agreed that his meager stipend should end if his discipline lagged. It was a period of willing self-exile. The fledgling writer had perhaps more to prove to himself than to his doubting family. Haig-Brown completed his first book in that chill London flat, the little manuscript that became *Silver*, the life story of an Atlantic salmon. The family was grudgingly impressed when *Silver* was accepted by a London publisher, and Haig-Brown had already started the story of the Nimpkish country that was titled *Pool and Rapid*.

There was newspaper work too, he said.

Did your family of gentlemen writers finally begin to have second thoughts, I interrupted, *when they saw you were really serious?*

They waffled a bit, he laughed. *It didn't seem like full-time work.*

What about your neighbors? I asked.

Here in Campbell River?

Yes, I said, *did they accept writing as full-time work?*

Well, Haig-Brown chuckled and filled our cups, *since it's not like plowing or chopping down trees or drift-netting salmon—my neighbors never really thought of writing as work.*

The Puritan ethic dies hard.

You're right, he said. *People looked at our twenty acres and were happier thinking about us as farmers—and when I finally became a court magistrate they were happier still.*

But you never went to a university or studied law, I stopped him. *How did you become a judge?*

He was elected, Callaghan said.

Anne Haig-Brown came back. *You mean it was an elected post?*

The town talked him into letting his name go on the ballot, she said gaily, *and when the dust settled—he was our new magistrate.*

I was stunned, he confessed.

Haig-Brown left his cold-water flat in London, and his family of reluctant latter-day Medici, and returned to British Columbia in 1931. Two years earlier, he had met the colorful Seattle girl who became his wife, and he was eager to find Anne again. Haig-Brown sailed back through the Panama Canal, husbanding his modest inheritance by booking passage on a tramp steamer. The little book *Silver* had reached the London booksellers before he arrived at Vancouver. Excepting the war years, when paper supplies were tightly controlled in the United Kingdom, that children's classic has remained in print almost sixty years.

It goes on and on, Haig-Brown said, *and I don't know why*.

It has a lovely quality, I suggested. *It never writes down to its audience—trying for the cute touches that mar so many books written for children*.

Well, he agreed. *I hated such books*.

Reading it again after so many years, I said, *I was struck by your speculation about the feeding grounds used by Atlantic salmon off Greenland—you guessed right about Greenland, thirty years before anyone else knew*.

But I had the wrong coast, he said, *and I was completely wrong about having Atlantic and Pacific salmon meet under the polar ice—that was pretty far off base*.

And your hen-salmon heroine spawned four times? I asked.

Pretty persistent, he admitted.

When he finally reached Vancouver, the city was tightly gripped by the Great Depression. The entire province lay stunned. Sawmills and logging camps and canneries had closed, and the ports were ominously quiet. Haig-Brown was held for several days in the immigration offices at the foot of Broad Street, and he was refused entry. Officials did not want immigrants with so little work available.

What will you do? they pressed.

I'm going back up the coast, Haig-Brown said.

But there's nothing.

Well, Haig-Brown told them stubbornly, *I'll hunt and fish and run some traplines—and try some gyppo-logging or beachcomb and salvage logs*.

You're pretty determined, they said.

Canadian immigration officials finally relented, and Haig-Brown traveled north to the logging camp at Menzies Bay. Almost primeval forests still cloaked most of Vancouver Island in those years, mixed stands of giant cedar, hemlock, spruce, sugar pine, and stately Douglas fir. The cedars were mossy trunked, thickly grown with fern thickets and devil's club, and tangled with hemlocks and Sitka spruce. The tracts of giant fir were relatively open and parklike, except for a few fern colonies and dense carpets of needles that reached for miles.

Haig-Brown had both intelligence and good judgment, and he found work quickly. His timber surveying experience on the Stillaguamish paid off. He was sent into the woods alone, which suited his temperament perfectly, as a timber cruiser. It is not easy work. Giant bears were still everywhere, along with cougars and wolves. But there were less obvious dangers in the work itself, and handling the calipers and tally books was not always simple. It often became dangerous. The trees were measured at diameter breast height on the bole, using big calipers and tapes. It sounds relatively easy, but it involved climbing, and clinging with badly chafed knees to reach the caliper height.

Getting back safely involved jumping down on slippery outcroppings and fallen trees, pitfalls hidden in dripping thickets of moss and ferns, and chest-deep bogs. Injuries on timber-cruising jobs are serious, because a tally man is often utterly alone. It is hard to calibrate trees with a swarming fog of biting *Simulium* gnats and mosquitoes, trying to balance on a slippery half-rotten deadfall, swaying unsteadily over a Hindu bed of thorny devil's club.

Haig-Brown was hired to find valuable tracts of Douglas fir, which supplies our finest structural lumber, and identified big stands in the Nimpkish country that held 120,000 board feet per acre. It was almost a pristine wilderness. Some big companies had shut down their sawmills and logging camps, but there were still enough gyppo- and skid-logging and high-lead operations on Vancouver Island to decimate its forests. It was difficult work that paid badly. Haig-Brown found himself clearing less than three dollars per day, since Delafield & Welsh deducted most of his fifteen-dollar daily wage for room-and-board costs. The men hooking and rigging logs fared no better. It was a tragic kind of servitude, but many were almost too grateful for any kind of work. The big companies were fiscally troubled too, but some merely took advantage of their workers. It was a time when radical politics filled the fishing villages and camps of British Columbia, and there were union agents and agitators everywhere.

Men who could really talk and debate and fight, Haig-Brown explained, *could get a big following in the timber camps.*

It happened in our country too, I said.

Sometimes the cut-over acreages caught fire, and the loggers were pressed into service as government firefighters. It paid only twenty-five cents an hour. *It was actually better pay*, he grinned, *but the hours got pretty long and it could get dangerous—some men got killed.*

Haig-Brown finally stopped working for the logging companies, when he found he could make better money working for himself at other things. There was summer work as a fishing guide trolling for spring chinook at the famous Tyee Club. He found plenty of fish and game, worked a trap line with various partners, salvaged stray logs from the beaches, and took summer jobs with friends on purse-seine fishing boats.

It's strange, he remembered happily. *It paid better than working.*

Although he had worked as a fishing guide for the famous Tyee Club at Campbell River, Haig-Brown had yet to fish the river itself. Zane Grey had come often to the Tyee Club in earlier years, to troll for the big chinooks migrating home through the Discovery Passage.

His early fishing for steelhead and salmon was limited to the Skagit and Stillaguamish, in the coastal mountains above Seattle, and the wild Nimpkish below the Queen Charlotte Straits. Local anglers already knew the Campbell was an excellent fishery, with fine runs of steelhead and salmon, and exceptional populations of sea-run cutthroat trout. Haig-Brown also found good fishing in other streams on Vancouver Island, but his lifelong affair with the Campbell still lay several months in the future. There were also several months spent working with Cecil Smith, a government cougar hunter who lived at Comox. Smith was a living legend, exceptionally skilled at his profession, and they hunted together in the foothill mountains between Buttle Lake and the Stamp River.

Cougar Smith was a character, Haig-Brown said. *Colorful and really good.*

Why did you work for him? I asked.

Money, he smiled.

Did you work just for wages, or did you already know you wanted to write about cougars? I said.

I wanted to write about cats, he confessed.

But why cougars?

Well, he replied thoughtfully, *I wanted to write about wild things and their behavior without a lot of sentimentality or faking—and* **Silver** *was only marginally successful—without any of the anthropomorphic tricks that try to portray animals thinking and feeling like people.*

Like **Bambi**? I interrupted.

Exactly, Haig-Brown continued, *but* **Bambi** *is not the only example— there's the awful Fortescue book about red stag, and a lot of Ernest Thompson Seton.*

Which Seton stories?

Lots of them, he said, *but particularly* **Wild Animals I Have Known**.

Do you think **Panther** *succeeded?*

I wasn't entirely happy with **Silver**, he said, *and it wasn't until* **Panther** *that I felt I was getting close to telling the story of an animal the way it should be told—without any faking.*

Did people like it? Callaghan asked.

Some people liked it, he replied grudgingly, *but the people who know little or nothing of wildlife—except for things like the **Bambi** stories—found **Panther** too filled with cruelty.*

It's hard to write about something like cougars without some cruelty, I nodded. *Were you upset?*

I was pretty irritated, he confessed.

What did you do next?

Well, he said, *I decided to write about something I really knew—so I started work on **The Western Angler**.*

Why did you pick a fishing book?

Because I was thinking about writing another nature book, he replied.

What kind? I asked.

Chinook salmon, he confessed.

*You mean you wrote **The Western Angler** just to establish your expertise about fish in 1939?* I interjected. *Just to make your critics accept **Return to the River** two years later?*

Yes, he laughed softly.

*But **The Western Angler** is still the standard work on the fisheries and fish species and techniques on the Pacific Coast!*

Perhaps, he said.

The book *Panther* was not written for children, like his earlier story of an Atlantic salmon, but it reached a wide children's audience. The edition published in Stockholm was titled *Ki-Yu*, and its Swedish publishers believed the book's original climax was too violent. It had the old cougar torn to pieces by wolves. The publishers argued that its death was too frightening for an audience of Swedish children. Haig-Brown objected strongly to changing *Panther* when it was first proposed, but the Swedish publishers stood firm, and he went steelhead fishing.

Finally, he continued, *I started to agree with their criticism—it seemed unlikely that an old cat would be killed by wolves.*

How did you change it?

The longer I thought about it, he replied, *it seemed better to have the old cougar crawl off and die alone—but I insisted on writing a preface to explain why.*

Did you write it? I asked.

Yes, he said, *because I think it's possible to conceal the cruelty of people from our children—only briefly at best—but it's a mistake to hide the cruelty of nature, because of its absolute truth.*

It's intriguing that **Panther** *is the story of a young cub orphaned and left to reach adulthood alone,* I said. *It's like your own life after your father was killed in France.*

Yes, he said softly, *isn't it?*

Haig-Brown finally ended his fishing-gypsy life in 1932, when he returned to Seattle to find Anne. They became engaged the following year. Haig-Brown went back to look for a place to live that offered more family amenities than the mills and logging camps on Vancouver Island. Such places lacked both schools and hospitals, and after their marriage in 1934, the young couple found themselves at Campbell River.

Had you decided to live here?

We arrived without intending to stay, he explained. *It was the end of the coastal highway in those days, and it was still close to the wilderness I loved, but it had hospitals and schools.*

How did you find the farm?

It was something like fate, Haig-Brown looked out toward the river. *It was simply for sale when we arrived—and I still had enough Cambridge money left.*

And no reason to leave, Callaghan added.

That's right, he said. *There are really two ways of thinking about a place for a writer to live and write—you can choose cities like Toronto or London or New York, because it might bring you more work—but it costs more to live.*

It's expensive in cities, I agreed.

We decided to live here in the sticks, he continued. *Perhaps I wrote less.*

You wrote quite a lot, I said.

More than most writers, Callaghan interrupted.

Some important American writers chose exile too, Haig-Brown agreed, *writers like Hemingway and Fitzgerald.*

Joyce left Dublin, I added.

Why do you think they leave? Callaghan asked.

I think they were looking back from Paris to understand their roots better, Haig-Brown explained, *but I chose another kind of exile—I wanted the excitement of a wild, new country few people had written about.*

Did you ever miss talking about your work with other writers? I asked.

Not really, he said.

Who did you talk to? Callaghan asked.

Anne was a pretty good sounding board, he replied. *She typed everything I wrote after we came to Campbell River—including* **Panther** *just after we married.*

Talking with her about your work is pretty amazing.

She's unusually articulate about your work and your sense of life, I agreed. *Some wives compete with the things their husbands love, but there wasn't a trace of that in anything she said—maybe she drowned her jealousy years ago?*

No, he said, *it's simply the way she is.*

But you never tried to talk about your work with other writers? I asked again. *Just to test things you were working on?*

Not really, he shook his head. *I've always agreed with Hemingway that it was possible to talk too much about your writing—because it wasted the pressures building inside you.*

He called it giving away juice, I nodded.

Exactly, Haig-Brown said. *When I was still in London, I knew lots of writers who talked and talked, but never actually wrote—except for precious things in obscure little periodicals.*

Where do you work? I asked.

Mostly sitting right here, he looked around his library, *but it depends entirely on what one means by working—one has to live and travel sometimes and see things worth telling about—things worthy of your intuition and skill.*

Like the book you're writing?

Yes, he said. *You can't write about fish and fishing throughout Canada without seeing all of the country—talking to people and fishing and getting the feel of things everywhere.*

How do you actually write?

You mean writing longhand or typing? he rummaged through his papers. *My work has always been written out by hand in these schoolboy copybooks, before Anne finally types it up.*

Are you disciplined? I asked.

I suspect you're asking if I can sit down and write when I must, he laughed, *or only when I'm in the mood—I write every chance I get, but I'm easily distracted.*

Does it come pretty cleanly?

I can usually write when I want, he nodded, *but sometimes I just sit here helplessly, although it comes without much changing when it comes.*

Did it always come like that?

Pretty much, Haig-Brown explained. *The early books were all copied out twice—I did that for two or three books—until I realized that I wasn't changing much.*

And when it stalls?

Sometimes I try a little fishing, his eyes twinkled with mischief. *Sometimes I work in the orchard or work at other things with my hands.*

What about beginnings and endings?

They're always difficult, Haig-Brown admitted. *I think most writers find them tough—I know I still struggle.*

You write first drafts in your head?

I don't think so, he paused thoughtfully. *Not consciously—but perhaps I play with them before I pick up my pencils.*

Well, I said, *they don't just happen.*

You're right, he said.

Haig-Brown first published *The Western Angler* in 1939, and it was dedicated to General Noel Money, and their steelhead fishing on the Stamp. Money had already operated his famous hotel at Qualicum Beach before the First World War but returned to fight with the British army in 1914.

Money was given command of a territorial regiment called the Shropshire Yeomanry and was promoted to brigadier while serving with his troops in the deserts of Palestine until the Treaty of Versailles.

Haig-Brown firmly believed that Money had been first to take winter-run steelhead on the fly, when an entire Pacific Coast believed that only hardware or fresh roe could get the fish to strike. Although he started fishing summer-run steelhead as early as April on the lower Stamp, Money did not fish them with the dry fly, as many western anglers believe.

The writer argued that point convincingly that wintry afternoon in his library, telling us that he had first demonstrated a floating-line wet fly to the old soldier, using the A. H. E. Wood techniques from Scotland.

I had been trying it, Haig-Brown said, *and I introduced him to the greased-line method first.*

It's a pretty method, I nodded. *I've fished with keepers who knew Wood, and I've fished his home water at Cairnton.*

It must be beautiful water, he said.

It is beautiful, I said. *Particularly pools like Grey Mare and Malt Steep and Canary—where did you try the greased-line with Money?*

It was on the Stamp, Haig-Brown replied eagerly. *It was quite hot, and although Money was a fanatic, he'd already quit fishing.*

Too hot and bright? I asked. *Too low?*

All three, he said. *But when I demonstrated the greased-line, I took two fish quickly.*

Money was hooked too, Callaghan observed.

You're right, Haig-Brown smiled.

The considerable scope of *The Western Angler* was quite remarkable when it was published in 1939, and it remains the fishing bible throughout the Pacific Northwest after almost fifty years. It consists of five major parts. The first described the fishes of British Columbia and their zoogeography of distribution, and the second discussed appropriate tackle and fishing in the interior of the province. The third explored the sea-run and nonmigratory trout of its coastal drainages. The fourth section was devoted to the five species of salmon found on our Pacific coast. The last was a mixed bag of biology and equipment and philosophical observations about fishing.

It was almost not published, because Haig-Brown's editors at Houghton Mifflin had already pigeonholed him as a nature writer after books like *Silver* and *Pool and Rapid* and *Panther*. It fell to Ferris Greenslet, a famous Boston editor who was himself a serious fly-fisherman, to reject the manuscript in 1938. Greenslet later wrote a charming autobiography titled *Under the Bridge*, which contained a surprising amount of fishing.

It must have been a bitter defeat.

It was bitter, he admitted, *but it led to Derrydale.*

The Derrydale edition was beautiful, Callaghan interrupted. *Its success must have erased the bad feelings about Greenslet.*

Not quite, he said quietly.

Haig-Brown was still licking his wounds and had started the manuscript that ultimately became *Return to the River*, when Eugene Connett offered to publish *The Western Angler* in a lavish two-volume edition at Derrydale. It included the beautiful color paintings of Thomas Brayshaw, another exile from the United Kingdom who had settled in British Columbia. Connett's books were elegant limited editions, and Derrydale printed only 950 copies of *The Western Angler*, but Haig-Brown was pleased that Connett agreed to print the entire manuscript with its intricate sections on taxonomy and ichthyology. It was an immense success, confounding the poor judgment at Houghton Mifflin, and Haig-Brown added these observations to the smaller edition later published by William Morrow:

The original success of *The Western Angler* has been a very pleasant thing. So far as I know, the book has been largely disregarded in British Columbia. Certainly I have not been able to detect any significant change in the methods of handling the game fish resources of the province. But I understand that it has been adopted as a standard reference work in many universities, and by several other fish commissions.

This is quite satisfying.

But even more so has been the response of individual anglers all over the United States and Canada. The book has brought me letters from New York bankers and Oregon pulp-mill workers, from Pacific Coast steelhead fishermen, from trout fishermen in England, speckled trout enthusiasts in the East, and Atlantic salmon fishers in Scotland and Maine and New Brunswick.

Ferris Greenslet also rejected *Return to the River* at Houghton Mifflin, after only a few chapters had been completed. Haig-Brown was angry and hurt. Bitterly discouraged and feeling betrayed, he remained deeply committed to the project, a book too compelling to abandon. Haig-Brown took refuge in his work. Stories about the manuscript had started circulating in Boston and New York, and Morrow suddenly offered a five-hundred dollar advance when it was desperately needed. Haig-Brown used some of the Morrow advance to travel south through the Columbia River country, gathering background material to finish *Return to the River*. The book was finally completed in spite of Greenslet in 1940.

War had already engulfed Europe, and when *Return to the River* was published the following spring, both the United States and Canada were threatened too. Its final title came from its publishers, after Haig-Brown had first proposed it for one of the chapters. The impact of *Return to the River* surprised its publishers. Superb reviews took the front page of the book supplements in both the *New York Times* and the old *New York Herald Tribune*, a major triumph for any writer, let alone storytelling about a salmon. It received other lavish praise in both the United States and Europe.

Like his earlier books *Silver* and *Panther*, Haig-Brown's remarkable story of giant chinook salmon in the watershed of the Columbia was a work of fiction, but it was firmly rooted in a knowledge of ichthyology and life.

It is a beautiful book. Its story begins with the egg laying of a big henfish in a September rain, and its pale ova lie hidden in the pebbles and pea-gravel, ticking like tiny clocks. The eggs finally hatch, and the baby salmon wriggle up into the light, schools of bright, heavily mottled fry hovering restlessly. The story follows a single, quicksilver smolt until it reaches the salt. The tiny female is nearly lost to pollution in the estuary, but finally escapes into the fertile Pacific. Haig-Brown describes its migrations northward along the coastal skerries, past Cape Flattery into the Strait of Juan de Fuca, where schools of big salmon gorge themselves on herring and sand launces and candlefish. Baby salmon are decimated too. The book follows their odysseys six hundred miles north of the Columbia, through the tidal currents of the Discovery Passage, and past the Queen Charlotte Islands. The fish were growing swiftly now, weighing ten to fifteen pounds when they reached the baitfish shoals off Skidegate Channel.

His big henfish starts home again in a spring storm that forced the halibut boats and purse-seine fleet and trollers to seek shelter. Its journey back is dogged by seals and killer whales and sea lions. Commercial fishing boats crisscross the migratory routes used by vast schools of salmon, filling their holds with thousands of big, silvery chinook. Pollution hangs thickly in the estuary at Portland, staining the tides between the Pacific and Sauvie Island, and the fish must still pass the concrete fish ladders of Goliaths like Bonneville and The Dalles.

Haig-Brown's big henfish finally arrives over the riffles where it was born, starts to carve its spawning redds in the gravel, and is quickly joined by its mate. Their spawning rites proceed in the shallows, mixed with other mating pairs, and the males quarrel in great roostertails of splashing. It is a season of old rhythms that have evolved across centuries and centuries. When his salmon have finished, their several redds hold a gleaming treasure of spawn, and Haig-Brown's story is winding down. *Return to the River* ends quietly, with its cockfish already gone and the spawning over. Its great henfish is dying too, in some of the finest nature writing in our language:

> The strong current caught Spring as she went down from the surface. It drew her to itself, rolled her over and swept her on, and she no longer resisted. Her tail moved once or twice, feebly, but all the urgencies, all the desires that had driven life through her were spent. So she lay quietly across the flow, drifting, as no strong salmon does; and the water opened her gill-plates and forced under them. And she died.

The book was a critical success, a wonderful watery parable of life itself, although Haig-Brown was subsequently convinced its story was flawed by a blind faith in technology. Haig-Brown was not alone in his guileless optimism about the power projects. Our entire society had gulled itself into believing that fish culture could totally compensate for drowned habitat. Both biologists and engineers believed that fish ladders were infallible, and that smolts could easily pass the turbines and spillways on their way to the ocean, mitigating the immense barriers of the dams themselves. The failure of hatchery genetics to restore wild fisheries has taught us that wild genetics are more priceless than we had fully grasped. The persistent runs of wild fish still teach us these truths. Fish sometimes refuse to ascend our carefully planned ladders, and millions and millions of smolts have been killed passing spillways and penstock chambers. Bonneville and its sisters have proved a mixed blessing. History has steadily eroded our blind faith in other technologies too, and the once-mighty Columbia is a cripple.

It is unfortunate that *Return to the River* had reached the best-seller lists only three weeks before the Japanese attack on Pearl Harbor plunged the United States into the Second World War, erasing all thoughts of fishing and the tragic poetry of salmon runs, and books themselves.

The Japanese sunk both battleships and our family's royalties at Pearl Harbor, Haig-Brown observed wryly. *Our royalties were smaller.*

Haig-Brown wrote three other books during the war years. His novel of steam-logging operations in the Nimpkish country was simply titled *Timber* and was published in 1943. Its British title became *The Tall Trees Fall*, and Haig-Brown completed the manuscript for *Starbuck Valley Winter* the same year, correcting galley proofs while still serving with the Canadian army. It was a story about running a trap line, in which a young orphan is tempered by the disciplines of winter trapping and evolves from boyhood toward manhood.

Panther explored the same theme, except it was a young cat.

You've got a theory that a lot of my work comes from the loss of my father, he chuckled, *and perhaps it's true.*

It's partially true, I suggested.

But that's a major theme in all storytelling, he argued persuasively. *The struggle to become an adult is hard for everyone.*

You're right, I said.

The success of *Return to the River* at the threshold of the Second World War led the publishers to suggest still another fishing book, and they offered Haig-Brown a contract before he left the army. The manuscript that ultimately evolved into *A River Never Sleeps* began while he was mending in a military hospital, and it has perhaps the best writing of his varied life's work. The soldier finally came home to his farm at Campbell River in 1946, and the book was published in time to reach the booksellers for Christmas.

Your army time was well spent, I said. *You did a lot of writing.*

Three books, he agreed.

Although it is largely a collection of fishing pieces, it is typical of vintage Haig-Brown that *A River Never Sleeps* is filled with observations about other things. It discusses some pitfalls of house hunting, picking favorite things, his boyhood tutelage under the watchful eyes of Major H. M. Greenhill, and a richly varied spectrum of similar subjects.

There is wonderful fishing too. Haig-Brown mixes Dolly Varden trout with his first steelhead in the Stillaguamish country, where a bear steals his breakfast. There is coarse-species fishing in his boyhood England. Haig-Brown gives advice on changing to dry socks after wading carelessly during a January spate, pike fishing in Europe, mountain lakes, and sea-run harvest cutthroats fresh from the tidal currents of the Discovery Passage.

Haig-Brown tells us about salmon alevins hatching in February snowmelt, his growing doubts about building big dams, his warm friendship with General Noel Money, fishing his beloved Campbell with his wife on a soft April afternoon, and a story of carrier fishing in the water meadows of Hampshire that ends with a hilarious rat-hunting episode at Headbourne Worthy.

The book offers perceptive speculations about our five species of Pacific salmon, the best times of day for fishing, best fishing light, his experiences trolling for giant tyee in saltwater, and hunting big chinook in the September rain. Haig-Brown lost his taste for shooting in his later years, but *A River Never Sleeps* has stories about ruffed grouse and snipe mixed with its fishing. There are speculations about pieces of ox horn in the fishing artifacts of prehistory, the extensive literature of angling, and the lifelong pleasures of exploring a single river and its secrets. The book is often eloquent, and the closing passages of *A River Never Sleeps* are always worth reading again:

> I don't know why I fish or why other men fish, except that we like it and it makes us think and feel. But I do know that if it were not for the strong, quick life of rivers, for their sparkle in sunshine, for the cold grayness of them under rain and the feel of them about my legs as I set my feet down hard on rocks or sand or gravel, I should fish less often. A river is never quite silent. It can never, of its very nature, be quite still; it is never quite the same from one day to the next. It has its own life and its own beauty, and the creatures it nourishes are alive and are beautiful also. Perhaps fishing is, for me, only an excuse to be near rivers. If so, I'm glad I thought of it.

The success of *Return to the River* and *A River Never Sleeps* encouraged Haig-Brown to revise his earlier book, *The Western Angler*. William Morrow was excited about publishing an inexpensive trade edition. It had been eight years since Derrydale published its expensive edition limited to only 950 sets. Morrow had its edition of *The Western Angler* in the bookstores late in 1947.

It was a great success and quickly took its place among the best fishing titles of our century. It was also published with the celebrated pen drawings and watercolors of Thomas Brayshaw, another legendary angler in British Columbia. Brayshaw was a superb mathematician and teacher, and a skilled fly dresser who tied his flies without a vise. His patterns spoke eloquently of his Yorkshire origins, with their slim wings and soft hackling. Brayshaw had come to British Columbia to work for the Yorkshire Trust, which held several large interests throughout the province. While still in the United Kingdom, his fishing friends included John James Hardy, Lawrence Robert Hardy, and William Hardy, three brothers who founded the storied British tackle house.

Brayshaw was a character, Haig-Brown poured himself a whisky in the late afternoon. *He liked to tell about sending a fully dressed British salmon pattern to Kelson for criticism.*

George Kelson was still alive? I said. *The British salmon-fly expert?*

They exchanged several letters, he said.

What did Kelson think?

Kelson liked Brayshaw's fly all right, Haig-Brown replied, *but he wrote back testily to tell Brayshaw that although he had tied the fly with authentic feathers—some of its exotic plumage had moulted.*

Pretty funny, Callaghan laughed.

Did you know Brayshaw well?

Brayshaw had lots of friends everywhere, Haig-Brown told us, *and I knew him and how well he fished and tied beautiful flies—but I didn't know about his painting and drawing.*

How did you find out?

Friends told me, he said, *but when I asked Brayshaw about illustrating* **The Western Angler** *he told me that he was not skilled enough to try anything like that—and sat right here right where you're sitting, just doodling the most exquisite fish sketches I'd ever seen.*

History tells us that Brayshaw became expert at everything he tried. When he returned to fight with his Yorkshire regiment in the First World War, his skill with a Webley service pistol kept him alive in the terrible fighting at Ypres. His ability with the Webley was so well known among his fellow officers that Brayshaw later wrote and illustrated a British army manual on combat pistol marksmanship.

William Nation was another transplanted British fisherman who had emigrated to British Columbia and had settled at Paul Lake, some 250 miles east of Vancouver. Nation was a legend among his fellow guides in the famous Kamloops lake district and was a skilled fly dresser and caster. His flies were strongly rooted in the Scottish loch-patterns, particularly the tinsel bodies tipped with bright silk flosses and ribbed with bright wire. Nation was a skilled boatman who was highly prized for both his humor and his intricate knowledge of the lakes, and his elegant flies were highly prized too.

Bill Nation dressed the flies in the limited edition of **The Western Angler**. Haig-Brown mixed another round of drinks.

He was good, Callaghan said.

Nation thought that patterns like his Nation's Blue imitated the bright damselflies called Bluets, Haig-Brown continued, *and that a scarlet-bodied species of Zygoptera was the prototype for his Nation's Red.*

Stretches hatch-matching a little thin, I stood up.

You're right, Callaghan smiled.

Bill was full of tricks, Haig-Brown was trying to control his laughter. *He'd row his paying sports along the shores, and let them flail away while he trolled a big fly along the drop-off—and caught fish after fish!*

Haig-Brown turned several times to fiction after the Second World War and completed two novels in the months that followed. The book *Saltwater Summer* was a sequel to his story of youth and winter trapping, *Starbuck Valley Winter*. Its young protagonist has grown older and has taken partners to operate a small salmon-fishing boat. The book's rich sense of detail was clearly drawn from the commercial fishing that Haig-Brown tried during the Great Depression, and I was browsing through a copy when Anne appeared. Haig-Brown stood to make his wife a drink.

You've been talking about fish, she said. *I'm not much for fishing.*

What would you like to talk about? I asked.

Italian art, she laughed.

We might work something out, I said, *and you're not alone about not liking fish—fishing wives suffer a lot.*

I studied her bookshelves of art and philosophy and religion, and the language books stacked on her worktable. *And the fish talk*, Anne continued gaily. *Rod wrote about all your fish talk in* **Fisherman's Spring***—you're always chattering and chattering in fish talk!*

Fish talk? I parried weakly.

You're always talking away about trying a little brown thing or a little red thing, she chided gently and cut some cheddar, *and failing until you finally try the little black thing!*

You've got us! I admitted.

Tell us, Callaghan interrupted. *What book is your favorite?*

My favorite book is **On the Highest Hill***, Anne replied quietly. It's such a lovely, somber story, and it's so filled with life—it's so filled with strength and probity and life, that I think it's the closest book to Rod's character of anything else he's written.*

It's not well known, I said.

It's still his best, she insisted firmly. *What's your favorite?*

Measure of the Year, I replied.

Haig-Brown published the wonderful collection of essays he called *Measure of the Year* at midcentury and readily admitted that essays had become his favorite literary form. His *Measure of the Year* is a rich trapper's stew of a book. It has observations on the circling seasons along the Campbell, trees, wildflowers, music, books, organizations and churches in country life, avifauna, the poetry of simple tools, orchards, working in the garden, and the problems of serving as magistrate.

The writer was elected magistrate at Campbell River in 1933, when Haig-Brown was only thirty years old. His election came at the instigation of its local detachment of Royal Canadian Mounted Police, and he served as stipendiary magistrate for another thirty-three years.

You begin to understand something about panic, Haig-Brown laughed, *when you stand behind the bench without any legal education or experience—and those big constables wearing those big flat-brimmed hats and scarlet tunics and boots tell the people that your court is formally in session—for His Majesty the King!*

I'll bet, I said.

Later that night, Haig-Brown brought out a small stack of copybooks filled with notes gathered from his thirty-three years as magistrate and sent me back to the hotel with some of his copybooks to read. The notes were filled with things not found in *Measure of the Year*, yet the writer who had published twenty-five books, and was still finishing *Bright Waters, Bright Fish*, was filled with beginner's doubt about transforming his notes into a book about his courtroom years. It was after three o'clock in the morning, with a chill February wind rattling the hotel windows, when I found this remarkable paragraph.

After thirty-odd years as a country magistrate in our fishing village in British Columbia, lacking any formal training in the law, I have reached the conclusion that most of our criminal and social problems stem from frustration—a frustration compounded by problems of liquor and sex, rather too much of the former and too little of the latter, each of indifferent quality.

Haig-Brown will never make a book from those spiral-bound copybooks, and we must content ourselves with the sampler of courtroom essays in his *Measure of the Year*. Others have published collections of early magazine pieces since his death, but Haig-Brown himself had grave doubts about those projects.

You don't want to publish them?

Well, he said, *when they asked me to cull through my files and think about such books, I began to worry.*

What kinds of worries?

Lots of things, he said. *One that you would appreciate was discussing selectivity in trout fishing—and arguing that matching specific fly-hatches did not really matter on our continent—that it was a European thing.*

But you were writing about fishing a dry fly on cutthroats, I said.

Exactly, he said. *That's my worry.*

They're not very picky, I agreed. *Excepting the cutthroats in the spring creeks at Jackson Hole.*

You're right, Callaghan said.

It's you people who began to make me wonder if I knew anything about selective fish, he explained, *and the fishing you showed me on Silver Creek and the spring creeks at Jackson Hole really surprised me.*

What about the Frying Pan? I asked.

The Frying Pan too, he admitted, *during our meetings at Aspen.*

And you've changed your mind?

I've begun to understand that most rainbow and cutthroat fisheries are just not difficult enough to matter, he admitted. *You can't know anything about selectivity until you've fished over selective fish.*

You don't want to publish old pieces like that today? Callaghan asked.

He's changed his mind, I said.

That's right, he nodded. *Some of those early essays were filled with mistakes—and I think they should just stay in my files.*

Although his fishing audience has largely settled on *A River Never Sleeps* and *The Western Angler* as its favorite books, Haig-Brown seemed to prefer essays like those found in *Measure of the Year*. It also held his thoughts on firewood and its burning qualities, children and their role in country households, visitors, the importance of books in backcountry farms, citizenship, the ethics of hunting, tides, the ecology of tidal flats, the impact of industrial growth and clear-cut lumbering, pipes and pipe smoking, children's games, the quiet pace of country life, and the changing rhythms of his beloved Campbell.

I know you believe that stories and novels are the pinnacle of writing, Haig-Brown said. *Earlier I might have agreed with you—but these last few years I've come to liking the essay better.*

You really think so? I asked.

Pretty much, he said, *but I've got some doubts too.*

What kinds of doubts?

Sometimes I think that I'm too afraid to let my emotions show in my writing, he confessed quietly. *Too guarded to write really good fiction.*

And that's why you like essays? Callaghan interjected.

Perhaps, he said.

Which book is your favorite?

It's a difficult question, he stopped to fill his pipe carefully. *It's easier to tell you which book I like the least.*

What's that?

Pool and Rapid! Haig-Brown laughed at his abrupt confession. *It was more widely translated than any of the other books, but I have serious misgivings about publishing it again.*

But people loved it, Callaghan insisted.

People were wrong, he said.

It's not the first time a writer has disagreed with his audience, I persisted. *Which book is your favorite?*

The book I'm working on, he laughed. *Wasn't it your Frank Lloyd Wright who always said that about his buildings?*

Yes, I said. *It was.*

There was a steady stream of books in the next fifteen years, after *Measure of the Year* was published, and its structural use of the seasons led his New York publishers to suggest a fresh series of fishing titles. The collection of essays titled *Fisherman's Spring* appeared in 1951, and it begins with Haig-Brown's thesis that he was a serious angler, although he was equally serious about many other points of his compass.

Fisherman's Spring includes a conscious exploration of fly patterns dressed to imitate the spates of salmon fry and smolts migrating downstream toward the sea. Five species of Pacific salmon are involved, each having smolts of discrete average size, color, configuration, and parr markings.

It's an exercise in matching the hatch, he confessed, *but our hatches are a little fishy.*

I'll let it pass, I said.

It was an intriguing application of Halford's fly-hatch theories to a coastal Pacific river, its forest drainages relatively barren of aquatic fly life. The migratory fish themselves are testimony to the infertility of most steelhead fisheries. Too sterile to evolve and sustain resident populations of big fish, they have evolved restless genetic strains that leave the rivers when they reach smolting size and grow to adulthood in the more richly fertile Pacific. Haig-Brown's concepts of imitating salmon fry and smolts, which are primary forage species for the cutthroats and rainbows and Dolly Varden char, were also subtly mixed with the color-and-spectrum theories of fly dressing introduced by Letcher Lambuth and Preston Jennings. Lambuth was a fishing friend of Haig-Brown's from Seattle, a richly inventive angler who experimented with the Devine patents for spiral split-cane rods and was famous for his streamside Old Fashioneds. Jennings was the author of *A Book of Trout Flies*, the first disciplined American work on aquatic insects and flies tied to imitate them.

Haig-Brown's essay on Charles Cotton had always intrigued me, since it has been his collaborator, Izaak Walton, who has been most celebrated by history. Walton was praised for his piety and contemplative wit, perhaps by subsequent writers in fiercely pious times, while Cotton was denigrated for his boisterous ribaldry and wit. It was grudgingly admitted that Cotton knew more about trout, but his obvious fishing skills did not bolster his literary status. Cotton had also written scatological dramas. Walton was once widely credited with inventing his pastoral dialogues of whole cloth, but since midcentury we have known that virtually all of his *Compleat Angler* was borrowed freely from earlier books. His knowledge of flies and fly-fishing comes from *The Treatyse of Fysshynge with an Angle*, written in the middle of the fifteenth century. Leonard Mascall was also among Walton's sources, since the mistakes Mascall made in borrowing from the *Treatyse* appear unchanged in *The Compleat Angler* almost two centuries later. Such facts have been known for many years.

But when a British antiquarian found a previously unknown fishing book called *The Arte of Angling* while settling an estate in 1954 and sold it to the wealthy American collector, Carl Otto von Kienbusch, it became obvious that Walton had invented neither the dialogue form nor the fishing content of *The Compleat Angler*. Scholars are still arguing about the unknown author of *The Arte of Angling*, with its origins still clearly in dispute and the book was published in 1577. Mascall published his *Booke of Fishing with Hook and Line* thirteen years later, and Walton's *Compleat Angler* was first printed in 1653.

Walton is more lyric and his prose is more polished, but the parallels between *The Compleat Angler* and those earlier British books are unmistakable. Mascall supplied the flies and fly-fishing passages. *The Arte of Angling* supplied the same cast of characters, and Walton reworked whole sections of his earlier sources only slightly. Walton is still admired for his lyric moods, but his literary stature has changed.

We'd call him a plagiarist, Haig-Brown observed thoughtfully, *but that's judging him in terms of our century*.

How's that? Callaghan asked.

Because taking freely from earlier books was commonplace in Walton's time, he explained. *It probably started before Hammurabi and Homer—plagiarism itself is a pretty modern concept*.

Stealing from one book is called plagiarism, I paraphrased jokingly, *but stealing from hundreds of books is called scholarship*.

Precisely, he agreed.

Some people were puzzled by your essay on Charles Cotton, I said. *You didn't give Walton equal time*.

I was more interested in Cotton.

But many fishing historians have attacked Cotton, I continued. *They sound almost worried that such a ribald wastrel could have forged such a close friendship with our saintly Father Walton.*

I liked his wastrel side! Haig-Brown grinned.

Anne came down the half-stairs into the library. *You should have known Rod when I first knew him*, Anne teased. *Rod wasn't always the soul of probity he seems!*

Wastrel! he laughed.

There were also several other books written in these years. *The Whale People* was a novel of the whale-hunting coastal tribes farther north, and there were three children's books about the history of British Columbia, books titled *The Farthest Shores, Fur and Gold*, and *The Captain of Discovery*.

Haig-Brown's next fishing book was *Fisherman's Winter*, a wonderfully evocative book that is not well known. It deserved a much larger audience. Many Haig-Brown readers were disappointed with *Fisherman's Winter*, perhaps expecting it to explore his experiences on winter steelhead rivers like the Nimpkish and Skagit. It has become a particular favorite of mine, because it captures a favorite part of my fisherman's world.

It was a wonderful trip to Argentina and Chile, Haig-Brown said. *It's a fascinating countryside to fish.*

When the first commercial flights to Chile and Argentina started, Haig-Brown was invited to sample their fishing. His expedition started with the Laguna de Maule, an ancient volcanic basin fed by thermal springs, lying at almost ten thousand feet in the heart of the Andes. It has since been reworked to store water for irrigation and power, drowning its food-rich shallows and spawning grounds. His first river fishing took place on the Rio Laja, which rises in the monkey puzzle forests west of Concepcion and is lined with slender Lombardy poplars in the beautiful farm country beyond the foothills. Haig-Brown and his party used horses to travel along the Laja and stayed at the old Palacio, using oxcarts to carry their boats.

The trip continued farther south, exploring the Quepe and Cautin and Tolten with skilled Chilean *boteros*, who worked their skiffs deftly through the chutes and rowed hard to fish the big, swirling pools. Haig-Brown was particularly taken with the Tolten, and his delight is obvious in these lines:

> On the first day we seemed lost, almost from the start, between green-forested walls that went straight up from the broad river. The growth was far heavier than along the Cautin and the Quepe, and its greens were impressively rich. Bird song was constant when one could hear above the sound of the river,

and at one place *bandurrias* scolded and complained from the high treetops about our passing.

The Villarica volcano rises at Pucon, where Haig-Brown fished the Trancura and Liucura. Pucon had been a famous summer-holiday village for many years and still has some of the finest small hotels in Chile. It later became a winter resort too, and it was skiing that brought the late Alfredo Heusser to Pucon, where he became even more famous as a fishing guide and fly dresser. Heusser created the Pancora, which is a workable imitation of the Chilean crayfish and is easily tied. His Trancura is the most famous trout stream in Chile, with the Liucura tributary that rises in the Mamuil Malal Pass into Argentina. The rivers join at the Martinez Pool, and Haig-Brown described it perfectly in *Fisherman's Winter*: "We left the Martinez Pool soon after that and I was sad to leave it because it is, without a doubt, one of the truly great trout pools of the world."

Beyond Pangipuilli, Haig-Brown took the little steamer up the lake to Chan-Chan. The late Kip Farrington, who is better known for his marlin fishing off famous Cabo Blanco in Peru, had a timber-country farm there with excellent trout fishing on the Enco and Fui. There were logging camps in the headwaters of Pangipuilli in those days, and the old timber tally-man from British Columbia described their operations with obvious knowledge and skill.

After sleeping all night on a timber packet that crossed Lago Riñihue, between the mouth of the Enco and the outlet of the San Pedro, he fished a large river that sluggishly reaches the Pacific at Valdivia. Haig-Brown traveled farther south from Los Lagos to Paillaco and turned east into the Swiss-looking countryside above Lago Ranco. The lake is an ancient caldera, with several islands at its center, weathered volcanic plugs that lie silhouetted against its silvery expanse. The caldera is still ovoid, its shape relatively unchanged by the later eruptions of Choshuenco and Puyehue. It is a wonderful fishing region. The Calcurrupe is among the finest trout streams in the world, rising in the fjordlike forests at Lago Maihue and flowing swiftly into Lago Ranco at Llifen. The Riñinahue, Ñilahue, and Caunahue also flow into Lago Ranco, and Maihue itself is fed by smaller rivers like the Blanco, Quinileufu, Hueinahue, and Carranleufu. Haig-Brown floated the Calcurrupe and fished the reedy outlet lagoon at Maihue. There was no chance to explore the Llifen region more widely. The beautiful little Cumilahue is probably the principal spawning tributary in the entire Calcurrupe watershed, and perhaps the finest fishery of its size in Chile. Haig-Brown did not fish anything but the Calcurrupe and did not discover the Cumilahue in his brief stay at Llifen. *Fisherman's Winter* tells us that he barely explored the Llifen fisheries, but his instincts told him that his expedition into the Calcurrupe country was too short.

Haig-Brown fished briefly at the outlet of Lago Ranco and traveled to Osorno and Puero Varas, with their lakes and beautiful volcanoes. He circled the big Llanquihue Lake, climbing into the forests to Petrohue between the snowfields of Osorno and Calbuco. The Petrohue is a beautiful river. It spills from Lago Todo de los Santos, gathering itself in a reedy lagoon before tumbling swiftly toward its spectacular falls downstream. The falls are formed by a fault line of deeply fractured lava outcroppings, a wild series of cataracts well worth seeing, roaring into a swirling, rocky pool the size of a stadium. Haig-Brown discovered a spring-fed stream that welled up from a fissure in the lava and found it like a British chalk stream except for its wild junglelike setting. Lago Todo de los Santos itself is surrounded by five volcanoes, its steep shorelines and narrow arms thickly forested in exotic beeches and *ulmo* magnolias and flame trees. The lake itself is a deep turquoise, carrying the glacial silts of its volcano icefields, and is among the most beautiful lakes in the world.

It's a wonderful country, Haig-Brown stared out through his orchard in the rain. *I always wanted to get back to Chile—to fish the Calcurrupe country at Llifen and explore the Petrohue.*

Crossing the lake itself, Haig-Brown spent the night at Peulla's charming mountain hotel, but it was raining hard and he did not try to fish the little rivers there, the Negro and Peulla. The border is finally crossed by bus, and a traveler must board another ferry in Argentina to sail to Llao-Llao on Lago Nahuel-Huapi. His fishing in Argentina was less leisurely, but Haig-Brown saw some remarkable country, fishing with men like Gustavo Schwed, Tito Hosmann, and Guy Dawson.

It surprised me, he confessed. *I expected more rain forests like Chile —but the big foothill country was more like Wyoming or Alberta.*

It's beautiful country, I agreed.

I went feeling pretty hostile toward the Peron regime, he continued, *but I found myself enjoying the people and country immensely and wanting to spend more time fishing it—particularly the salmon on the Traful.*

It's still there, I said.

There was fishing in the jungle-looking forests along the Rio Manso too, south of San Carlos de Bariloche, and at its Laguna de las Moscas. Tito Hosmann showed him the arid rock-chimney valley of the Limay. The roads were poor in those days, clinging to the steep bluffs at the Anfiteatro del Limay and winding north through the Valle Encantado. Hosmann took him farther north to Meliquina, where the fly dresser José Navas lived above the lake, and Haig-Brown left wanting more time to explore its weedy shallows and the Bocas del Hermoso.

The beautiful *estancia* called La Primavera has landlocked salmon transplanted in 1904 from Sebago Lake in Maine. Its Rio Traful is incredibly crystalline just below its lake, its pools so clear that wading is almost dangerous, since it is difficult to estimate their depth. Haig-Brown found them challenging sport and fell in love with pools like the Campamento and Horseshoe, and the swift Pool of Plenty.

Guy Dawson took him to fish the Collon Cura and Quilquihue, and to the wind-polished basin of the Chimehuin, the most famous trout stream in Argentina. Haig-Brown would be stunned at the fishing pressure along these rivers at Junin de los Andes today, anglers booked primarily through outfitters in the United States. He might have felt a measure of guilt for first writing about the wonderful fishing in Patagonia and starting the steady pilgrimage of trout fishermen into these latitudes. It is country I have fished often over the past thirty-odd years, and I have come to treasure *Fisherman's Winter* for its capacity to awaken happy memories of its people and its places.

The book is wonderfully evocative, I said.

It had a strong impact, Haig-Brown admitted. *It's a pretty exotic world. And you even had the taxonomy right.*

Taxonomy is a particular concern of mine, he nodded thoughtfully. *I really think that a man who could walk through a new country without wanting to know about its trees and wildflowers and birds might as well fish blindfolded.*

Not just in a strange country, I said. *Most people don't care about knowing taxonomy at home.*

People are pretty lazy, he agreed, *and sometimes I think Walton was wrong about fishing—it's just too intense to contemplate the countryside.*

Or anything else, I said.

Haig-Brown published *Fisherman's Summer* in 1959 and followed it two years later with a kind of biophysical survey of British Columbia he titled *The Living Land*. It explored the topography, climate, geology, soils, watershed, agriculture, timber resources, minerals, industry, energy projects, fisheries, wildlife, demography, and future problems of the entire province. Its unflinching commitment to thoughtful development and wilderness did not find much support in a government aggressively pledged to timber and industrial growth and fisheries. British Columbia has been largely myopic to ecological values over the past half-century, its first priorities given to industrial development and growth. Haig-Brown was not discouraged when officials at Victoria largely ignored *The Living Land* and its thesis.

But I didn't expect to change Victoria, he said. *I thought it needed writing—and perhaps I finally wrote it for myself.*

It's a good reason, I agreed.

The little beginner's manual titled *A Primer of Fly Fishing* appeared in 1964. It is probably the least successful of Haig-Brown's many books, its contents pared down to basic concepts by a writer too thoughtful and perhaps too richly experienced to write a beginner's text. It is like finding a pianist doing a simple exercise when his earlier performances have celebrated Mozart and Bach.

Was the primer your idea? I asked.

No, Haig-Brown replied. *My publishers were the ones who pushed it pretty hard—I never liked it much, and it didn't feel right.*

Were you working on another book?

I'm always working on another book, he laughed. *Aren't you?*

Yes, I admitted.

The other manuscript was *Fisherman's Fall*, which also appeared in 1964. Haig-Brown suggested it was his last fishing book, but that sad prophecy was not entirely true. He wrote the copy for the lavish portfolio prepared by the government at Ottawa for the International Law of the Sea Conference. Haig-Brown managed to complete his manuscript for *Bright Waters, Bright Fish*, which surveyed sport fishing throughout Canada, only a few weeks before he died.

There was a surprising tribute paid to Haig-Brown in 1970, when he became chancellor of the University of British Columbia. It was an event more unexpected than his election as stipendiary magistrate at Campbell River many years before. Haig-Brown stayed at his university post three years, and after working on the government folio designed to get other governments to participate in salmon treaties, he also served six years on the International Pacific Salmon Fisheries Commission. But the university post was a surprise.

Well, I said, *it's pretty ironic that the boy who failed to get into Cambridge became a university chancellor at Victoria.*

It is ironic, he said.

Things come full circle, I agreed, *but how did it happen?*

It was simple enough, Haig-Brown chuckled. *People put my name on the ballot again and I won.*

It was another elected post? I asked.

That's right, he smiled.

Before we left Campbell River, Haig-Brown and his wife joined us for dinner at a charming inn along the estuary. We all decided on the rare prime rib with Yorkshire pudding, which was served in almost indecent lumberjack portions, and the cellar had a Chateau Gloria.

We talked about ichthyology and aquatic entomology, and the manuscript that ultimately became *Bright Waters, Bright Fish*. We talked about the decimation of salmon throughout the Atlantic and his extraordinary knowledge of the Pacific species and their cycles. His insights were both complex and simple, mixing the perceptions of the poet with the probity of science.

Where did you study biology? I asked.

I didn't study it formally, Haig-Brown replied. *I simply studied it by myself—not at college or anything.*

But you really know aquatic biology.

Amateur knowledge, he said. *But it makes a point worth making—the term amateur has evolved a curiously negative connotation over here.*

How's that? I asked.

The amateur is considered inept, he explained, *but it didn't always have that negative connotation—its Latin roots come from love of something.*

Love? Callaghan said.

Love is the root, Haig-Brown nodded. *Somebody who loves something—and its British connotation has usually been somebody who loves a subject, yet has the skills to pursue it professionally.*

But happily chooses to remain amateur? I asked.

Exactly, he said.

It was not just fishing talk, since Anne had joined us at dinner and fishing talk bored her. Our dinner talk ranged freely. We talked about Mozart and Vivaldi, wines and single-malt whiskies, languages, the labyrinths of recent Chilean politics, unions, the bitter politics of the logging camps in the Great Depression, urban planning, dams, the coastal tribes of British Columbia, drift-netting, stress analysis in building and bridges, roads, clear-cutting, the impact of fish hatcheries on genetics, Italian painters, Piero della Francesca, Verdi, the hill towns of Tuscany, Venice, Brunelleschi and Bramante, the Uffizi Gallery, the church of San Miniato al Monte, and the richly decorated bell tower of Giotto.

Anne could happily live in Florence, Haig-Brown teased his wife gently. *Too bad they don't have steelhead in the Arno.*

Fish talk! Anne parried.

Haig-Brown had fished with us briefly that afternoon, walking down through the orchard to the river. He took a few small cutthroats at the Line Fence Pool, a taking-lie he first described in *A River Never Sleeps*, and rolled a bright steelhead that failed to rise again. The fish were arriving to spawn and to gorge themselves on the pink salmon fry that would migrate downstream soon. He seemed quite happy in his fishing, although he tired quickly. His health seemed better since his back surgery in 1965, and Haig-Brown confirmed that judgment, walking back through grape arbors and orchards alive with grosbeaks.

Our last evening in his library, where we stopped off for a nightcap, he was quite jovial. There was a salmon fly painted by Charles de Feo over the whisky table. His talk was filled that night with the books he had written, his recent trips to other parts of his adopted country, and the books he still wanted to write. There was both probity and fire in his voice. Anne suggested that it was getting too late for her favorite writer, and we tried several times to leave. Haig-Brown protested vigorously each time. It was obvious that he wanted to talk, and the room was filled with his laughter. When I asked him to record the last pages of *A River Never Sleeps*, he read in a soft voice that trembled with emotion. Haig-Brown was filled with life that February night, and he would turn sixty-eight in only a few days.

Roderick Langmere Haig-Brown died on October 9, 1976, after suffering a heart attack while tending the lawn that reached down from his writing desk window to the river. The orchard was stripped bare in the wind. His pencil box and typewriter and copybooks lie abandoned now, like his noisy desk chair, after twenty-six books in a lifetime that has been compared with Walton and Thoreau. His devoted wife, three daughters, and a son survived him. His daughter Valerie has been editing and publishing his papers. It was a remarkably productive life at the simple farm along the Campbell. His work mixed the disparate worlds of writing, ecology, fisheries management, farming, jurisprudence, lumbering, hunting for cougar bounties, journalism, university life, and fly-fishing with his skills at observing people and wild things and life in the swiftly changing world called British Columbia.

His beautiful book *A River Never Sleeps* includes a moving essay on death and dying, which speculates on rivers that had caught his imagination across the fly-fisher's world. It begins with these sadly prophetic words:

> If one has to die, I should think that November would be the best month for it. It is a gray, stormy month; the salmon are dying and the year is done. I should think there is nothing very sad about dying, except for the people one has to leave and the things one hasn't had time to do. When the time comes, if I know what it's all about, I suppose I should think, among other things, of the fish I haven't caught and the places I haven't fished.

Fishing Luck

Winter is always a good time to think about fishing luck. It is usually a curious subject. Folklore is filled with fishing luck stories, but over the years, I have seen luck play a surprisingly small role in fishing. Luck is obviously involved in blind trolling and stumbling into hatchery trucks, unless a friend on the hatchery crew has given you a fish-stocking schedule. Throwing hardware at a reservoir and mindlessly cranking it back involves luck too.

Watching a red-and-white bobber floating in a muddy creek depends on fishing luck, and I tried it often when I was small. It seemed a workable solution to those childhood times when we were not in trout country.

But there are many kinds of luck.

Once I went fishing under a railroad trestle in late April. Big jetty-sized blocks of limestone protected its abutments from spates. There were sunfish and smallmouth bass and pumpkinseeds, but in the spring they were mixed with a few listless hatchery rainbows. It was the trout that I really wanted. It was the first hot day that spring, and there were big bull snakes sunning themselves everywhere, still filled with winter torpor. The snakes were sluggish after their hibernation among the rocks, ugly and coiled, enjoying the late April sun.

It was horrible and I was afraid. It was five miles back to town on my bicycle, but I pedaled home without fishing. Thinking back through the years, it was another kind of fishing luck.

Bad luck still happens sometimes. Jock Fewel and Ben Bachulis once took me fishing for steelhead on the lower Deschutes in September. It was unusually hot in Oregon that week. The fish were there all right, seeking respite from the lukewarm impoundments on the Columbia. The river above Bonneville Dam became a tepid lake. It was simply so hot in the canyon under the Pictograph Cliffs that we languished and took sweaty naps like beached whales. Bachulis took an aluminum beach chair from under the dining fly at our spike camp and sat neck-deep in the river. It was too hot for anything until twilight, but I fished through the long riffle called Watertower that evening, moving six fish and hooking five.

Our outfitter had several tents at his scrub oak site, but it was too hot to sleep there. We lay outside on canvas army cots with a few misgivings about Oregon desert rattlesnakes. The outfitter had been trapping magpies, intending to teach the birds to talk, and had transformed his biggest tent into an aviary. Its floor was littered with bird droppings. We moved the dining fly farther away from the magpies, and supper was surprisingly good. I rummaged through my duffle after supper, tied a few Green Butt Skunks, and fell asleep with images of snakes and steelhead.

After midnight our camp became a wild explosion of noises. Birds were screaming and people were flailing around in the dark. The pot rack came down in a cacophony of skillets and saucepans. Something was in the tent with the magpies, and whatever it was, it was terrifying them.

What the hell's going on? somebody yelled. *What's all that racket?*

Spotted skunk, the outfitter said.

What happened to the magpies? I asked sleepily.

It killed them, he said.

Killed them all? Fewel asked.

Every one.

Well, Fewel said drily, *think of the bright side—you won't have to teach all those magpies to talk*.

The river was high and milky in the morning. The hot weather had triggered a cloudburst over the snowfields on Mount Hood, and their chalky melting kept the Deschutes unfishable for days. We buried the magpies and left after breakfast.

It had been an unforgettable night. Sometimes fishing luck can get a little strange, but heavy rains and high water are not always bad. Spates are usually good on the small salmon rivers of Scotland. Some years ago, I flew to Prestwick to join some British friends on a small spate river that rises high in the barren moors at Kingshouse Bridge.

It was raining hard when I arrived.

Sheets and sheets of rain came in squalls off the Irish Sea, and I stopped happily for the night in the little Tudor hotel at Troon. The heavy rains and fatigue after a long flight were too much, particularly when added to the disciplines of shifting gears with my left hand and driving on the wrong side of the road. Scottish golfers are famous for their hardiness. Having invented the game, they are often found playing in doubtful weather; and it has been said that if they always waited for good weather, they would seldom play golf. Since I could see no golfers playing the Royal Troon, which lay beyond the croquet lawn and gardens below my room, it was likely that the forecast was bad.

It was still raining in the morning. Other travelers were grumbling when I stopped for a lunch of smokies and shepherd's pie and ale beside Loch Lomond, but after almost forty years of salmon fishing, the rain was welcome. The tea-colored burns spilling into Lomond were bank-full and roaring, staining the lake with their pigments where I turned into the highlands toward Bridge of Orchy.

The road wound high into the wild Moors of Rannoch, and it was still raining heavily when I finally stopped for directions at Kingshouse Bridge, in the headwaters of the Etive. The little country hotel there is the oldest in Scotland, and both the hotel and its stone-arch bridge are found in a famous watercolor painted by the late Ogden Pleissner.

The little Etive was running quite high, and long before I found the postmaster who serves as its riverkeeper, it was a torrent. The old man could scarcely contain his excitement. *'Tis been fierce dry for weeks*, he babbled. *Fierce dry—but the bright fish will be coming now!*

Our first morning, I drew the Iron Fence Pool just a mile above the sea loch. The mountains on the Etive are unusually beautiful, perhaps the most beautiful in Scotland. The Iron Fence is a sweeping bend bordered by a thick copse of conifers. Its cast-iron fence is almost a relic. The river slides past a series of outcroppings and ledges there. Some outcroppings were used as casting platforms, sculptured out and bridged with masonrywork.

The first time through the pool, carefully fishing a low-water Blue Charm, I thought a fish pulled at my fly. I have spent so many happily fishless days in Scotland that I easily dismissed it. Past the little stonework bridge to the last outcropping of ledges, there was a boil behind the fly sixty feet out.

Sea trout, I thought and cast again.

But I was wrong. Teasing the little Blue Charm through its swing, I saw a bulging wake in the shallows and hooked a twelve-pound hen salmon. It bolted downstream, leapfrogging and stripping line shrilly from the reel.

Salmon! I thought excitedly. *Maybe I'm not really in Scotland!*

It rained hard all night. It was still raining softly in the morning, and the entire week fished well. The rain had changed everything. Ankle-deep shallows were transformed into taking lies as the gentle Etive rose three feet. Our third morning, the sky grew black in the steep mountain glens, and we stopped fishing to escape a blinding rain in the ghillie's hut.

When the rain stopped, bright salmon were rolling everywhere, and I hooked four salmon in six casts at the tail of the Big Pool. It was a pod of bright fish that had just arrived on the spate, and I took sixteen that week on the Etive.

Weather changes play a considerable role in fishing luck. Several years ago on the Grimsá in Iceland, Robert Buckmaster and I arrived during the worst drought in more than a century. The Grimsá held plenty of fish, but it was reduced to a trickle. Salmon holding in the fjord refused to cross the shallow flats at its mouth. The river has sixty pools, but only six or seven were really fishing well. The beautiful Laxfoss Pool, where a series of chutes and waterfalls spill twenty feet down both sides of a lava outcropping, is the site of the fishing house on the Grimsá. The pool usually produces almost a thousand salmon itself each summer, more salmon than all the rivers we have worked to restore throughout New England together, but it was reduced to an unfishable trickle. Strengir is a famous pool too, its stairsteps worn in the smooth rhyolite ledges that reach three hundred yards below the boiling chutes at its throat and it holds the best fly-water on the entire Grimsá fishery.

Strengir was not holding fish. Few were able to traverse more than a dozen waterfalls to reach its cooling-fault pools, and its other fish had seemingly left. It produces almost as many salmon as the Laxfoss, yet our party had not moved a fish there all week. Few had been caught by midweek. The river has averaged better than a hundred fish per week to its ten-rod parties over almost twenty seasons, but our week was not fishing well. The drought broke at midweek in the only lightning storm that anyone in the entire Borgarnes region could remember. Our party took almost thirty fish the day after the storm, and we had superb fishing.

Geoffrey Thomas is a fishing friend in New Zealand who insists that I have always lucked into their best weather each trip, in a string of good fortune reaching back a dozen years.

It's uncanny, mate! Thomas laughs. *We don't really want to fish with you people—we just want to know when you blokes are coming down, so we can finally schedule our family vacations.*

Thomas reminds everyone of the trip when storms along the Southern Alps had literally drowned the airport at Invercargill. The *Otago Daily Times* had a photograph of a boatman rowing past its ticket counters.

And you blokes were fishing happily on the Greenstone and Caples, Thomas rests his case, *in the only bloody sunshine anyplace*!

Last February I lost a big rainbow on a small pumice-gorge river in northern New Zealand. The fish was so strong that it left me shaken. Peter Church had spotted it cruising a big pool under the cliffs, using a big *manuka* tree to see into its emerald depths. I was fishing a big nymph tied on a heavy sproat hook. When the fish took the fly, it exploded in wild gyrations on the bottom. It never jumped or porpoised. We had already released a ten-pound rainbow that morning, but this fish was uncontrollable. The rod simply hopscotched and danced wildly with its head shaking, and suddenly it was gone.

Broke me! I sighed.

But the fish had not broken off. The big nymph was still there, attached to the six-pound tippet, but its hook had been twisted open.

Sometimes luck is a happy surprise. Twenty-five years ago, I was exploring the salmon rivers in the Sognefjord. The trip was ahead of schedule. Since I was interested in the stave churches of Norway and had already photographed the famous churches at Borgund and Vik, it seemed like a good time to visit the beautiful little stave church at Urnes.

Urnes dates to the early twelfth century. It is believed that the sixteen-pillar church that still stands in the mountains of Sogn, in a steep meadow above the fjord, has incorporated parts of a much older church from the same site. The first church at Urnes was probably built in the eleventh century, and some scholars believe it might have been the oldest in Norway. It stands in a stone churchyard, across the fjord from a small village hotel. There is no road to the church. The village across the fjord seemed empty, and it took fifteen minutes to find anyone at its small hostelry. It was a young girl with surprisingly long blond pigtails and a minuscule Carnaby Street skirt. She spoke some English, and with my halting Norwegian, we succeeded in starting lunch. It was warm and still, and I decided to eat outside in the garden. Lunch was smoked salmon, hard-boiled eggs, and a tomato-and-onion salad with a bottle of Piesporter Goldtröpfchen.

My boyfriend will row you across the fjord to Urnes, the pigtail girl explained. *But you must bring plenty of beer*.

What kinds are there? I asked.

Ringnes and Hansa.

Hansa, I said. *Can we take some ice to chill it?*

Ja, she smiled. *I'm coming too*.

Sognefjord was perfectly still after lunch, and we rowed across slowly, our wake gently disturbing the mountains and forests in its mirror. The girl sat in the bow, trailing her fingers in the water. Her boyfriend was a tow-headed giant who wore nothing but faded jeans. Our boatman spoke no English. It seemed possible that he was a mute, because I did not hear

Norwegian either, and the girl with the pigtails just giggled. We finally moored the skiff at a stone jetty, and when I started up the steep meadow toward the stave church, they were both giggling and drinking beer.

Urnes was worth the trip. It looks tiny and quite ordinary at a distance, its timbers warping with time and its steeple leaning slightly. The stone wall surrounding its churchyard was mossy and thickly dappled with lichens. The low picket gate has a little roof of hand-split shingles. Its treasures are not obvious. Fragments of the earlier Urnes church are found in its dark little nave, a belfrylike space framed by Viking shipwrights at the scale of a doll's house. Its carved wooden capitals and arches are unmistakably Romanesque and quite old. The crucifix is clumsy and primitive. Its crucified figure has a rib cage that looks more like a codfish than a man, and its wood is shrinking and split under faint traces of pigment, but it has a curious power. The plan of the church is roughly cruciform. Its facade has carved treasures too. The timber pilaster supporting the northeast corner of the choir is obviously from the old church at Urnes. Its carvings seethe with intricately twined demons and reptiles, and the north portal is even more spectacular. Its carvings are a richly worked motif of mythic beasts, mixing snakes and serpentine dragons locked in mortal combat with a strangely graceful lion. The work has a powerful sinuosity. Its images struggle and writhe, mixing old mythologies with medieval Christian symbols, in carving as tormented as the brushwork of Van Gogh.

Who carved such things? I thought.

The beer was gone when I returned to the jetty. The girl giggled and buttoned her blouse, and the boy just laughed. The trip back went haltingly, because the oars kept slipping from the wooden oarlocks, and we kept drifting off course. It was still early, and I decided to drive the mountain road to Mørkrid, a village lying at the head of the fjord. Its hotel is comfortable and small. The porter saw my fishing tackle and told me that a beat was available on the river. The angler had fallen and could not fish. Most of his allotted time was already gone, so the fishing was relatively cheap, and I decided to try it.

You have been fishing? the concierge asked. *What rivers have you fished? I'm leaving for Laerdal tomorrow.*

It's the Queen of Rivers, he was obviously impressed with my fishing arrangements. *You must not expect too much of our little Mørkrid.*

The Mørkrid rises in the huge glaciers of the Jøstedalsbreen. It is strangely milky and blue. There was only a single pool in my beat, where a steep glacial tributary spills under the road into its throat, and its tail shallows gathered smoothly under the alders downstream. The current was too milky to read its secrets easily, and just when I had rigged my tackle, there was shouting downstream. I drove back and found two Norwegians struggling with a salmon.

How big is it? I asked.

Ten kilos, they said. *We have been fighting it almost an hour.*

What are you using?

Worms.

The Mørkrid obviously held fish, and when they finally dragged the salmon out on the stones, I drove back to my beat. There was only an hour left before dinner, so I fished down the pool quickly, covering it with concentric fly-swings.

Just above the tail of the pool, the fly stopped swinging, and I had hooked a fish. It bulldogged straight upstream into the rapids at the throat of the pool. It tried to hold there in the heaviest currents and spent itself quickly, wallowing and weakly drifting back. It could not see me clearly through the milkiness, and I beached it easily, carrying it quickly back to the hotel. The concierge was dumbfounded when he saw the fish, and a small crowd gathered. It weighed almost twenty pounds. The porter stood grinning and carried it into the kitchen, and when I came in to dinner, the serving girls applauded.

You were lucky at fishing, they said.

But the biggest surprise came when I stopped to settle the bill after breakfast. The owner had taken the fish for the hotel kitchen and had left a fat envelope with my account. It was thickly stuffed with Norwegian *kroner* notes.

But I don't understand, I said.

It's quite simple, the concierge explained. *The hotel owes you money.*

But why? I protested.

It's the fish, he said. *We bought your fish for the kitchen last night—and it's worth more than your hotel bill.*

And my bar bill too?

That's right, he said. *The fish even paid for the fishing—with your kind of luck, you could pay for your entire holidays.*

It's worth a try, I said.

Fishing luck is not always fickle. Norman Rockwell once painted a famous cover for the *Saturday Evening Post* of a city fisherman with his pipe turned down in the rain. Calendars have always depicted city anglers furtively buying fish from farmboys. We love such myths and stories.

Fishless days are common. Such days can persist stubbornly in the memory, and I remember several miles of hard canoe work with Charles Dibner in Maine. We were prospecting a tributary of Sebago Lake for spawning smelt and landlocks, but we caught absolutely nothing.

Well, Dibner laughed when we finally racked his canoe back on the car, *it's a good thing I wore my lucky fishing shirt.*

Lucky fishing shirt? I protested.

You should see how bad the fishing gets when I forget it, he said.

A River for Christmas

El sueno de la razon produce monstruos.

—GOYA

Huge mountains filled the moonlight, and their icefields glittered at day-break. Chocolate mountains rose through the coastal fog, treeless and still sleeping at breakfast, trapped between the Andes and the Pacific. The capital lay ahead in its amphitheater of foothills. The fog grew patchy and thin, and the silver 707-320 was throttled back, starting toward the airport at Pudahuel.

We were still at ten thousand feet. The biggest peaks towered above the plane, and where the fog had cleared beyond its starboard wing, we could see Zapallar. The coast ahead grew sunny and clear. We could see the empty beaches at Viña del Mar. There were several ships in the harbor, sharply etched against a pale morning sea, and the rooftops rose steeply above the circling waterfront at Valparaiso.

Abroche su cinteron, the pilot announced. *Fasten your seatbelt.*

Our silver 707 settled steadily, its engines running lean and its big flaps lowered. Large patches of fog still filled the valley. We could see small *fundos* and truck farms, and tall windbreaks of eucalyptus trees and pop-lars. It was late spring and men were working. The beautiful Central Valley

193

of Chile is remarkably fertile and is famous for its vineyards. Its eucalyptus groves were brought from Melbourne and Sydney, like the trees of California, and the coastal foothills are not unlike the wine country above San Francisco.

Santiago de Chile is a city of 2,925,000, sprawling along the Rio Mapocho and surrounded by huge snow-covered peaks. It is less famous than other cities below the equator, its qualities less obvious. Santiago is less seductive than Rio de Janerio, with modern towers rising along its sweeping Copacabaña, and less bustling than São Paulo. Lima is much older and remains richly primitive. La Paz seems scarcely changed since its sixteenth-century origins, lying at more than twelve thousand feet in the treeless *Altiplano* of Bolivia. Buenos Aires has more than 12,000,000 people and is among the world's most sophisticated cities.

Santiago is seemingly dour and stolid, but such perceptions are wrong. The city has been plagued by earthquakes since it was founded in 1541, so few of its colonial buildings survive. Its modern architecture is almost grimly built of stone and concrete to withstand centuries of seismic activity. Only the old cathedral, with its red fortress-thick walls and Renaissance bell tower, remains from its civic beginnings. Santiago is a wonderful city, but it displays its charms grudgingly. It is difficult to know, since the city is less gregarious than the Chileans themselves.

Its site is spectacular. The city lies primarily south of the Rio Mapocho, a stream bed so empty of water throughout the year that its dry gravel is the butt of continual joking, and small trees grow thickly between its concrete walls. The principal axis of its core is the Alameda Bernardo O'Higgins, a magnificent twelve-lane boulevard lined with Spanish chestnuts and *jacarandas* and acacia trees. It is named for the Irish soldier of fortune who fought for independence from Spain, with the help of an Argentine army led by José de San Martin. The old cathedral of San Francisco is there. The Calle Ahumada is the busy center of commercial activity in the city, and the Plaza de las Armas is the principal seat of the government, with the Corinthian portico of the Congreso Nacional in its gardens of palm trees. The National Academy of Arts is aggressively French, with classical facades and pillars, and its bulging mansard roofs. The Palacio Moneda was built in 1805 and stands in the windy Plaza de la Constitucion. It is the presidential palace and has many important government offices too. There are several small volcanic hills in the city, which have been planted as botanical gardens, and there is a small funicular to the summit of San Cristobal. Beyond the circular Plaza Banquedano, the lovely Avenida Providencia leads into the beautiful suburbs called Barrio Alto, the Providencia and Las Condes and Arrayan. I once found an authentic Thonet rocking chair in a junk shop at Arrayan and a vintage rifle hung from a big nail. Its stock was split and its forepiece was missing, but its octagonal barrel was not too badly pitted, and its brass action still gleamed. It was a frontier 1873 Winchester, the rifle the Sioux called the Yellow Boy, and I wondered what it was doing in Chile. I should have bought it, in spite of its forepiece and stock, but there was no way to manage the Thonet.

The Andes seem to surround Santiago and its suburbs, which lie at approximately 2,000 feet. There is skiing at Farellones in the winter, just north of the city. Aconcagua is not visible from Santiago, but its summits lie at 22,835 feet, a mountain so formidable that it has a full-blown volcano on its lower slopes. It is 2,515 feet higher than Mount McKinley in Alaska. Santiago itself lies in a half-circle of mountains, Tupungata and Farellones and Maipo, averaging 16,000 feet. These ranges are higher than anything in Colorado and California, a massive wall rising 14,000 feet above the city. The Andes are spectacular in themselves, but their magic is not fully understood until twilight. The optimal place to witness such magic is the Piscina, the rooftop bar at the old Hotel Carrera, overlooking the Plaza de la Constitucion and the Moneda. After sunset, when the city is already slipping into darkness, the entire *cordillera* still holds the light on its steep mountain walls until Santiago is awash in lavender and rose.

The same staff was employed in the reception at the Carrera, and the concierge remembered the old days when I worked in Santiago and kept a small suite at the hotel before taking a tiny apartment in the Avenida Bulnes. It was wonderful to see old faces smiling. The rooms are spare but comfortable enough, and after a leisurely bath to escape the sluggish effects of flying all night, I took a three-hour nap and completely missed lunch.

Thunder woke me suddenly. The spring storm broke fiercely across the city, its sheets of cold rain sweeping through the narrow streets, erasing the mountains from the sky. Such squalls are often a prelude to summer, which arrives just before Christmas. The storms mist restlessly along the Andes, stirring in the windbreaks that shelter the vineyards at Maipo and San Felipe. The rains pass quickly, darkly wetting the freshly tilled soil. Some rivers still run milky with snow. Several weeks will pass before the trout finish their spawning and the best fishing begins. The Chilean spring-time has unpredictable moods.

The brief squalls still rattled on the windows overlooking the plaza. Gum tree leaves scuttled across the cobblestones, past the sentries guarding the Palacio Moneda. Its huge courtyard was still gutted and filled with scaffolding, after the air strikes that shattered the Allende government three years before. Its solemn facades were still heavily scarred by the smallpox of small-arms fire.

Fitful periods of sun coaxed hundreds of people into the streets, until the bitter *puelche* winds returned swiftly, emptying the streets and stone-work benches again. The storms finally passed, surrendering the city to the people, its streets shiny and wet in the afternoon sun.

I took the elevator to the Piscina and found it empty. I ordered a *pisco* sour and walked around its parapet wall looking at the city. The swimming pool was still covered. The Moneda lay below, and there were workmen swarming in the scaffolding.

It's all changed, I thought sadly.

The streets quickly became busy again. The old waiter brought my drink to the parapet on a silver tray, and I paid him, leaving the change with a tip. The old man thanked me and smiled. I was still tired from flying all night, but it felt good to come back to Santiago. I sipped the smooth *pisco*, cautiously testing its strength, and watched the people below. It was several minutes before I sensed the waiter behind me.

Not yet, I raised my half-filled glass.

You were in Chile, señor?

Yes, I said, *I was here often in the last years of the Frei government.*

Eduardo Frei Montalvo, he said softly.

He was a fine man.

Perhaps too fine, the old waiter said. *It was not a gentleman's game.*

No, I agreed.

It's sad to see our Palacio Moneda standing empty, he sighed. *She's like an old corpse without eyes.*

It's still a beautiful building, I said.

The attack was very good, the old man brightened. *They say the fighters fired eighteen rockets at our poor Moneda—and not a single rocket missed!*

Good pilots, I nodded.

Many people think they were not really Chilean pilots, because they were so skilled, he said. *Do you agree they were not Chilean?*

You think they were gringos? I smiled.

What do you think, señor?

They were Chilean.

The darkly painted Hawker *Hunters* had flown from Los Cerillos when Allende went on the radio to refuse surrender. The president promised to sacrifice his life defending the revolution. The troops waited almost an hour past their eleven o'clock deadline. The two fighters took out the massive richly carved doors on their first gunnery pass. There were seven runs, and eighteen AGM-12 *Bullpup* rockets were fired. Both the Hawkers and their small missiles were British-made and had done their work too well. Huge fires boiled up from the gutted courtyard, and other smoke billowed high from the shattered portico. The pilots had spent only fifteen minutes over their sad target. The guard detachment of *carabineros* had refused to defend the Moneda against the troops surrounding them. Allende permitted them to leave, along with a team of federal investigators, although their former commander, Eduardo Paredes, was a long-time political ally and chose to stay.

The Moneda was defended by Allende and other armed political colleagues, who carried AKM-47G automatic weapons manufactured in East Germany. These weapons were not Chilean military issue. Daniel Vergara was a communist political ally of Allende throughout the electoral campaign and was rewarded with a key position in the Ministry of the Interior. Vergara was involved in several political quarrels and clandestine incidents that ultimately served to weaken Allende's popular support. The AKM-47G weapons in the Moneda that tragic morning were flown aboard a Cuban cargo plane into Chile on March 11, 1973. Vergara had used his authority to load thirty crates of armaments directly into trucks at Pudahuel, weaponry weighing more than a ton, and forced them past angry customs officers without inspection. The weapons were also distributed to the paramilitary civilian guard Allende called his Grupo de los Amigos, and it was these political *guerrillas* who ultimately defended the Moneda, along with snipers in the government offices around the palace. The infantry encircling the Moneda had still not attacked the thick-walled palace but were returning sniper fire aggressively.

Brigadier Javier Palacios was leading the army units surrounding the palace. Palacios waited another seventy-five minutes after the air strikes to demand Allende's capitulation and attack the Moneda.

Four political advisers close to Allende had left the Moneda when the Hawkers broke off their attack, crossing the street to the Ministry of Defense, and tried to negotiate a peaceful solution. The narrow streets rattled with gunfire. The snipers loyal to Allende kept them pinned down in the portico of the Defense Ministry, unable to return or telephone their beleaguered leader. The attempt at armistice had failed. Allende sent a number of staff members and colleagues from a side entry just before Javier's troops attacked. These civilians were also pinned down by sniper fire, huddling pathetically on the sidewalk with their white flag. Troops vaulted over them swiftly to enter the building. When the firing stopped, Salvador Allende sat dead on a brocade sofa in the brightly painted Sala de la Independencia.

Did he commit suicide? I asked.

I believe it, the old waiter nodded sadly. *He told us that he would on the radio just before the planes attacked—and he told us earlier, in his last speech to Unidad Popular.*

You believed it? I pressed.

Si como no! he said. *I was there listening that night.*

You were Unidad Popular?

Yes, he said.

Why did Allende fail? I asked.

Because he was a fool, the old man sighed unhappily, *and he filled his government with charlatans and fools.*

But you supported him?

It's simple, he said. *Allende was not the only fool in Chile.*

The little bar downstairs was empty too, except for the old piano player in the corner, practicing his songs softly. The government buildings and offices would close in another two hours, and the bartenders were preparing for the crowds. The bar was strangely quiet.

During the campaign and the weeks that followed the narrow Allende plurality, the moods of the capital mixed anger with triumphal excitement and fear. The empty little bar across from the Moneda had been a hotbed of intrigue for many months. Both the military at the Ministry of Defense and the proposed cabinet officers of the fledgling Allende government were being lavishly courted. There were British arms merchants who hoped to sell *Centurion* tanks, and the F-6 *Lightning* to replace the outmoded Hawker *Hunters* based at Los Cerillos. The French wanted to sell their Dassault-Breguet *Mirage* 5, a sleek delta-winged jet fighter. Czechs were usually found at the corner table near the piano, selling beautifully made Kalashnikov AK-47G automatic rifles. British friends pointed out a famous American arms dealer having lunch with some Chilean army officers in civilian clothes. Soviet officers in badly tailored suits stopped off too, along with the furtive Cubans, who sometimes carried both diplomatic passports and weapons like the elegant little nine-millimeter Makarov pistol.

The newly appointed Cuban ambassador, Luis Fernandez, was seen meeting a colleague at Pudahuel, and escorted him blithely past customs and immigration with the help of Daniel Vergara. The visitor was Manuel Piñero, who was director of the secret police in Havana.

It was pretty exciting, I thought while the bartender mixed another *pisco* sour. *It was like a bad Humphrey Bogart picture.*

Pardon, señor? he asked.

Was I talking?

Yes, he said. *I believe you were.*

I was here when Allende was inaugurated, I said. *I was thinking back.*

Strange day, the bartender nodded and wiped the bar.

Were you there? I asked.

It was impossible to get into the plaza itself unless you were Unidad Popular, he shook his head. *Many tried to get there, but there were political thugs controlling who actually got in.*

To create a completely loyal crowd for the television?

Si como no! he said. *But there were three candidates who split the election pretty evenly, with less than 2 percent of the vote between Allende and Jorge Allessandri—two Chileans out of three voted against Allende.*

Were you working that day?

No. He laughed caustically. *I stood along the Providencia and O'Higgins with the people who voted for Allessandri and Tomic—and thousands stood there crying when the car carrying President Frei went past.*

Too bad he could not run again.

The law is the law, he shrugged. *Frei could have easily carried 80 percent of the vote.*

What happens now?

The junta is also the junta, he laughed. *It's a beast with too many feet and too few brains—but there was no other choice for Chile.*

Think they'll let go? I asked.

The air force brigadier seems to understand conciliation and healing, he said. *He seems to understand that Unidad Popular is finished—and that the time for military repression is past.*

Gustavo Leigh?

Yes, the bartender was shaking another *pisco* sour. *Leigh understands that Unidad Popular ran things so clumsily that it finished itself—the army simply provided the pallbearers.*

But what happens now? I persisted.

Leigh thinks the junta should try to heal things quickly and stop the tight control, he said. *They've won, but they're still too harsh.*

They can't wait too long, I agreed. *Frei and the other leaders are getting old—and if the junta won't let go, there won't be anybody qualified to run the country in a few years.*

Allessandri and Frei are too old already, he agreed. *Tomic is a fool.*

And Leigh himself?

He's a thorn in Pinochet's belly, he said. *But he's interesting—he might resign and try politics.*

Think Pinochet will let go?

Quien sabe? the bartender laughed. *Looks more like a bulldog every day.*

The shopkeepers and clerks crowded the Providencia buses at twilight, milling at the boulevard stops near the cathedral of San Francisco, sheltering their heads with wet copies of such newspapers as *La Nacion* and *Mercurio*. Others met with friends in small coffee shops and bars, and some waited for the squalls to pass in the shopping arcades and porticoes that line the Alameda O'Higgins.

The bad spring weather can last for weeks. Its dampness seems to impregnate the massive buildings themselves, streaking their somber facades with rain. Their wet masonry glistens when the sun comes back, and walking the narrow streets surrounding the Moneda, it is possible to retrace the rifle and machine-pistol fire that had raked many windows and roof parapets and doorways. Pockmarks had chipped and riddled the walls where the snipers had fired on the troops below and had drawn heavy small-arms fire in return.

Still tired, I thought.

I took dinner at the Piscina instead of going out to Providencia. The restaurant I liked there could wait until tomorrow. The meal was chilled *almejas* on their tiny shells, and perfectly grilled crayfish with a Cousiño chardonnay. The *postre* was a pale caramel *flan*, and I sat a long time over coffee, watching the lights of the city and its mountains. The times that I had worked in Santiago, in urban planning and airport work for the Frei government, had been pleasant in spite of the political turmoil of the Allende campaign. We spent happy times at Viña del Mar and Riñaca, eating seafood at small cafés and exploring old waterfront restaurants such as Menzel's in Valparaiso, and friends from the embassy had taken a little steep-roofed summer cottage on the coast at Zapallar.

But there were troubled times too. The political quarrels were heated and erupted often among the architects and engineers at my office. The people were inexplicably changing. Chileans had always been a happy people in the past, but they were becoming curt and short-tempered and cruel. Their political debates had flared into sharp disputes, bitterly dividing old friends and colleagues, and entire families were torn apart. It was raining again at daylight. I took a breakfast of croissants and coffee in my room, watching the wet city streets. There were patchy scraps of overcast hanging over the peaks.

The weather was better before lunch. I waved the doorman off when he pointed to a taxi and walked past the Moneda to catch another myself in the Alameda O'Higgins. The bright sun was happily welcome. The boulevards were lined with flowering trees, beautiful *jacarandas* and *ulmos* and Spanish chestnuts, and the streets and sidewalk cafés filled quickly at noon. Old photographers with ancient box cameras on wooden tripods worked at San Cristobal around the heroic monuments, and wrinkled flower sellers hawked violets to laughing young couples along the Providencia and the tree-lined Mapocho.

The capital almost seemed itself. It was still early and I told the driver simply to drive around. The funicular still climbed its steep rails, straining to carry loads of schoolchildren to the shrine at San Cristobal. The beautiful eucalyptus trees were leafing out along the Pedro de Valdivia, and the walled gardens were bright with scarlet *copihue* blossoms. The taxi waited while I circled through the Prince of Wales, searching the old club for familiar faces, where spectators were sipping their drinks under the Tudor half-timbered gables of the clubhouse. Several tennis matches filled its courts. There was a pickup *chukkar* at the Polo Club, where I had watched an ironic match on the eve of Allende's inauguration, where grooms were still walking the sweaty horses.

It felt strange, I thought. *Like hearing tumbrils rumble in the Paris streets—or waiting helplessly for Shanghai or Singapore to fall.*

The Providencia was filled with shoppers when I finally reached the restaurant. The smoky old Parron had opened its courtyard to welcome the Chilean springtime. The tiny darkly paneled salon still had its zinc-topped bar from Paris. Several old men sat playing dominoes and cards. Wonderful cooking smells drifted through the rooms into the courtyard. The old Parron was still itself. Its patrons still gorge themselves on meat and roast *cabrito* and seafood under the grape trellises in the spring, and I took my *pisco* through the bar into its sunny courtyard.

Señor? the headwaiter asked.

Penso aqui, I pointed to a table dappled in leafy sunlight. *Gracias.*

Si como no, señor! he said.

The waiter came swiftly across the courtyard. *Algo de bever?* he asked.

Vino, I said. *Cousiño Macul.*

Blanco o tinto, señor?

Blanco, I said.

The old headwaiter stood watching me curiously when the waiter left. The vines were alive with finches. The headwaiter came back.

You were here in the old days, he told me. *You came often to the Parron in those times.*

Yes, I said. *I had an office nearby.*

It is a fine time to come back, he said. *It is springtime in Chile.*

Tiene tiempo macanudo, I agreed.

You've been gone several years, he continued. *When were you last with us in Santiago?*

Three years ago.

We have seen some hard times, the old man said quietly, *and things are still not good, but we are still Chileans—we still have hope.*

It will take time, I said.

Life goes on, he smiled. *Did you see any pretty girls in the Providencia?*

Didn't see them, I joked.

You are getting old, he laughed. *But you always worked hard—you sometimes made little diagrams and drawings at lunch.*

Those people at Obras Publicas had me pretty busy.

Springtime is bad for working, he said.

You're right, I agreed.

The waiter brought a bottle of Cousiño Macul in a pewter ice bucket and carefully poured me a glass, rolling his wrist deftly. It was perfectly chilled, and I nodded happily and took another sip. The brightly colored finches were quarreling busily. The waiter spoke briefly with the old headwaiter, glanced across the courtyard to my table, and came back smiling.

Lunch, señor? he asked.

Tiene erizos hoy?

Si como no, senor! he looked surprised. *You like our sea urchins?*

I learned to like erizos, I said. *I like them now.*

Something else?

Perhaps an omelet with mushrooms, I studied the menu, *and a tomato salad—are there fresh chirimoyas?*

Not yet, señor, he shook his head.

Flan and coffee, I said.

The old headwaiter drifted back to talk, and I shared my wine. *Some things have not changed*, he said. *The Cousiño is still very good.*

It's excellent, I said.

Are you working here? he asked.

No, I replied, *I'm going south to try some trout fishing.*

I'm from the south, he said.

Valdivia? I asked.

How could you guess that? he asked.

Your accent, I said.

Where will you try the fishing?

Lago Ranco, the young waiter brought my sea-urchin eggs in a chilled broth with finely diced onions. *I have old friends who have a pretty farm at Llifen.*

It was not taken? he interrupted.

Taken? I asked.

Our agrarian reform almost exploded into a civil war, he explained. *It was particularly sad in Linares and Cautín.*

Their farm was too small, I said. *Only farms larger than eighty hectares were taken under the agrarian reform.*

I believed that once too, he said, *because I was Unidad Popular—but because I'm from Panguipulli, I know the truth.*

What happened? I asked.

Our agrarian reform began with Frei, he glanced furtively around the courtyard, *but we changed it into something evil.*

You were Unidad Popular?

Yes, he admitted sadly, *but we lied about agrarian reform in the Allende years—and the lies helped to destroy us.*

What happened? I asked.

President Frei expropriated 1,408 farms legally during his term, he said. *It was his law and the owners were compensated fairly—he took most of the farms that qualified, about 15 percent of our tillable land.*

What happened with Allende?

The Congress was overwhelmed with allegations of illegal expropriations, he replied. *Its investigations found that more farms were taken illegally in Allende's first two years than Frei took legally in four—and the police were completely forbidden to interfere.*

How many were taken altogether?

Allende took 3,570 farms before the military coup, he admitted sadly. *About 35 percent of the tillable acreage in Chile—after Frei had taken 15 percent legally.*

My friends had trouble too.

I'm from the south, he nodded. *Many farms and lumber mills and vineyards were stolen—roving bands of guerrillas and workers just nailed the Chilean flag to the gates—and took them in the name of the people.*

Did the owners fight?

Some fought back and some simply left the country, he said. *Many were killed—and there were political murders in many towns.*

It was a bitter time, I said.

What happened to your friends? the old man asked.

The valley had a band of heavily armed men taking farms, I replied, *and nobody knew who they were.*

Probably not Chileans, he interjected.

Who were they? I asked.

Cubanos, he said.

Cubans?

Yes, he confessed. *I listened to the Marxist politicians and voted for them, but I'm still a Chilean first—and roving paramilitary groups led by Cubans and terrorists were hard to accept.*

It happened, I agreed. *My friends were warned that they were going to be killed—their children were on the death list too.*

Who warned them? he asked.

It was one of their workers, I said. *His brother had attended the meeting that drew up the death list—and he warned them.*

Did they try?

My friends armed themselves and told the leader they would kill him if he tried to take their farm, I replied. *They never came.*

Did anything happen? he asked.

Their worker was drowned in the Calcurrupe, I nodded sadly. *It's strange that he died in the river—he was a skilled botero and knew the river well.*

You fished with him? he said.

We fished the river several times, I responded. *He was very good.*

They killed him.

The Parron was not busy that afternoon, and many tables in the court-yard were empty. We simply sat and talked. Lunch lasted three hours, with another bottle of wine and several pots of coffee. Pigeons scuttled in the eaves. The shadows worked across the courtyard, leafy patterns flickering on the gravel. The old men were laughing in the bar, and the finches were hopscotching among the empty tables, foraging busily for crumbs. The young waiter brought us two cognacs.

It's Quinta Normal, the old headwaiter raised his glass. *Welcome back.*

I remember it well, I said.

I've enjoyed talking, he said. *It helps to talk sometimes.*

What was it like in Santiago?

It got embarrassing for a loyal Marxist, he said wryly. *There were huge demonstrations of Chilean workers against Allende—copper workers and farm workers filling the streets in protest—it was hard to explain.*

Workers are supposed to support a Marxist state, I laughed.

It's the theory, he admitted ruefully, *but the workers' strikes really opened my eyes—and then we had the Marcha de las Cacerolas Vacias, with thousands of women protesting.*

The March of the Empty Pots?

It happened the first year, he explained. *Thirteen months after Allende became president, and there were thousands of housewives beating on pots outside the Moneda—protesting the food prices and shortages.*

Did it happen again? I asked.

The march was broken up when thugs from Unidad Popular attacked the women with chains, the old man said angrily. *It was a terrible day—and it finished Unidad Popular for me.*

What did the women do next?

They were afraid to march, but Allende got a little crazy after they protested, he continued, *because they beat their pots every night at ten o'clock—and you could hear pots banging all over Santiago.*

That's a wild story, I said.

It was all a Marxist fairy tale, he said wryly. *Now we're stuck with soldiers—and the country needs Walt Disney.*

Walt Disney? I puzzled.

It's just a Chilean joke, he laughed. *Disney has experience with getting animals to talk.*

Chile is both varied and quite beautiful. Its startling beauty seems a curious background for its recent history of political strife. But Chileans had surprised themselves and surprised the world too, with the quarreling that had lurked behind their happy faces. The geography of Chile is unique. The country lies along twenty-eight hundred miles of the Pacific, reaching from Bolivia and Peru past the Strait of Magellan to stormy Cabo de los Hornos, the fabled cliffs and skerries at Cape Horn.

Chile is less than 150 miles wide, lying tightly pinioned between the Andes and the sea. Its configuration is difficult to fathom, and its sprawling ropelike length looks impossible to govern. Yet the mountains are giants, a barrier so formidable they serve to unify a people clinging to their slender Pacific wall, and Chileans in the northern deserts and at the Strait of Magellan obviously share the same fierce pride.

It's hard for others to grasp, explained a Chilean engineer who worked with me in planning a new national park at Torres del Paine. *Think about a 150-mile strip against your entire Canadian border, with the world's longest mountain range on one side and the Pacific on the other.*

Strange piece of property, I agreed.

Think that Seattle is Arica, he continued, *and Kennebunkport is Cape Horn.*

I'm thinking, I said. *It's hard work.*

Arica lies at the northern frontier with Peru. It is still an astonishing fifteen hundred miles from the trout-fishing country, the distance from Boston to Denver. Its northern coasts are treeless and stark, but their rocky beaches are teeming with life. The coastal seas are quite cold. Chilled by the icy Humboldt Current, which wells up from Antarctica to flow past the equator, the Pacific is still fifty to sixty degrees off Ecuador and Peru. The current is more than a hundred miles across, saturated with rich nutrients from the latitudes below Cape Horn. Such mingling currents always offer unusually fertile fishing grounds, sustaining big condor rookeries along the coast and unthinkable colonies of sea birds.

The chill coastal seas affect the climate of the entire continent, shrouding the northern coasts in almost continually overcast skies. The hot deserts and arid foothill ranges lift them slightly. Their moisture is trapped and rising. It soars and billows upward across the *cordillera* of the Andes and falls again in heavy rains in the jungle headwaters of the Amazon and Parana.

The coasts are parched and barren. Few streams reach the sea, and even their highest *arroyos* and gullies are usually dry. Water is precious and scarce, and its existence is obvious at thirty-five thousand feet. The mountains are dry and brown, and there are faint patchwork traces of cultivation in some valleys. Cultivation dwindles quickly below Tocopilla, until the empty Desierto de Atacama lies under the plane, a desert so bitter that it receives absolutely no rainfall. Its only moisture hangs in its thin wintry mists. The primitive Atacameño tribes buried their dead wrapped in woven fabrics, with colorful pottery and woolen bags filled with fish hooks and utensils and tools made of stone and poorly worked bronze and bone. The dry soils and parched air preserved everything, and the corpses were steadily dessicated and mummified. It is not atypical to find sardines from the Pacific, brittle and still surprisingly silver, lying with brightly colored toucan and parrot feathers from Bolivia.

Such burial sites tell us something about Chile today, a Chilean anthropologist told me at Santiago. *These ancient people traveled.*

But what about today? I asked.

Shriveled fish and brightly colored feathers tell us they fished and had frequent contact with jungle tribes across the Andes, he explained. *You are not hungry when you can fish.*

But now? I asked again.

It is the same in Chile today, he said. *We have poverty, but we live too close to the sea to have terrible hunger.*

The Desierto de Atacama is a puzzle, both a dead landscape and terribly rich. Its vast deposits of sodium nitrate once supplied the fertilizer called Chilean saltpeter to the entire world. The mines were swarming with workers, and the seaports thrived. Almost 70 percent of Chile's exports consisted of saltpeter until the First World War. The German chemists Wilhelm Ostwald and Fritz Haber developed methods of manufacturing synthetic nitrates and plunged Chile into a terrible depression when its exports of saltpeter withered. Its prosperous northern seaports ebbed swiftly into poverty, only to flourish again when American metallurgists found techniques of extracting copper from low-grade ores. The entire Atacama region held immense lodes of relatively poor copper. Big mines at Potrerillos and Chuchiquimata were swiftly developed, rivaled only by the mines at Rancagua sixty miles south of Santiago. Chuchiquimata quickly grew into the biggest copper mine in the world, its profits erasing any thoughts of the idle saltpeter pits at Maria Elena and Pedro de Valdivia.

Small ports like Iquique and Antofagasta and Tocopilla, which had busily loaded ships with chalky sodium nitrates, became prosperous loading copper. The Atacama finally withers in increasingly fertile valleys below La Serena, a beautiful Spanish colonial city founded in 1544. The Chilean rivers hold water again, draining the snowfields of the high *cordillera* at Aconcagua, and there are big farms and vineyards at San Felipe.

The beautiful Central Valley of Chile sprawls more than two hundred miles below San Felipe, past Santiago and its suburbs to San Fernando. The spreading capital has taken too much of these fertile lands. Roderick Haig-Brown loved what he found surrounding Santiago and described it perfectly in his book *Fisherman's Winter*:

> We were swiftly free of the great city, and here was the fertile Vale of Chile, lovely irrigated farms, tiled cottages with gardens full of blazing geraniums, handsome houses with cool, flower filled courtyards and delicate wrought-iron gates under arches, water-filled ditches flowing everywhere and great mats of blackberry vines, called the curse of Chile, tightly grown into hedgerows. On the roads one met huge tank trucks, wooden instead of metal, carrying wine instead of gasoline. On the dusty side roads, and on dusty tracks beside the main roads were horsemen and horse-drawn wagons and oxcarts. The farms everywhere were lovely, looking old and cherished and rich.

There are big palm trees lining the streets at Ocoa, and it is surprising to find rice paddies outside the capital at Batuco. The principal vineyards of the Rio Maipo and some of their wines are justly famous. Farther south at Angol, there are livestock farms and grain fields in the coastal mountains. Concepcion is a university city founded in 1550 and has become a center of commerce and industry too. Arauco is a commercial fishing port, lying under a foothill copse of pines with white rollers breaking on its beach. Talca and Temuco are major provincial cities, serving a region of prosperous farms and livestock *fundos*, and there are still large populations of the Araucan and Mapuche tribes at Lumaco and Lago Budi and Llifen. The volcano Llaima rises east of Temuco, surrounded by beautiful monkey puzzle forests and snowfields. There are trout in the rivers between Santiago and Temuco, particularly in the Laja and Bio-Bio, which was the perilous frontier of Araucan territory in Spanish colonial times.

Villarrica is the threshold of the lake district, a favorite summer region for city-bound Chileans between Christmas and Lent. Lago Villarrica is a beautiful lake, with its conical white-hatted volcano smoking steadily in the distance. Pucon is a major vacation center with several first-rate hotels, including the famous Hotel Autumalal.

The lake district lies between Villarrica and Puerto Varas, a wonderfully pastoral country with strong echoes of southern Germany, and boasts a dozen big mountain lakes scattered along a hundred miles of mountain wall. Its strong echoes of Europe are not mere chance. The region was heavily settled by Germans, not the Germans whose politics forced them to hide after the Second World War, but people who came more than a century ago seeking religious and political freedom in Hapsburg times. The trout fishing in Chile is their legacy. The German immigrants first settled between Villarrica and Puerto Varas because the countryside reminded them of home, and their husbandry has only strengthened that sense of place. The big lakes and streams could obviously support trout, and it was the transplanted Germans who first introduced trout to Chile. Their tenure is already quite old, and I have fished with young *boteros* on several rivers that had obviously German family names but spoke and understood not a scrap of the language. Their character is obvious in the tidy farms, neatly fenced and well tended, and in the steep-roofed attic dormer windows and millwork of their houses and outbuildings. The faintly Rhenish echoes of their church towers are obvious at Panguipulli and Calafquen, and at other places throughout the region. Both Osorno and Valdivia have old German populations, and Puerto Varas has a German citizenry too, its tidy streets all looking at the Osorno Volcano across Lago Llanquihue, the biggest lake in Chile.

Puerto Montt is the terminus of the Pan American Highway, a bustling port of almost sixty-five thousand and a sheltered harbor filled with fishing boats. Its stone quays are a collage of drying nets and crabbing traps and boats listing on their keels at low tide. Fish buyers gesture and haggle over freshly caught *congrios* and long-legged crabs and shellfish, and on the beach of the clapboard restaurant at Pelluco, a small flotilla of skiffs was moored high above the water and the men were patiently drying their nets.

Farther south, the Chilean coast is almost roadless and totally wild. The Andes themselves plunge steeply into the sea, deeply scarred and fractured by immense seismic fissures. The coast is a broken jigsaw puzzle of fjords, narrow passages and sounds, a world of only partially charted islands and skerries. The mountains are still heavy shrouded in icefields, relict glaciers of the mammoth icefields that helped to shape the entire southern Andes. There are few trout in many rivers that drain these glaciers, rivers too cold and silty to support much life. The watersheds that offer good sport are only partially born in melting glaciers or have lakes in their drainages that precipitate out most of their milkiness. Such rivers include the Petrohue, Puelo, Negro, Abascal, Toro, Barcelo, Reñihue, Amarillo, Yelcho, Corcovado, Tic-toc, Palena, Pico, Aisén, and the Rio del Cisnes— the poetically named River of the Swans.

Few settlements are found in these chill latitudes. Big sheep stations like Sotomo and Chaparrama and Yelcho are bigger than the handful of tiny fishing villages on these coasts, in the entire two hundred miles between Puerto Montt and Aysen. Puerto Aysen lies at the mouth of the Rio Simpson.

Beyond the Simpson, which has been aggressively logged and settled since the Second World War, the steep mountains and glaciers spill directly into the salt, calving off immense shards of ice. Some of these icefields measure almost a hundred miles in length, slipping patiently toward their iceberg-filled *esteros* and fjords. Few settlements exist in the 250 miles of broken coasts between Aysen and the meat-packing *frigorificos* at Puerto Natales, on the Seño de Ultima Esperanza—the mountainous Sound of Last Hope.

The brushy hill country of Magallanes has few settlements, but it has the largest sheep stations in the world. Punta Arenas is the provincial capital of Magallanes, a windswept city of more than sixty thousand on the Strait of Magellan. The western sea lanes leading into the *estrechos* lie in a 250-mile fault. Its fissures lie between Isla Desolacion and Isla Riesco, passing south of Dawson Island and including the faulting rift that holds Lago Fagnano on Tierra del Fuego itself. The fault rises steeply from the immense lake, displaced southward across the Sierra de Valdivieso into the famous Beagle Channel, where Darwin passed aboard the HMS *Beagle*. Farther south lies the Chilean naval station at Puerto Campbell, on the barren Isla Navarino, where Mision Inglesas is virtually the last outpost in Chile. Sixty miles farther south lie the Wollaston Islands and the Cabo de los Hornos.

Santiago lies half-forgotten there, back along more than two thousand miles of empty coasts, mountains, immense glaciers, lakes, rain forests, and almost fifty Fujiyama-perfect volcanoes—less a country than a slender journey of the mind.

The concierge sent his night porter upstairs for my luggage and fishing tackle at six o'clock and had a battered taxi waiting. The narrow streets were almost empty before breakfast. The driver plunged into the intersections with a challenging flick-flick of his lights, and in the outskirts of the city, there were filmy layers of fog. The poor visibility had no obvious effect on the driver. We seemed only to drive faster. The parkway was not fully built, and warning barricades and painted barrels passed in a foggy blur. I paid the fare gratefully when we finally reached Pudahuel and the porters took my baggage.

Puerto Montt? I asked.

Aqui, señor! the porters gestured. *Aqui!*

Mil gracias, I said.

It was another hour before the rose-colored mist lifted enough to fly, and we were driven out to the Hawker-Siddeley sitting on the ramp. The military government had curtailed service to Valdivia, maintaining its policy of postcoup austerity, and had grounded its domestic jet aircraft in favor of the sleek British turboprops that were cheaper to fly.

The Rolls Royce engines hummed smoothly when we taxied out, holding briefly at the runway threshold while the bright orange Braniff DC-8 landed, after flying all night from Miami.

Our plane swung into position and started its takeoff roll, its engines rising in a shrill turbine whine, and we gathered speed to rotate off smoothly. The truck farms and rice fields lay under the patchy fog, and against the mountains lay the city itself. Breakfast was *chirimoyas* and croissants and coffee, and beyond the vineyards stood the Maipo volcano. It was clear after Rancagua, and volcano after volcano stood shining in the sun—Maipo, Descabezado, Chillan, Antuco, the sharp-peaked Velluda, Longquimay, Llaima, Villarica, Mocho and Choshuenco, Puyehue, Calbuco, Puntiagado, and the beautiful Osorno.

Beyond Villarrica, the big Chilean lakes lay against the foothills. Calafquen lay beyond Villarica itself, and I could see the timber-cutting camps and sawmills at Panguipulli and Enco, and log rafts floating at the head of Riñihue. Lago Ranco lay ahead, its watery caldera dotted with volcanic islands. Llifen was clearly visible from ten thousand feet and the city of Osorno lay ahead. Petrohue lay hidden between its volcanoes, beyond Puerto Varas. We were descending rapidly into Puerto Montt now, and the pilots deployed the flaps, our shadow sailboating quickly across Lago Llanquihue.

Alberto Schirmer was waiting at the baggage claim, and the cool wind smelled strongly of the sea. The baggage and tackle arrived, and we drove into Puerto Montt. *We'll have lunch at Pelluco*, he said, *and then drive to Petrohue.*

Pelluco, I remembered the old restaurant. *Still good?*

Simple and good, he said.

• A RIVER FOR CHRISTMA

Pelluco is a fishing village on the sound eas⌐ head of its shallow seas, a world of shoals and that dwarfs Chesapeake Bay. It is famous in a c⌐ *mariscos* and other seafoods. Its seafood is ha⌐ The big clapboard restaurant is almost plain and simply ⌐ gravelly beach is crowded with skiffs and drying nets and traps. is best known for a huge, steaming hot dish of shellfish and *chorizo* sausages stacked high around an armature supplied by a Chilean barnacle, a species several inches high and shaped almost like an artillery projectile. The dish is preceded by its own rich broth. It arrives piping hot, shaped like a wicker beehive, and breathing clouds of steam. The barnacle stands at its core. It is mostly inedible and is eaten last, since one must eat through the armor of sausages and shellfish stacked and layered around it. The spicy little *chorizos* and bigger sausages are used to wedge and key everything together. There are mussels and rough-shelled oysters and several species of clams, including a species the Chileans call *zapatas* because they seem as big as work boots.

Such a dish is almost an ordeal of eating. The broth stands in a big tureen, impossible to eat in small portions like the hot bread, and there are platters for the landfill-sized piles of empty shells. The barnacle is finally pulled apart to reach the fleshy muscle attached to its single claw. It tastes exactly like a Kennebunkport lobster.

Hungry enough? Schirmer laughed.

I'll try, I said. *It's just too good to pass Pelluco without eating.*

Some white wine? he asked. *Concha y Toro?*

Cousiño Macul, I said.

Our lunch lasted almost three hours. The fishermen worked busily on the beach, and a flotilla of skiffs was silhouetted a mile offshore. It was sunny and cool. The Hornopiren volcano stood on the mainland across the sound, and the light was almost silvery. Maillen and its sister islands lay retreating toward the horizon, sharply outlined like ships, with the biggest islands off Calbuco as pale as smoke from Mapuche fires.

The wine was good and the talk was better, filled with firsthand stories of the troubled Allende years. There had been a lot of violence in the Llanquihue country, and Schirmer had lived through difficult times.

It seems like a nightmare, he said gravely. *We went from the happy Chile we had always known to an armed country—filled with strangers, openly carrying Soviet weapons.*

Who were they? I asked.

Some were obviously Chileans, he replied, *but many were not.*

Cubans?

were Cubans, he nodded, *and their weapons came mostly through*

How did the weapons come?

Secretly, he said. *The arms arrived in small shipments and were cached in the hills—the police found many weapons in many places.*

How did the Cubans come? I asked.

Los Cubanos all came openly, he laughed. *They carried diplomatic passports and arrived in Chile with Allende's blessings—Castro sent us the biggest army of diplomats in history.*

Were there lots of weapons?

There was a Cuban freighter at Maullin when Allende died, Schirmer said. *People testified that it was filled with arms.*

What happened?

When the military took the Moneda, he continued, *the Cubans weighed anchor and sailed without unloading their cargo—and when they were ordered to stop they simply refused.*

Did they try to stop them? I asked.

Chilean pilots followed them out, he said, *but they should have sunk them—so the world could see what they were really carrying.*

Were there caches near here?

There were weapons found on the Rio Chamiza, he said. *Guerrillas killed the lumber-camp overseer there—but there were big guerrilla camps farther north.*

Where? I interrupted.

The biggest was at Panguipulli, he replied. *Guerrillas took the old Kenrick place at Chan-Chan and had a big campamento in the hills.*

Rio Enco, I said. *I've fished it.*

It was a timber-cutting farm of less than five hectares, Schirmer said angrily. *Our laws stipulated that only tracts over eighty hectares were subject to agrarian reform.*

But they just took it? I said.

It happened often, he said. *They took fundos that were beautiful and prospering and remote—legal or not!*

Who was leading these things? I asked.

Commandante Pepe, he said. *Commandante Pepe was a Chilean named Jorge Gregorio Liendo—and he was actually given government trucks to help his guerrillas occupy almost fifty farms here.*

What about the police?

The carabiñeros were ordered not to interfere with the people's will, he fumed, *and there was chaos!*

Who gave the orders? I interrupted.

José Toha was Minister of the Interior, Schirmer explained, *but his liaison with Commandante Pepe was Daniel Vergara.*

What were they like? I asked.

Toha was a strange one, Schirmer continued. *Tall and skeletal and pale, with a heron's beak and a greying beard to hide a weak chin.*

Communist? I asked.

Toha called himself a socialist, he said. *But our communist party grew out of the Socialist Party in 1921—he was certainly a leading Marxist.*

What about Daniel Vergara?

Vergara was a protégé of Luis Corvalan, Schirmer rolled his eyes, *and Corvalan led the Chilean communists when Allende was president—Corvalan and Toha were close political allies, and Toha appointed Vergara to his ministry.*

What happened to Toha? I said.

Toha was impeached for his unwillingness to police illegal expropriations and his government help to Commandante Pepe, he poured himself some wine. *His successor Hernan del Canto was a Marxist politician from Valparaiso—he was impeached on the same charges, and Toha killed himself in 1974.*

Who controlled agrarian reform?

Jacques Chonchol! Schirmer growled. *Chonchol was a leading young Christian Democrat throughout the Frei years, and a popular protégé of President Frei—but Allende quickly appointed him Minister of Agriculture, and Chonchol took control of CORA personally!*

CORA? I asked.

Corporacion de la Reforma Agraria, he explained.

You think he was secretly a communist?

Chonchol vanished completely during the coup, Schirmer said drily, *and he surfaced again in Moscow.*

The weather was changing again when we left Pelluco, and it was raining when we stopped at Puerto Varas. The Osorno and Calbuco volcanoes were hidden in the overcast. Llanquihue lay leaden and almost still, with showers working darkly across the water. The volcanoes lay only thirty-five miles away, but sprawling Llanquihue seemed to reach completely to the horizon.

We circled the lake toward Petrohue in the rain, passing through Rio Pescado and Los Riscos. It is a beautiful drive in good weather. The road follows the lake through a countryside of small dairy farms and orchards, working directly toward Volcan Osorno. The Bahia del Volcan lies between Osorno, crossing the steep Rio de las Nutrias. Big rainbows ascend these

little tributaries to spawn each spring. The little German hotel at Ensenada
had been closed since Allende's election, and I stopped briefly because
Haig-Brown had once stayed there. Haig-Brown had found the place hope-
lessly Teutonic, lacking a bar to soften its ruthless discipline and silence,
and empty of laughter. Haig-Brown found small signs posted throughout
the hotel, proclaiming its philosophy of strict rules. It was not a typically
Chilean *hosteria*, and in his book *Fisherman's Winter*, Haig-Brown offered
an atypically blunt judgment:

> When I came out after dinner I found a broad tweed-skirted German lady
> poking a powerful leather shoe at my lovely catch. "Fish," she said, with
> enormous disapproval. "Fish and blood."
>
> Her eyes swept her resting compatriots on the veranda in search of
> sympathy, and I withdrew quietly. I felt I was living up to the motto of the
> hotel, hanging in printed cards on every wall:
>
> *Silencia de cada uno asegura el reposo de todos.* The silence of each one
> ensures the peace of everyone; more freely, one corpse makes a whole cem-
> etery.

Rural strife had closed the little *hosteria* on the Bahia del Volcan, and
it stood empty in its silence now. Its *reposo* was finally complete. The road
climbs away from Llanquihue into the beech-and-bamboo thickets that lie
between the volcanoes. Flocks of parakeets darted into the trees, and a
big black-and-white crested bird flew clumsily across the road like our
pileated woodpecker.

What bird is that? I asked.

Carpintero de Magallanes, Schirmer smiled. *Magellan woodpecker.*

The Sierra Santo Domingo filled the sky ahead, and the Rio Petrohue
lay tight against its steep hillsides. Their summits were lost in the rain. We
circled upstream along the river to his little Hosteria Petrohue, at the outlet
of Lago Todo de los Santos. The little *arroyos* that plunged down past the
narrow road were murky with glacier melt and black volcanic ash. Immense outcroppings of fractured lava blocked the river diagonally, and
great flumes of turquoise water roared through the fissures and faults,
spilling into the Cascadas del Petrohue.

It's still beautiful, I said happily.

Five volcanoes surround the lake, but they were still hidden in the
clouds. The beaches are gritty and black with their particulates. Great
alluvial fans of sooty ash lie under Osorno. Cerro Puntiagado merely
echoes its volcanic origins, its 7,653-foot peak partially the igneous core
of ancient eruptions. Calbuco is a conical volcano formed of stratigraphic
layers, similar to Puyehue and Osorno. Such volcanoes are the most ex-

plosive when they decide to erupt. Cerro Tronador rises almost eleven thousand feet across Todo de los Santos, towering above its four sisters to define the Argentine frontier. Its shattered summits tell us it was once a larger, stratified volcano that violently tore itself apart.

I've always liked its name, I said quietly.

What's that? Schirmer asked.

Tronador!

Tells us something about its ancient past, he agreed. *Thunderer!*

It must have been a giant volcano.

Osorno is only nine thousand feet high, but it rises almost from sea level. The little Schirmer *hosteria* is almost precariously sited, pinioned on the gritty beach between the beautiful lake and the volcano. It is not the highest volcano at Todo de los Santos, but its symmetry is nearly perfect. It fills the sky and one's thoughts. Osorno is both beautiful and frightening, its snowfields starting at approximately four thousand feet, looming just above the inn. It stands alone, a snow-capped pyramid rising from its immense conical base, roughly circular and fifteen miles in diameter. The volcano separates Llanquihue from the fjordlike Todo de los Santos.

Its snowfields cover thick glacial tongues, and immense blue-green fractures and folds are visible at its summit through binoculars. Steam and urine-colored stains are visible too, particularly in cold weather. Climbers report the acrid smell of brimstone on still days. Melting snow glitters in the steep ravines and vanishes in the alluvial fans of abrasive ejecta. No stratified volcano is ever totally benign, but Osorno has been sleeping peacefully since our Civil War.

We carried my baggage upstairs and I hurriedly unpacked the tackle. Schirmer came back when I had found everything. *We've still got time for some fishing*, he said. *The rain has stopped.*

Where should we go? I asked.

We've got two choices, he replied. *We can stay here and fish the Boca Petrohue—or we can take the launch up the lake to Cayutue.*

Cayutue? I asked. *What's Cayutue?*

It's a stream that comes from a small laguna, he said. *It's beautiful.*

How long does it take? I said.

It's sixteen kilometers, he pointed. *Takes an hour.*

Let's fish here, I said.

I'll have to row, Schirmer smiled. *You'll just have to trust me above the outlet rapids—tomorrow I'll get you an honest botero.*

I'll trust you, I laughed. *Don't lose an oar.*

The lagoon above the Boca Petrohue is a still-flowing arm between the inn and its ferry landing and a pretty little dairy farm across the water.

The lake itself is slightly murky and turquoise with silt from the big glaciers. Its steep shores are quite rocky, except for the grassy pastures across the water and dense beds of tules downstream. Steep cypress and *coihue* forests rise above the swift outlet on both sides.

It is difficult to judge its depth. Its turquoise flow is simply too opaque to see the bottom clearly, although great boulders lie under its smooth face, half-seen and betrayed faintly by its lazy eddies and boils.

Haig-Brown fished the outlet his first afternoon on the Petrohue, with a bright-eyed boy as his boatman thirty-five years ago. They anchored just above the rapids and caught nothing, but when they went ashore and fished the river itself, Haig-Brown took a bright four-pound rainbow that jumped and fought well. Wading the fast chutes just below the lake, he took three more fish, including a bright hen rainbow that went almost five pounds.

Schirmer held us deftly above the outlet without anchoring. It was cold and felt raw, and we caught nothing there. He rowed skillfully while I steadily cast and cast and told me a disconcerting story of two children who had lost an oar there years before. Unable to control the boat, they were caught in the rapids just below the outlet and killed in the terrible cataracts downstream.

The bodies were never found, he said.

It was too rainy and raw to put ashore and fish the swift pools below the lake. We rowed back up the lake while I cast patiently to the shore. There were big sedges scuttling and fluttering in the tules, and I changed flies, picking a big bucktail caddis dressed by Polly Rosborough in Oregon. It took nothing until we had decided to quit. When we had almost reached the dock, and I was simply trailing a few feet of line behind the skiff, a good fish took a hatching sedge just beside our starboard oar. I hurriedly dropped the fly in the ring and hooked a four-pound brown.

Finalmente! Schirmer said. *Tiene suerte!*

Tenemos suerte, I agreed.

It was raining again when we reached the inn, and its fireplace was welcome. Schirmer motioned me over to the tiny bar. *Frio*! he shivered. *Let's have a drink and celebrate—what would you like to toast our fish?*

Tiene Quinta Normal? I asked.

Cognac, he nodded.

Did you have problems here before the coup? I took the cognac gratefully.

You mean here at Petrohue? he asked.

Yes, I said. *Any problems?*

Not really, he raised his glass and we drank to our single fish. *Our problems were mostly with paying guests—we didn't have any!*

Nobody came to fish?

Nobody came for anything! Schirmer laughed bitterly. *We had to sell our boats and motors and let most of our boatmen go.*

What happened to them? I asked.

Many just drifted away, Schirmer continued. *The boy you will fish with tomorrow lives at the farm across the outlet—others had no reason to stay.*

But you kept your property, I said.

We were lucky, he shook his head sadly. *Others were not so lucky.*

Was there lots of trouble?

We had some bad times, he nodded. *People were killed defending their farms—there was an old woman who died here when guerrillas surrounded her little fundo and refused to let the doctor through their barricades.*

Did that happen a lot?

It happened enough that we finally helped each other arm ourselves, he said. *We used small planes to drop food and ammunition and medicine when guerrillas tried to blockade a friend's farm.*

Did guerrillas come here too?

Some men came once, he said, *carrying Russian automatic rifles.*

What did they want? I asked.

They made me take them all around the lake in the big launch, he said, *looking into all its arms—and they particularly wanted to see the Edwards house at Playa de los Ciervos.*

Agustin Edwards?

Yes, Schirmer said. *Allende's people hated Edwards and his family— not just because they were wealthy and controlled banks and newspapers, but because of their intelligence and quality—they burned his beautiful house.*

Didn't they own **Mercurio**?

It's still the best newspaper in the country, he nodded. *It's always been honest—and the truth is still a weapon in a world of lies.*

Did the guerrillas stay long?

They stayed a few days, he said, *and they never offered to pay us.*

Didn't you give them the bill?

No, Schirmer confessed. *They had too many AK-47 rifles.*

But why were there guerrillas in the countryside? I protested. *Allende was sitting in the Moneda, and they'd already won the election.*

Not quite, he said. *Not quite.*

Why not?

Because military and police promotions were still outside political control, and Allende failed to win control of the congress too, Schirmer reached for the cognac bottle, *and the old president of Chile was still the most respected politician in the entire country.*

Eduardo Frei Montalva, I nodded.

Frei was elected to rejoin the senate in 1973, he explained, *with 387,637 votes—the biggest plurality in the history of Chile!*

But why were there guerrillas? I interrupted. *Who supported them?*

Who do you think? he asked.

Were there many?

Thousands, Schirmer exclaimed angrily. *Every faction in Unidad Popular had its own little political army of thugs before the coup—and the right wing had its own idiots armed to the teeth.*

What were they for? I asked.

Che Guevara believed in killing off ability and intelligence and skill to create a vacuum of leadership, he said. *It's a strategy that works.*

Were they planning such tactics?

Political thugs from the Vanguardia Organizada del Pueblo killed Edmundo Perez in 1971, he replied, *and there were other killings—the killers had a list of targets, including your ambassador and our Cardinal Silva.*

Who was Perez? I frowned.

Frei's Minister of the Interior, he said. *Many hoped he might become president if Chile ever held another national election.*

Guevara's theory, I nodded.

Perez had quarreled with Allende's henchman, Coco Paredes, Schirmer explained, *and with Jacques Chonchol.*

I met Chonchol once, I said absently.

Where? he interrupted.

It was a big party, I explained. *Given by a Chilean sculptor.*

What did you think?

Too smooth, I replied. *Intelligent and articulate and a little too oily—untrustworthy and something else.*

What else? he asked.

I'm still puzzled, I said. *I saw a big cobra once in the border jungles of Nepal—and that's how I felt meeting Chonchol.*

Too bad you're not a Chilean, Schirmer laughed bitterly. *It took Frei and his Christian Democrats twenty years to see Chonchol clearly.*

You think Chonchol and Paredes were involved in killing Edmundo Perez?

Paredes was, he said.

But what were the guerrillas for? I persisted.

They were guilty of several political killings, he said. *It's common knowledge they were planning to kill key commanders in the military and police—they killed an important naval officer after a reception at the Cuban Embassy and murdered a chief of the carbiñeros at Concepcion.*

Some people think Frei was like Kerensky in 1917, I said. *Too soft and well meaning to deal with his times—you agree with that?*

Not entirely, he said.

Did they get most of the guerrillas during the coup? I asked.

Between the carabiñeros and the army, he shook his head, *most were killed or caught in the coup—there were lots of them caught at Panguipulli.*

But what were they for?

Allende had some dangerous bedfellows in Unidad Popular, Schirmer explained. *He was not actually a communist, but he was pretty naive in his dealings with his own political crazies—I think he was a popular well-meaning socialist—they were using him and just waiting.*

You think they were getting ready to dump Allende? I gasped.

I think Allende was our well-meaning Kerensky in Chile, he nodded, *and I think they would have displaced him conveniently—like Benes and Masaryk in Czechoslovakia in 1948.*

You remember some history! I said.

Chileans have just taken a bath in history! Schirmer said wryly. *We've had too much history lately—and we've been vaccinated!*

The rain lasted through the night, but the weather was clearing and the lake was perfectly still at daylight. The volcanoes were sharply reflected in its mirror, disturbed only by the feeding of two black-headed swans.

The *boteros* had already loaded the skiffs on the truck before breakfast, and they scrambled up with their boats when we carried our tackle from the inn. The clouds were burning off. The big launch from Peulla came steadily down the lake, a lazy wake shattering its perfect mirror, and the *chunk-a-chunk* echoed in the hills. The schoolyard beyond the boat landing erupted in a happy clamor.

Schirmer clambered into the driver's seat. *It's finally clearing,* he said. *Looks like a great morning to float the Petrohue!*

Can't wait, I said.

The little Rio Maquina plunged past the road, gritty with snowmelt and ash. Osorno was still completely hidden in the clouds. Spray rose from the Petrohue falls and drifted upstream across the road. Beyond the *cascadas* themselves, which are completely impassable in boats, there is a great turbulent pool that Haig-Brown fished thirty-five years ago. It is a pool that fishes well in early spring, and through the heat of the summer, because it is fed by a cool spring creek that flows at fifty-odd degrees all year. Its effluents are warmer than the river itself before Christmas and are much cooler in January and February, in the fierce heat of the Chilean summer.

We left the Puerto Varas road, turning sharply left into the woodcutter's trace and fishtailing in its bright-colored mud. The big *coihue* trees and bamboo still glistened in the sun, dripping with rain. The boatmen unloaded their skiffs from the truck, and we helped wrestle them down to the river.

Lucho Liedtke! It was the thin blue-eyed boatman with a shock of wheat-yellow hair. *Soy su botero en el Petrohue hoy!*

He shook hands almost shyly.

Liedtke? I repeated his name. *Können Sie ein bischen Deutsch?*

Liedtke knew I was speaking German but obviously failed to understand it. *No, señor*, he grinned sheepishly. *No entiendo aleman.*

Lucho has no German, Schirmer shrugged.

I know, I smiled.

Ragged clouds still drifted through the tall beeches and *colihue* and flame trees. Liedtke worked deftly with his oars. We ran the swift chutes between the waterlogged trees, and he back-rowed skillfully to hold our boat against the current while I cast to likely lies.

It's a beautiful river! I thought.

The first mile was swift and strong. Its currents were broken by the tangled logs and big stones, and dark pockets and seams that held shoals of greedy rainbows. The fish were mostly twelve to sixteen inches. They fought hard and spent their strength foolishly, with mindless cartwheeling and jumping. We fished carefully through the morning. There were several deep cliff-face pools hung with scarlet *notro* and trailing vines and elephant ears, but the bigger fish proved stubborn. Twice we rolled big browns under my bucktail, but both were sluggish and missed.

Los languidos, Liedtke grinned toothily.

Several times we worked good-looking holes without any sign of fish, and the young *botero* took us into the next chute, shaking his head unhappily. The overcast was completely gone and I shed my rain jacket. We took several skillet-sized rainbows in the long riffle where we stopped for lunch. The boatman killed a half dozen and dressed them quickly. Schirmer and his boatman had already built a cook fire, and I rummaged through my boat duffle for a fishing thermometer.

What is it? Schirmer asked.

Forty-six, I said. *It's still too cold for really good fishing.*

Some sun should help, he said.

The smoke from our cook fire drifted upstream lazily, and we sat in the warm grass. The little river meadow lay tucked under a copse of big *coihue* and tree ferns, and a clump of elephant ears. It was sunny and almost hot.

Bad fishing, Schirmer sighed.

But it's a wonderful day, I accepted a wine glass, *and the fishing will get better when the river gets warmer*.

The weather improved steadily. We had freshly broiled trout *meunière* with a chilled chardonnay after a hot milk broth with *mariscos*, and then there were fat *lomos* of beef grilled over an open fire. Schirmer produced his last bottle of old cabernet from the years before Allende.

La ultima botella, he said.

It's Antiguas Reservas! I studied the dusty bottle. *How old is it?*

Twelve years, he smiled.

The boatmen were stripping a thick stalk of elephant ear, chopping off the giant leaves and cutting away its stringy skin, leaving smooth banana-length pieces. *Why are they cutting up nalca?* I asked.

Dessert, Schirmer said.

I didn't know you could eat it, I said. *What does nalca taste like?*

It's related to rhubarb, he laughed.

Rhubarb ten feet tall with leaves as big as a kitchen table, I said. *That's a lot of sour taste.*

Try it with some rose-hip jelly, he suggested.

It's pretty good, I admitted.

Finally we loaded the boats again and pushed off. It was getting sunny and clear. The river grew even more beautiful downstream, and the big volcano towered behind us, its perfect snow-capped cone reflected in the still flats. The swift, blue currents eddied through dark channels in the stones, under lava cliffs hung with flame trees and *ulmo* and flowering vines, with immense labyrinths of water-logged trees breaking the flow.

The fishing went better.

The first deep run under the brushy cliffs produced a fat three-pound brown, and we picked up a steady drumfire of rainbows in the riffles and pockets. Some fish were rising in a big flat, and my boatman muted his oars to stalk them. We could see every stone on the pale chalk-colored bottom, but the fish were invisible. The first fish was working above a tangled jam of *coihue* trees. It refused my bullet-head bucktail on the first cast, and I cast quickly again. The fish ignored it too, feeding steadily.

Selective, I thought.

The rises were gentle, almost interlocking bulges and swirls, like trout feeding on spent mayflies. Sporadic hatches had been coming all morning without triggering a rise of fish. Bank swallows had been working high over the riffles, wheeling back and forth to catch the dancing flies.

Mating swarms, I thought.

Selective feeding is seldom a problem on such big Chilean rivers, and I was not really prepared for it. There was a single box of dry flies in my boat duffle, and several polywing spinners were tucked into one compartment. I picked a small rusty brown pattern, and a fish intercepted its first float.

Muy bien! the boatman grinned.

We went ashore and I quickly wrestled into my waders. Liedtke told me excitedly that he had never seen the *mosca seca* fished before, and he was fascinated with the dry fly. Wading is considerably more efficient than floating, and I took six of the seven fish we saw working, including a silvery sea-run brown of eighteen inches that jumped crazily.

Gusto la mosca seca, Liedtke laughed.

I like the dry fly too, I said.

Our best fish came later on a bucktail. It was lying just behind a mossy boulder, tucked under the elephant ears and *colihue*. It took the fly savagely. The boatman worked hard, pulling his heavy oars to hold us against the current, and we circled into a still backwater. His shrill laughter echoed from the cliffs, almost a girlish cackle, when he finally saw the fish. It was a sullen fight that carried us fifty yards downstream, and it showered us both with water when I released it. The big fish went six pounds.

It was a fine stopping place, and the young *botero* sat smiling while I broke down my tackle. We sat without talking and just drifted the last mile, happily content with our fishing and enjoying the river and its volcano, and its wild jungle-looking forests.

Mil gracias, I thought.

During our trip north to Lago Ranco, we sat watching the beautiful foothill country and the high snow-covered mountains in the distance. The dairy herds were mixed. Fat Holsteins grazed with brown Swiss and palomino-colored Guernseys. The fields were pale green and lush, and in the rolling country beyond Frutillar, the fields were saffron-yellow and the orchards were blooming. Memories of other Chilean springtimes crowded my thoughts as we passed Paillaco.

The weathered clapboard houses and outbuildings stood in wind-breaks of poplars and pines. Moss grew thickly on the split-rail fences and posts, and on shingle roofs and chimneys and anything else facing south. The wooden houses were silvery grey with the salt carried on the Pacific winds. Puffy clouds hung against the mountains. Lago Ranco lay ahead, its sprawling drowned caldera glittering beyond the dairy farms and rolling hills. The mountains had turned almost black with spring squalls. There are several tributaries feeding the big lake, including the large river called the Calcurrupe, which rises in the Lago Maihue.

Why are you smiling? Schirmer asked.

Was I smiling? I said. *Guess I'd forgotten how beautiful this is.*

It is beautiful, he nodded. *Chile lindo.*

Lago Maihue itself is drained through a narrow half-mile lagoon, weedy and thickly bordered with reeds. There is a little clapboard school at the outlet, with a pretty farm on its south hillside too, and a trout lake in the steep notch beyond. Its upper end is like a jungle fjord, fed by icy little rivers called Blanco and Hueinahue and Currinhue. The lake is weedy and fertile, its aquatic growth crawling with scuds and dragonflies and other nymphs. Its big rainbows are quite silvery, with pale olive backs and delicate spots scattered across their dorsal surfaces and tails. Such fish are slabsided and deep, shaped more like smallmouth bass than trout, and rise quite freely. The Maihue gathers itself slowly in its stadium-sized outlet. It spills past a huge cobblestone shoal into a churning flume, tight against towering thousand-foot cliffs. The swift birth of the Calcurrupe is frightening.

The Calcurrupe itself boils with spume, spilling deep and strong in a circling chute against the mountain wall. Like the lake that gives it birth, the Calcurrupe swiftly drains a seismic fault, with steep mountains rising to its south. Its highlands are occupied by small bands of Mapuches, who cut the brush and berry thickets in the spring for planting and burn the thickly piled cuttings. Their smoke hangs across the valley in the mornings, and the mountains glow with hundreds of fires at night.

The Calcurrupe flows approximately ten miles to Lago Ranco at Llifen. Its first mile winds through a series of brushy channels, between the outlet and its Cumilahue tributary, where I had once taken a twenty-eight-inch brown six years before. The river is almost like a lagoon downstream, thickly bordered by tules and cypresses, and with entire forests of water-logged trees tangled thirty feet down. The sunk forests were ghostly and skeletal straight under our skiff, great structures hung with undulating fountain moss and weeds.

The river is too formidable to wade in most places. It is almost entirely fished on day floats with skilled Chilean *boteros*, although there are shallow riffles and bars that a bold fisherman can attempt wading. Its Contessa Pool is wadable at its throat, and its primary tongue reaches a quarter mile downstream in early spring. Another wadable stretch lies off the grassy little meadow where we stop to enjoy midday *asados*, a gravelly shingle I called the Playa de los Almuerzos. Another reach of wading water lies just above the Llifen ferry, across from the beautiful Hadida farm. Its mouth at Lago Ranco is boat-fishing water, usually fished at twilight and before breakfast. It is almost an estuary and surrenders immense trout, but I have never wanted to fish there.

The Cumilahue is different, we passed through Futrono and circled the lake. *It's a pretty wading-sized river—it's a river worth traveling almost six thousand miles to Chile.*

It is crystalline and richly fertile, with hot springs in its headwaters on the Choshuenco volcano, and miles of pale pea-gravel riffles. The Cumilahue is a primary spawning ground for both its own fish and for spawning runs from the Calcurrupe and Lago Ranco itself. Big browns arrive in the fall and stay to winter over, and silvery rainbows swarm upstream in September and October. Both species are still in the river when the season opens and can stay for weeks during a rainy year. The hot springs sustain heavy populations of crayfish and transparent little *Galaxias* and fly hatches. Spawned-out kelts mend and recover quickly, and the fry that drift back downstream toward Lago Ranco grow swiftly too. Its fly-hatches are excellent, and the Cumilahue is famous throughout Chile.

The Cumilahue flows into the Calcurrupe about a mile below Lago Maihue, but several other rivers flow directly into Lago Ranco itself.

The Quiman and Caunahue drain the high rain forests that surround the Choshuenco volcano. The Furaleufu is a strange little brown-trout river, with marshy lagoons and fallen trees. The Ñilahue is a large river, rising in a world of barren ashfields and pumice chimneys and deeply eroded fissures. The valley floor has collapsed below its falls, and huge clumps of *nalca* and flowering vines hang from niches in its postpile cliffs. Beeches and flame trees and bamboo grow thickly, and we climbed down a big *rauli* to reach the valley floor. The Riñinahue is a glassy little river with a charming backcountry hotel. Its big waterfall stops the spawning runs, over almost a mile of butter-colored gravel above Lago Ranco, and the big lake itself is a remarkable fishery.

We had lost sight of the lake when the road dropped down the mountain to cross the Caunahue on its timber trestle. The little river is a wild flume there during snowmelt, when it forces through seismic fractures a hundred feet deep and less than twenty-five feet across at the bridge.

Haig-Brown traveled to Llifen thirty-five years ago to gather material for *Fisherman's Winter* and would still recognize its simple houses and post office and the headquarters of the *carabiñeros* above the lake. The simple country hotel where he stayed to float the Calcurrupe is gone, lost in a tragic fire many years ago, and its foundations are hidden in brambles. His other observations about Llifen in *Fisherman's Winter* remain true:

> I first learned about Llifen and Lago Maihue and its Calcurrupe country from my friend Edouard de Rothschild when we were fishing a swollen British Columbia stream in May. When he heard that I was going to Chile, Edouard wrote to urge me again not to miss the place. He was quite right. Although my time there was far too brief, I believe that Llifen could well prove the most important fishing center in Chile.

The perspective of thirty-odd years has largely proved Haig-Brown's judgment correct. Its fisheries offer decent sport throughout the season when the summers are not too warm after Christmas, and when there is sufficient rain to keep the rivers cool. Other fisheries exist farther south that might rival those at Llifen, but most are anadromous fisheries based on migratory sea-trout runs that last briefly.

But over the years, I believe the Llifen region has fished best in the Chilean springtime, during the several weeks before Christmas.

We circled the pretty lagoon at Llifen, past the stony alluvial fan of the Caunahue, and entered the dusty streets of the village. The little post office and boat landing were unchanged, like the *confiteria* and the police barracks, and the little clapboard grocery run by the pretty young girl we called the Dama de las Cebollas. There were several Mapuche fires clearing the mountains beyond the Calcurrupe, and their filmy haze hung between the hills. Bigger mountains lay toward the north, still holding big pockets of fresh snow. Several steep monoliths rise just beyond the village, thickly covered with vegetation, shaped like giant thousand-foot bollards and capstans. The valley floor itself is a fertile patchwork of dairy farms and orchards and thickly grown forests. It is strange that Haig-Brown made no mention of the Cumilahue in *Fisherman's Winter*, although his party had to cross it in making two floats on the Calcurrupe from Lago Maihue. The big tree-covered monoliths were behind us now, like the steep pinnacles in a painted Chinese scroll.

We reached the little Hosteria Cumilahue in late afternoon, swinging the truck under its massive timber gate into a lane of flowering *copihue* trees. Its gardens had grown more beautiful in six years. Schirmer's men were already unloading my baggage, and the sturdy Chilean maids were laughing and helping. Flocks of *tricaques* chattered noisily in the trees, scolding a big hawk that rode the thermals overhead, and a great flock of

Chilean lapwings wheeled past. Adrian Dufflocq was in the flower gardens below the house, helping another guest with his casting, and he ignored my outstretched hand.

Ernesto! Dufflocq almost crushed me with a wild *abrazo* hug. *It's been almost seven years since we've seen you at Cumilahue—welcome home to Chile!*

I'm happy to come home, I bear-hugged back.

Dufflocq! he introduced himself to Schirmer respectfully. *I know who you are—and your troubles with the CORA guerrillas.*

You had your troubles too, Schirmer said quietly.

Have you time for a whisky?

Mil gracias, but it's several hours back to Petrohue.

We all shook hands warmly. *Gracias por todo*, I said. *Muchisimas gracias por la pesca and everything else!*

Por nada, Ernesto! Schirmer said.

Dufflocq hugged me roughly as Schirmer left in his truck. *Let's have a drink*, he said happily, *and tell me about everything!*

I'll try, I said.

Dufflocq is the son of a famous Chilean professor, the scholar who wrote the best-known reader used in Chilean schools. He is vigorous and good looking and articulate, with strong opinions and loyalties. His friendship is warm and intense, and I would not like to challenge his dislike. Dufflocq's ancestors were French, from the Basque country in the foothills of the Pyrenees, and his character still echoes the humor and fierce pride of such mountain people.

His ancestors were probably fishermen too, having come from the Gave d'Oloron country, where there are still a few Atlantic salmon. The cathedral at Oloron Sainte Marie still has a salmon fisherman and his catch carved into its weathered stonework portico. The alpine forests and big Chilean lakes and rivers have fascinated Dufflocq since his boyhood, and trout fishing is an obvious footnote to his Basque blood and its passion for the mountain country that lies on the Spanish frontier.

His apprenticeship began at Lago Villarrica in those childhood summers, when the family tried to escape the February heat of Santiago. There was fishing there in the Tolten, and in the big lake itself under the smoking volcano. But the principal fishing center was Pucon, where the Zapata family had been fishing *boteros* for generations on the swift Trancura. Alfredo Heusser lived at Pucon too, the best-known angler and flydresser in Chile. Dufflocq completed his apprenticeship under Heusser, fishing and making flies and guiding parties in the summers. His lessons were mastered well. Heusser is gone today, having lived well past eighty years, and Dufflocq has since become the most famous trout fisherman in Chile.

How's the fishing? I asked.

It's been pretty good, Dufflocq replied, *but the Cumilahue has changed.*

What's happened?

You'll see, he explained. *We've had some terrible floods that filled many pools with stones and hurt the fishing—and it tore out the new bridge to Lago Maihue just last year.*

Had many guests? I asked.

We had almost no guests from other countries after the Allende inauguration, he said. *Mostly embassy people—but more people are coming again now.*

What about the fly-hatches?

The high water hurt them too, Dufflocq shook his head sadly, *but they're still pretty good.*

You had the best in Chile, I said.

We lost a lot of small rainbows in the floods, he said. *Lost some freshly hatched brown trout too.*

It held mostly browns in the old days, I said. *Is that changed?*

They're coming back, he smiled. *We don't see as many of those lavender, purplish old browns with bright magenta spots—but they're coming back, and we still get big silvery rainbows and browns running up from the Calcurrupe.*

Are there big rainbows now? I asked.

We're getting some good fish these days, Dufflocq said. *Getting some six- to eight-pound fish too.*

Is there still time to try them?

Si como no! he said.

We walked through the gardens to the big meadows upstream after I had quickly rigged my tackle. The pool behind Bernardino's farm was my favorite. It was less spectacular than the big cliff pools nearby, with their bald exfoliated rock dwarfing the little river, but it had great beauty in its flowering trees and bamboo. The meadows were beautiful too, with a few big *coihue* trees standing among acres of wildflowers, and we walked upstream slowly.

I hear they tried to take the farm, I said.

They tried, he said. *You remember the night General Schneider was killed?*

Yes, I said, *we checked and cleaned your guns.*

And carried them to bed, he said.

You had trouble later?

We had some armed troublemakers in the valley for several months, he continued. *They took some farms—and we were on the death list too.*

Where were the police?

Allende's people ordered them to permit the will of the people, he explained, *but these people were not from Llifen—and many were not even Chileans.*

What did you do? I asked.

Loaded a shotgun and went to see the leader at three in the morning.

Was he Chilean?

No, he said. *I'm still not sure what he was!*

What the hell did you tell him?

I told him I wanted him to understand me, he laughed darkly, *and that I knew his men could take my farm by force, but I told him that I was a simple Basque with strong feelings—and that I would kill him myself if they tried.*

Did it work?

They never tried, he shrugged. *Guess it worked.*

Did you mean it? I asked.

I don't know.

The mountain rose steeply across the river, an impenetrable forest of beeches and Chilean bamboo, mixed with flame trees and magnolias and bell-flowered *ulmos*. There are beautiful *pelu* along the Piedra Pool, and we stopped to admire them. The Chilean rain forests are wonderful before Christmas, and it is easy to understand Darwin's fascination with the exotic species found in these latitudes.

The bird life was everywhere along the river too. There were gaudy scarlet-breasted flickers and *checau* birds. Chilean ousels were busily collecting caddis grubs in the riffles. Flocks of black ibises passed overhead, and their cries echoed from the mountain. Mockingbirds warbled and trilled from the bamboo thickets, and big *carpinteros* hammered at dead trees. Kingfishers darted among the cypresses along the water, and when we crossed through the orchard to the river, a big flock of black-and-white *queltegues* rose noisily from the shallows.

Correntino! I pointed.

We watched the torrent duck slip from a big stone and swim swiftly upstream, streaming bubbles and working its tiny wings like fins. *Correntinos kill fish,* Dufflocq smiled, *but I love them too much to care.*

They're wonderful, I agreed.

The pool behind Bernardino's farm comes down swiftly past thickets of *colihue* and shelves off under the trees and vines, spilling from the deep whirlpool under the big cliffs upstream. But it had changed in the floods. It was not as deep as I remembered it. The steep mountain wall was an exotic curtain beyond its glassy flow, but the cypresses and beech trees had been stripped away, like the mossy logs layered in the swift currents.

What should I fish? I asked.

Dufflocq suggested a small Muddler tied with olive-dyed bucktail and turkey. It was a pattern I had dressed for many years to suggest the darkly mottled Chilean crayfish, after dyeing a half-dozen Muddlers in a saucepan years before.

I found an olive Muddler in my vest, and my fingers were shaking slightly as I fastened it to the leader. The river flowed swift and smooth, and I slipped into the current, still feeling the old shivers of anticipation. The fly dropped against the bank and settled into its teasing swing. I took a shuffling step and repeated the cast, placing the Muddler under the trailing vines. I fished through the pool without moving anything and waded quietly back upstream. *It hasn't fished well since the worst flood*, Dufflocq said, *but don't give up on it yet—try that little polar-bear bucktail you used to tie, the little silver-bodied Puye.*

I might still have one or two, I said. *I'll look.*

Fish it down into the shallows.

The tail-shallows looked too thin and exposed to shelter a good fish. Every stone and pebble was clearly visible. Nothing came to the slim silver-bodied fly until I had fished through again and stopped casting.

Don't stop yet, Dufflocq called.

There was a small branch caught in the smooth current, broken and still connected to its roots, its leaves wet and still green. It had probably snapped in the last storm and was still alive. I dropped the sparsely dressed bucktail just above the branch. It worked through its swing. I cast again, dropping it closer and working the fly past the leafy shadow. It still looked good, and I cast back to the partially drowned branch, teasing the fly well back under the snag.

The current bulged, lifting the entire snag slightly and sending a huge swirl downstream. There was a fish ghosting behind the fly. Its swelling swept into the riffles and died, and the fish was gone.

Try him again! Dufflocq yelled.

We decided to rest the fish. Several minutes later I repeated the cast, and when the fish bulged again, I slowed the fly quickly. Its bow wake suddenly dissolved into a rolling splash, and then I felt its weight.

The entire shallows erupted in a wild cartwheeling jump, and the fish shot downstream. It held briefly in the riffles. The swift current boiled up across its back until it looked like a stone breaking the flow. It exploded again, showering spray in the twilight until it almost reached its sheltering branch. Several times I forced it away from the snags, feeling the leader catch like a straining guitar string, but the big fish came free. It finally circled, just beyond my reach, and when it surrendered, it threshed wildly.

You were right! I babbled excitedly.

Four kilos, he guessed.

Eight or nine pounds seemed about right. We stood admiring its silvery length in the shallows, and I stooped down to remove the fly. *It's a beautiful rainbow,* I stroked the fish gently. *No puedo matar—she's too beautiful!*

Let's go home and celebrate, he suggested.

Si como no! I said.

We released the fish carefully and stood watching while it gathered its strength. The current slipped over its dark shoulders. Its gill covers worked steadily. The trout lay quietly for several minutes until it simply drifted away.

It's still some river, I sighed.

There was a big fire in the grate when we finally reached the house, and a grinning boy was bringing more wood. Patricia Dufflocq was busily lighting the lamps and candles. The Mapuche serving girl brought the whisky tray and the ice bucket, and Dufflocq poured me a drink.

Dinner, Patricia called.

Our dinner began with tiny shrimps and *almejas* in a white-wine sauce, and the serving girls followed with a broiled *trucha criolla,* the succulent Chilean perch. The chardonnay from Maipo was wonderful, and when the girls brought a crown rack of freshly killed lamb, Dufflocq returned with a dusty bottle.

Ernesto! he said. *You remember your last stay at Cumilahue?*

Si como no, I said. *Perfectly.*

You remember the wine? Patricia asked.

You still have it?

We have all the bottles you signed, Dufflocq laughed. *We told you we'd keep them until you came back.*

I'd forgotten, I admitted.

Dufflocq carefully opened the bottle, trimmed the foil to hold its cork, and poured it.

Welcome home, they said. *It's been too many years.*

Antiguas Reservas, I said. *Gracias.*

We fished together for several days, and the Cumilahue surrendered good fish every time we tried it. Good rainbows seemed to hold in the likely places, bright fish mixed with strong well-mended kelts that had spawned in September and had fattened quickly on crayfish. Several times I hooked fish that seemed like big browns, but I lost them quickly.

Nothing wrong with big rainbows, Dufflocq laughed.

But where are the browns?

They're still here, he teased. *Not like the old days—but they're here.*

No se puede, I said.

It's possible to catch them, he said, *but browns are never easy.*

You're right, I agreed.

Our last day I decided to fish the long pool below the old trestle bridge. The curving reach of water lies under a high cutbank of chocolate-colored soil, its cornices so alive with nesting swallows that I call it the Golondrinas.

It lies on the Yugoslav dairy farm two miles above the Hosteria Cumilahue. Its owners had fled Europe in 1940, when the British were driven from the beaches in northern France, and they left the country when Allende took office thirty years later in Chile.

Were they worried about expropriation? I asked. *How big was their farm?*

Too small to qualify, he said.

Why did they go?

They left suddenly, Dufflocq explained. *Said they'd seen it all before.*

Tito too, I nodded.

The Golondrinas flows two hundred yards under its soft cutbank cornices. Its throat lay under a thick clump of *mimbres*, where a deep hole had scoured out under the roots, and there were other sheltered pockets downstream. Still farther down, several holes had formed between two large stones, and there was a deep run under the trees at the tail. The run had given me a six-pound brown many years before.

Dufflocq watched from the high trestle. I chose a darkly hackled Pancora, the dense palmer-tied wet fly carried by most Chilean fishermen and developed by Dufflocq's master at Pucon. I dropped it twice, letting it settle deep past the roots. It was taken hard, and the reel started shrilly as the fish hooked itself.

Rainbow! I shouted to Dufflocq.

It went twenty-four inches, with a red stripe fully three inches wide, and it doused me with water when I released it. I wiped my sunglasses and watched a big mayfly hatch from the shallows at my feet. The fish had fought hard along the roots, and I moved nothing when I fished it through again.

Farther downstream, under the cornices of busily nesting swallows, there was a strong boil behind the fly. The fish rolled again without taking. It took the third cast solidly and quickly stripped the reel into its backing, jumping like a tumbler. It took several minutes to control the fish. It bolted several times, and twice it frog-walked me into the backing again. It was a fine cockfish, almost completely recovered from its spawning, and it shot back into deep water.

Thirty yards more I hooked and lost another big rainbow above the boulders. It took the fly aggressively, hopscotched wildly back upstream, and almost dry-docked itself in the shallows.

It's stuffed with big rainbows, I thought happily.

There was a quiet splash in the tail shallows in the smooth run under the *cipreses* trees, and I turned to watch. Big mayflies were hatching more steadily now. The fish came again, porpoising to take a yellowish mottle-winged drake. I studied the smooth current until I could capture a specimen. It proved surprisingly like a yellow-mottled hatch common in Catskill country, although none of our fly-hatches is found south of the equator. I changed the sinking line and added a fresh 4x leader before rummaging through my flies for a likely pattern. There was a single Yellow Drake in the big Wheatley box, dressed with pale yellow-dyed grizzly and delicately flecked wood-duck wings.

It looked perfect and I gently preened its feathers. The cast worked out and settled. The fly rode nicely just above the trout, its wings cocked and floating well. The smooth current bulged under its drift. The fly drifted through the fish's lie and I teased it off, dried it with a few quick false casts, and cast again. The trout took it softly and shook itself when I struck.

Big brown! I thought excitedly. *Big brown!*

Its bulk and coloring were unmistakable. The fish shook its head, probing deep along the bank, searching out hidden roots and snags. It bolted sullenly upstream. I felt the nylon grate briefly and slip free, touching a big stone. It held and the fish porpoised, shook itself angrily, and bolted back past me. It forced me to follow, stumbling in the twilight among the stones, and took the fight to the Cane Weaver's Cottage. It was getting dark and I netted it gratefully. It writhed powerfully, twisting in the meshes, and I admired its twenty-six inches. It lay gasping in the shallows, facing into the flow, while my pulse and breathing settled. The big fish finally drifted off.

Hasta pronto! I whispered.

The lights in the trees were welcome when we reached the farmhouse, and the Southern Cross glittered in the sky. The soft wind smelled like rain. Dufflocq was preparing to broil the meat in the fireplace, but there was still plenty of time for a hot bath, and when I was soaking he brought me a glass of wine. Supper was quite late. Patricia served marinated *mariscos* and a thick lentil soup with freshly baked bread, and when the meat was served, Dufflocq opened another dusty bottle of Chilean cabernet.

I've got a fresh case of Antiguas Reservas, he said. *Sign them with some sketches of flies—and they'll wait in the cellar until you come back.*

I'll be back, I said.

The ragged clouds pushed into the narrow valley, drifting in thick layers against the steep mountain walls. The stars were gone. It started raining before we left the supper table to gather around the fire, softly at first, and then drumming steadily on the roof as the storm gathered strength.

The sullen *puelche* wind rose quickly in the darkness, driving the bad weather deep into the Andes. It blew pebbles and dust in the village streets until they grew wet and shining in the lights from the houses. There was heavy static on the radio at the headquarters of the *carabiñeros*, and the roads were empty. It was snowing on the volcano. Angry whitecaps rolled across the big lake, breaking across the shallow bar off the Calcurrupe's mouth.

Our supper was finished. Coffee cups and wine glasses were scattered on the stone hearth, and the fire felt good. The *puelche* grew stronger in the darkness, sighing past the eaves, and the fire sputtered and flared as the wind licked past the chimney. Our candles guttered briefly too, and my trip was almost over. It was time to start for Santiago in the morning, and we sat talking of other seasons, sipping cognac while the fire settled in the grate and died.

You're leaving already, Dufflocq and his wife protested. *You always leave too soon—our best hatches are still coming.*

What are they like? I asked.

We've got a big yellow mayfly that you've never seen, he said, *and a big orange stonefly with parrot-green wings!*

You're joking! I protested.

Ernesto, Patricia said gravely. *Adrian never jokes about fishing.*

When do they hatch? I asked.

Christmas, he said.

The dying fire flared again briefly when she gathered its embers, and Dufflocq brought more wood from the porch. The wind moaned softly outside. Patricia added a fresh log and worked the bellows.

Christmas is still two weeks away, I said unhappily, *and I can't stay—those hatches are something for another time*. Rain rattled across the big windows. The fresh log had started to burn brightly, and I swirled the cognac in my glass, smiling and staring into the fire.

What are you thinking? he asked.

Nothing, I sighed. *Just thinking what a fine present the Cumilahue would make—and about getting a river for Christmas!*